Blood Covering
El Paso
Trail

BILL HANDY

Acknowledgments

First and foremost, I need to thank God the Holy Spirit for the inspiration of every story inside the pages of this book. Thank you, Christian Faith Publishing, for the help in bringing my work to life.

Special thanks to my wife, Mandi, for all the contribution, help, and details of the storyline. She has corrected and driven creativity along the way.

Chapter 1

You never knew how hurt a woman can be until you look into her eyes and see the pain she feels for a man she really loves, a man who is a cheater and a liar, a man who would take his paycheck once a month and spend it on alcohol and women. In the twelve years they have been married, his wife, Martha, would have to continuously bail him out of jail again and again. She has had to live with this kind of discontentment for most of their relationship and may have to live in this for the rest of her life. Martha was a true and good woman. She always did her best to be a good wife even though this would happen every month with no hope in sight.

Don Jamison was a hardworking man most of the time until payday when he would come to town and worry only about himself and the good time he could have. After working five and six days a week at the local sawmill, he would not worry about his family or how they would survive the rest of the month without two pennies to rub together. It was payday, and it was time for him to have a good time! He would always show up at Rowdy's Tavern, have that good time, and then end most nights in a fight where he would get himself arrested and end up in jail penniless. He'd have to sleep it off. You would see the true disappointment in Martha's eyes the next day when she would show up to pick him up once more. She had learned to hold back the tears because she had cried too many times. When she would show up to pick up this drunk husband of hers, you could always see the heartbreak. There was no reason why she had to go through this. She was a good woman, and because she loved him, she would do this over and over again. This is how it is in the hard South after the war has damaged so many, or at least right now in Chattanooga, Tennessee.

We were forced to move the jail to a temporary location last spring when the Tennessee River rose over fifty feet and washed it away. Poe's Tavern was the acting jail and courthouse until we could rebuild. The flooding would happen quite often. Until we could raise the money to fix the problem, this was the only solution we had.

When I arrested Don for disorderly conduct and fighting, l knew Martha would show up to pick him up. She always knew if he didn't make it home, he was probably in jail. If he was not at our normal jail location, she would need to come to Poe's Tavern. She had come searching many times and was no stranger to all the usual places. I hated to arrest Don because it was not always his fault. The other men knew he was an easy target after he had been drinking. They would pick at him until he got aroused into a tizzy and ready to take on the world. They knew he was a drunk, a rabble-rouser, a hot head. Oh, the demons he battled every month on payday. Just a little drink and the demons would take over, and he would forget all the normal ways of thinking. When you're ten feet tall and bulletproof, you can fight the devil and win. That's what your half-thick drunk brain would tell you.

My name is Elijah Adams. I'm the deputy sheriff and in charge when the sheriff is away. I will have peace when I am in charge. I held that sheriff's badge in the town I moved here from. It was a small town just outside of El Paso, Texas. Traveling here while I was in the war fighting for the South, we moved with our troops all the way from Texas to Chickamauga battlefield where many battles took place near Chattanooga. Having family members living here and fighting for their rights to maintain their ways of life, I had felt the need to help out in the effort. Once the war was over, I stayed in Chattanooga, not knowing whether I wanted to return to Texas or not. A lot of my family members from my mom's side are living in McMinn County in a small town just north of here called Athens.

It was time to make my rounds through town. I made my way through the streets and local businesses. Everything was calm until I got to Rowdy's Tavern again. When I was almost there, I noticed another fight was happening. This time, it seemed like a minister was trying to exorcise the demons, I guess. When I walked in, the normal troublemakers were holding the reverend. When they saw it was me coming in the door, they immediately dropped him to the ground. They know I am all business and take my job seriously. I asked what in the hell was going on, and no one answered me except for the barkeep. "Get that preacher out of here before he gets himself killed!" he exclaimed. The preacher looked up at me and said he was trying to save these lost ingrates.

"This isn't the church, preacher," I said as I picked him up and asked, "What are you doing in a bar? Who are you and why are you here?"

He dusted himself off and replied," I am Reverend John Williams and I have been sent here to speak to the sheriff. I have been reassigned to a church in El Paso, Texas. I was told to find the sheriff, and he would be able to assist me. Someone else told me this place here is where he would probably be. These gentlemen here were being loud and rude to the ladies as well as pushing this young picker around, so it was my place to help and enlighten them as to what the Word of God says about their behavior. They have no right to be carrying on so. The wages of sin is death, they need to know these things!"

I looked him over, put my hand on his shoulder, and answered, "Yes, they do need to hear that, but it ain't your place to correct them on their behavior toward women or pickers! This isn't the place for a sermon! That's for church on Sunday. The local tavern is to help relieve them of some of the meanness these men have built up. You will have to take this somewhere else before you get hurt. You, Reverend John, is it? Well, you come with me to the jail for a cup of coffee and tell me *exactly* what this is all about."

We made our way down the makeshift walkway to Poe's Tavern, "our temporary jail." It was a tough walk; since the flooding, there was nothing but mud everywhere. It has been raining nonstop from the beginning of February till mid-April.

"Reverend John, my name is Elijah Adams. I'm the deputy sheriff in charge while the sheriff is gone to investigate a shooting outside of town. Would you like to explain exactly what you're doing here and why you are looking for the sheriff?" As I walked behind my makeshift desk, bar counter, the reverend took up a stool, leaned forward, and began to explain.

"As I told you at the bar, my church headquarters has asked that I travel to El Paso and take over the pastorship of a church recently vacated by the death of the former preacher. The governor has given me papers for your sheriff to help me with my passage. Maybe to help me hire a guide or to have the sheriff assign someone to help with this long trip to El Paso."

I shake my head. "Reverend, not sure what to tell you. The sheriff should be back later tonight if you would like to wait. We have two cells in the back if you would like to wait or sleep in one of them. One cell is occupied, but the other is open. You can keep the other occupant company. His name is Don Jamison. A decent guy but a drunk. He shows up once a month and causes trouble at the bar with that rowdy crowd you met earlier. He always ends up here. You go right ahead and spend the night if you'd like. The door will be open, so you can go get a bite or a coffee there at the store. We just hold a place with a cot for those who we are trying to keep from getting hurt. Stay or go, it's up to you. There is a motel up the street if you would prefer, but a man of God is welcome anytime. My dad is a minister, and I do appreciate what you do."

Soon after, I left to make my rounds as I was trying to do earlier. As I was leaving, the reverend shook my hand and asked, "Have you heard of a man named Mr. Siskin?"

Yes, I had heard of the Siskin family. The Siskins are definitely known for their helping Christian causes.

"This family is supporting my travels through one of the parishioners of my fellowships. I am authorized to offer a guide fair wages to help in my efforts for safe travels. I would like to ask you to accompany me on this journey."

Not sure how he knew I was from that area, but for the last few weeks, I had been missing my homeplace and my parents. Money would not be the only deciding factor here, but an overwhelming feeling of missing my parents was a different thing altogether. "Not sure, Reverend, if I'm up for that task. I have settled here after the war and am trying to make Chattanooga my home now."

In the silence, I began to think. I liked living here in Chattanooga, but when the flooding happened, it flowed all the way to Missionary Ridge where it washed away my settlement and changed my plans. *I do have distant family in McMinn County that I see once every six months or more often if I can make it. Mom and Dad in El Paso have been tugging at my heart pretty strong for a while now, so this gives me something to consider. Also considering having a traveling partner, not sure how good of a partner he would be, though.*

I said good night to the good reverend to make my rounds with a few more things on my mind this time. I thought of how much I miss my parents. They were in pretty good health when I left, but it has been several years since I last saw them… I have a new life here. I could do more with myself in El Paso. After all, I was a sheriff there, and here? Just a deputy sheriff. Not sure if I want to travel with a preacher trying to save the world. I remember my dad dragging me from town to town, trying to save the world when I was a kid. Never knew if the world really wanted to be saved! He still is a pastor just outside of El Paso right now. When the sheriff returns, I will talk with him about this situation and get his input.

After making all my rounds of checking all the local businesses for locked doors, I go back to the tavern where all the fights had happened earlier to clean up the riffraff that was still hanging around. I make my way down main street where everything is clear and all is well. *Kind of looking forward to talking with the reverend again.* Brings back memories of my dad when I was a kid, always preaching at me or to me. My dad is a great man. He's in his late sixties now and getting older. I know my parents could use help since they are up in age. The thought of an old girlfriend crosses my mind. She may be married by now, but I think about her often. As a matter of fact, I still have a photo of her in my wallet. Tammy sure was a pretty little thing.

Returning to Poe's, I saw Martha, who had come to retrieve Don. As I passed her to head inside and retrieve the keys, I asked, "Hello, Martha, how are you? I know Don has let you down again. I'm sorry you're having to go through this all the time. You deserve better. I do know there's nothing you can do about it.

She looked up at me with sad eyes and sighed. "We all have our crosses to bear, and this one must be mine. If my husband were more like you, Elijah, we would be better. He seemed to be doing okay until the flood came and took our crop and fields. After that, he gave up and turned to drinking way too much. Every time he gets paid, he just wants an escape, and I can understand that."

I furrowed my brow. "Yes, Martha, we all lost a lot when the flood came, but that's no excuse for his behavior. Drowning yourself in a bottle is not the answer. Come on in, I'll get him for you, and you can take him home again."

As we walked through the door, I yelled out to Don Jamison, "Your wife is here to take you home!" No response. I yelled once more. Again, no reply. As I walked closer to the holding cells, all I could hear was a faint cry like that of a child. I know Don and the reverend were here when I left. The closer we got to the back, the louder the crying got. It was weeping coming from the cell! I had only been gone for forty-five minutes or so. What could have happened? Did he hurt the reverend, or did the reverend do something to him? Don had never been a violent man outside of the bar. Who could have known how he would take to a preacher? Preaching might have been too much for him. Fire and brimstone may have pushed him over the edge. If anyone was to tell me Jamison was the kind of guy that could be converted, I would have not believed them. He was a drunk, a fighter, and a brawler! Once a farmer and a decent person, but not now. We looked inside the cell, and with amazement, we found Jamison on the ground and the preacher standing over him, praying for this weeping man. Jamison was crying like a baby. Preacher man must have been witnessing to him. Apparently, Jamison was a ready soul, and the preacher must be the real deal. A different preacher than what we were used to around here. Different than any I had known. Even when I had spoken to this man of God, I felt a fire inside my chest touching my heart as well. He would bring tears to my eyes as he would speak to me. Even at the bar when I first met him. There was definitely something different about this preacher being able to touch a no-account drunk's heart and have him on his knees, crying out to God literally! *The Jamison I know is not the kind of man to do as what is happening right before my eyes. I think I have truly seen it all now!*

I gestured for the preacher to step out of the cell and asked, "Reverend, what has happened here?" still in shock from what I was seeing! "Yes, go ahead, Martha. You can see what's going on with him."

As she pushed her way around me to get to her husband, the reverend stood up with tears in his eyes as well. He replied, "Deputy, I think this man is ready to spend some time with his wife and kids. I think he's tired of the bars and the fighting. No more time for Satan. Think he's ready for time with our Father God! Our Lord Jesus Christ!"

As the reverend and I walked toward the front with Don and Martha shuffling behind, I asked, "Reverend, I have only been gone forty-five minutes, what happened?"

The reverend smiled at me. "Son, it's not what happened in the last forty-five minutes, it's what's been happening for the last few months. The Holy Spirit has been dealing with this brother for quite a while now. You never know how strong the power of God is and how long He has been working on someone's life." *No man comes to the Father unless the Holy Spirit draws him! Brother Jamison has been drawn into the family!*

"Deputy Adams," said Jamison with tears running down his face, "I am sorry about the problems I have caused you around town. For the last couple of years, I've been an embarrassment for my wife and family. Nothing but hanging out at the bar every time I got paid, drinking every dime away. I am so ashamed of myself! So sorry for making it hard on you. Deputy Adams, you won't see me like this again. God has been dealing with me for weeks. This preacher has opened up my eyes as to why I have been feeling like this for these last few days. As the preacher said, God has planted a seed in my heart, and this brother has watered that seed. If you don't see the water, just look what's coming out of my eyes. God has truly changed my heart and changed my life, and I can't stop crying! I've never felt anything like this before. God has changed everything. You will not see me back here the way I was before."

He let go of his wife and started toward me with his arms opening. As he got closer, he asked, "If you don't care, I would like to hug your neck." So with his arms around me and him smelling of stale beer, old dirt, and other things with tears still in his eyes and a good honest smile on his face, he whispered, "Thank you for always treating me with respect even after you would pick me up off the floor of the bar and drag me here and waking me up with coffee when I deserved nothing!"

Then he released me and turned to his beautiful wife, Martha, who also had tears filling her eyes. "Oh, Martha, I'm so sorry. So sorry for letting you down. I'm ready to be the husband you married and the man you deserve. To be the father and the man I am supposed to be."

Tears running down both sides of his face, he turned toward the preacher and extended his hand, saying," Thank you so much, preacher. By the way, what is your name?"

The reverend grabbed his arm, pulled him into a hug, and smiled. "My name is John, John Williams. I am traveling to El Paso, but I would like to correspond with you and Martha to see how things are going. When I come back to this area, I would like to come check on you also if you don't mind me doing so?"

As he hugged the preacher's neck, he said, "I do appreciate that. Thank you, Preacher John." He then turned to walk out, holding Martha's hand, and continued, "Our lives will be better from here on out." He looked up at me and said, "Thank you so much, Deputy Adams. I will be going now." He turned to his wife, who was also crying now. "It's hard to get rid of these tears, Martha."

As I walked back toward my desk, I yelled, "You take him home, Martha. I think you got the husband you need back. You know where you can find us if you need us."

As the Jamisons left, I could feel a presence in this jail as I had never felt before, especially in a jail or a bar. Maybe in a church meeting or a tent revival when I was a child. Both people were wiping tears from their eyes, and I was sure when they get home, the kids would be too. Hard to believe this had happened. There was something truly different about this preacher. A fire in his words I had not felt before. I've known many preachers, including my own father, but this preacher? Just something different about John Williams! I had felt this since I had met him even in the bar. His words had power behind them. I could feel a difference in my heart as well.

I got up from my makeshift desk and headed around the reverend toward the windows that overlooked the town I had been trying to make my home for the last few years. Out of the corner of my eye, I saw the reverend pull up a chair at one of the small tables that were just inside the door. He pulled out a small pocket Bible and put a canteen of water on the table and began to relax. I put my hand to the window frame and let my head fall forward. Then turning toward the preacher, I started, "I have been thinking about what you asked me before. About needing someone to go with you to El Paso. My homeplace is just outside of El Paso. My parents' farm is there. They are getting older and they must be needing help with the farm. My heart has been telling me I should go with you, Reverend. Actually, I have been thinking about this for the last few months. As I was walking on my rounds, I wasn't sure what I should do until I saw what happened with the Jamisons. Now I know! I'll be your guide, Reverend John."

The Reverend John clasped his hands together and bowed his head as if saying a prayer. Maybe he actually was when he raised his head and looked to where I was. "Deputy Adams, if that's what God has spoken into your heart, then you are definitely the man I need with me. I'll feel safer because you're coming with me. Before, when I was asking for the sheriff, I was told you are a good man and that the sheriff would help in anything I needed. I do know God's hand is in me meeting you, and our friendship is from above. I would love for you to come with me on this journey."

"It's been a long time since I have made this trip, and it will be a tough trek. I do hope you know what you are getting yourself into. It is going to be very tough. I have my horse and a mule full of supplies. I know it would be quicker on a train and not to mention more comfortable."

"Yes," said the reverend, "but I feel we are supposed to travel by horseback."

I looked at him and nodded my head. "As long as you know what we are up against. Life on a long trail is very harsh, sleeping under the open sky and sometimes the rain or the wild. Animals and snakes make life interesting, to say the least."

"God has work for me, and because He has put our paths together, you have work also. My Aaron in the wilderness, Elisha to my Elijah!" The reverend raised his hand to heaven.

I smiled at the reverend and placed my hand on my holster. "Not sure of all that, but I will be your gun since you don't carry one."

He looked at me and clasped his hands together. "God will open doors for us along the way. To lead us to the right brethren to help on this journey. God will change lives and drive the enemy off the battlefield before the battle ever takes place. Driving the Philistines from the battlefield right before our eyes! You shall see, brother. If God be for us, who can be against us!?"

I walked back to my desk and shuffled some of the papers there into better stacks. I grabbed a stray piece of paper and began to list my thoughts on what I wanted to take on the journey while answering, "I know what you're saying is true, Reverend. God has always taken care of me. When my friends died all around me in the war and I escaped unharmed, I knew then I had something else to do with my life. Even when I have been distant from Him for such a long time, not knowing where I stand with the Lord right now, I'm sure I will find out on this journey with you. I'm ready to see my parents whom I have been missing a lot lately. We corresponded over the years. Dad would always say his words through Mom, but every month, I would have a letter waiting for me. But not this month for some reason."

Standing up and heading toward the door, I turned, saying, "I'll be ready to go as soon as I can talk to the sheriff. I will close out my affairs here, and we can get on the road soon after. Let's go get a bite to eat and a good night's sleep and start in the morning."

Later that night, Sheriff Tate arrived at the jail. I introduced him to the reverend and told him how I had agreed to travel with him to El Paso. As we sat around a table, he was more than encouraging me to go and to come back to a job that would always be available to me if I decided to return, assuring me he would send my pay when it came due. We reminisced over some of the situations we had been in and out of together through the years of friendship.

"Sheriff Tate, you have been a good friend, and I have learned many things from you. I hope you will be able to find another deputy soon." He grinned and placed both hands on my shoulders, squeezing slightly.

"I may find one soon enough, but it sure won't be easy to replace your service or loyalty, son."

Chattanooga had been a great place to live for a while. Ever since the flood and me losing my small spread, I had been shuffling in my mind whether I should rebuild or not. Now I have my answer. Sometimes it takes a fifty-foot flood above normal all the way to Missionary Ridge to show us God's desire for us to move on! Reverend John said, "Sometimes one door closes so another door can open." I always wanted to go to the top of the mountain to see all the states. I heard about it since I had been here but never got to witness it myself. They say you can see seven states. I was not sure if that is true, but I knew you could see one! Tennessee and maybe Alabama? I was about to see plenty of Alabama as we headed to Texas. Interesting how our dreams change when a flood comes and changes the dream to a nightmare! I thought about Noah and his plans changing when the angel told him of the upcoming flood and how the farm he had been working on for a hundred years was about to be washed away. *Is this my ark full of animals to contend with? We shall see.* I know I wouldn't have the faith of Noah to believe in the word from that angel. Maybe that's why I wasn't told of the flood before it came.

I had been feeling something sent to me, maybe from that same angel that spoke to Noah. Maybe it was preparing my heart to go back home, to give protection to the good reverend and maybe also for my protection. *Who knows if I had traveled without this preacher, I may not have had this protection that I'm sure the reverend has. And now I will have it as long as I am with him. I guess in the morning, we will find out whether this is God's plan or not. I am stepping out in faith, of the reverend's or mine, I'm not sure of which.*

As we were heading out toward the hotel I'd been staying at since the flood took out my place the sheriff thanked me for everything I had helped him with and sent us off with God's speed on our journeys. He lightly chuckled. "You may need it with this Reverend John Williams, not sure of the experience he has on the road and in the wilderness."

"Thank you, Sheriff Tate, we will see what I've got myself into as the days forward will tell. I am about to find out. It was a tough road coming here, but I was with my regiment from Texas at that time. Sure, it will be even tougher without the backup I had then. If God had truly been preparing me for the coming of this minister and our journey together, then He will give us everything we need on this journey. If not, I guess we are in for it."

The next morning, I checked out of the motel and said my goodbyes so we could be on our way. I headed down to the local stables to retrieve my horse and settle my account with the stablemaster. I met up with the Reverend John in front of the bank. He asked me what kind of horse I had and if she would be ready for such a long journey. Old Rosie, I explained, was ready for everything we could come against. Rosie, being a seven-year-old Quarter Horse that made me train her from a touch-me-not horse to one that did everything I asked, was truly a loyal horse. She was a rough ride but very fast when the time was needed, and I preferred speed over comfort any time, and she truly had it!

I walked over to the First National Bank to close out my account. While I was there, I bumped into Janie. She was a very pretty woman, a pretty little redhead I had fun and a few drinks with at the tavern these last few years.

"Hey, Elijah, I heard you were leaving town. Were you even going to come say goodbye? When will you be back?" she asked. I could not rightly tell her. "How about one more time before you go, something to remember me by?" She slid up beside me, ran her hand down my arm, and batted her long lashes at me.

"Well, Janie, I don't think I have time for that right now, maybe when I return," I said hastily as I took a small half step back out of her reach. Hoping that I didn't offend her and knowing that actually something had been taking place inside of me and that I couldn't do those things any longer, I decided to tell her the truth. "Janie, I'm heading to El Paso with a preacher that hired me to keep him safe. I'm not sure I would feel quite right about visiting you before I get on my path. I will look you up when I return."

She gave me a sweet yet sad half smile and replied, "I do understand, but please don't forget about me." With tears in her eyes, she hugged me and walked away. I know what we were doing before wasn't right anymore, and for some strange reason, it meant something now. Not a hundred percent sure yet, but maybe I would know by the time this journey is over. Time will tell.

As I moved to mount up on my Old Rosie, I took one last look around at this big beautiful town. Chattanooga was a wonderful place to live. I looked at the sidewalk where many people had been hurt and that I had to rescue, seeing and remembering all the people I had to arrest for breaking the laws I had to uphold and the bloodstains on those walkways from the battles and fights I had broken up, (some I had taken part in). I was going to miss it here. I turned toward the reverend, nodded my head, and we slowly rode out of town.

Chapter 2

While riding from Chattanooga and out of Tennessee into Alabama, we came to a small town we later found out was called Jackson. We ended up at a rather large plantation that was located right in the middle of this town. Drattens Hall is what they call it. What a large beautiful plantation, with a large white house in the distance and many cotton fields as far as the eye could see and many picker people still working these fields even though Lincoln had freed all Black persons from slavery. So many are still working? Freed slaves? Maybe they stayed because this was their only place to go?

We rode up to a couple of older picker men. They looked at us as if we were hunting runaway slaves or the sort. The reverend and myself were just passing through and hoped no one would mind us doing so. As we approached, one of the old men asked what we needed here at Drattens Hall.

"Just passing through and admiring this beautiful plantation. We had taken notice of this beautiful artwork on the buildings."

With a deep and strong Southern drawl, the picker man explained, "Yessir, dis has been in da family for a long, long time. Da same man dat built dis home also built da courtshouse dat we have n town. Massa said the first one was builts in 1738, or dat's what massa tol' us anyhows. Someone by da name of Palatine, was dat man's names, dat came up wit it. Dat all I know, sir, and I've lived here on dis plantation my whole life. Even doh President Lincoln, he free da slaves, I jus' din' have da heart ta leaves. Where else would I's go? Dis is mah home. Dis is why everyones is still here an we call dis home. So we stay on. We have never been treated badly by da massa and his family. Dis is all I ever known as home. Whom might yous peoples be and where are yous from."

While he had been speaking, the reverend and I dismounted our horses. The reverend wanted to be at eye level so we could show him some respect. He took a step forward and held out his hand to introduce us.

"Well, I'm Elijah Adams" I spoke up! "And this here is the Reverend John Williams. We are just passing through, headed to Texas. As long as no one minds, we would be appreciative if our horses could get some water, and maybe we could lay our heads down for the night?"

He smiled at me, saying, "Well, yessir, yous won't have a problems heres waterin' yous horses and sleepin' in da barns as long as yuhn checks with da massa at da big house."

We nodded in agreement and grabbed the reins. "Thank you, kind brother," said the reverend. The picker man decided to accompany us, and slowly we made our way along the fields and up the long drive toward the plan-

tation house.

He was a very kind sort and as soft-spoken of a man as

I thought I had ever met. As we made our way to the big

house, it became clear that we would be welcomed here.

There were actually no other whites here that we could see

except for one older man sitting on a rocking chair on the

porch drinking a glass of tea.

Later on, we found out the older black man's name was

Silas. When we arrived, he walked us right up to the front

porch steps to meet the owner of the plantation. He said,

"Massa, dis here is Mr. Adams and Reverend Williams.

Deys be passing through, wonderin' if dey could water

deir horses and maybe find a place to lay dey heads for the

night?"

The older man sat forward in his chair, looked at our

guide, and then looked us up and down. He closed his eyes

for a moment, and then in a stronger voice than I thought

would come from a man like him, he began, "I am Mr. Dratten, and these are my former slaves. They work for me now, for a salary, of course. Not sure why you are here on the plantation, but as long as you don't cause any trouble, you can sleep in the barn, and I'm sure Silas can rustle you up something to eat. We never mind company as long as you boys aren't looking for trouble. The only thing is, *boys*, you do right by me and my former slaves, then we'll do right by you and not have any problems. These pickers are a part of the family, and we won't tolerate them being treated wrong.

"Some of these workers were actually born here on the plantation, and Silas belonged to my family before I was born. His family belonged to my parents. It's like we are actually family ourselves. Pops always told me never treat anyone badly if you could help it, and I never saw him mistreat a slave unless drastic measures required him to, even though there are people around here that think all pickers should be run off. When the union arm came through, trying to push their will on all of us, we didn't fight, we just stayed. This is where we were born and raised. This is where we and the pickers are supposed to be."

The reverend spoke up and said, "Your father was a rather wise man seeing that this is exactly how God speaks of every man in the Bible. It does the heart good to know your two lives have knit together in such a troubled world as we have lived in for the last decade."

I started rubbing my chin and looked over to the barn. I started thinking of what the reverend had just said. When he said it, it had sounded strange to hear a white man speaking this way about a picker. It was sort of confusing the way he spoke! I had never thought of the pickers like this. I always knew they were human, just another form of people. Just a step above a horse or a beloved dog. And now these two are speaking about them as if they are no different than we are, to say the least!

I spoke up and explained that we would not be here more than that night, and we told him how much we appreciate the kindness. The truth was, I was ready to move on right now! Away from this confusion that I was hearing. But the reverend seemed more than content to stay here for more than just a night.

The reverend spoke up and said, "Good to know there are decent people still in this world, right, Mr. Adams?"

I nodded my head in agreement yet went on to explain, "Well, I did fight for the South, but only because I objected to Lincoln trying to dictate how we live our lives. I have no feelings whatsoever about slavery. I did object to all the lives that were lost because of such a wrong cause! I think we should bury the hatchet, let bygones be bygones, and put the past behind us." But in my mind, I never thought of it the way these two were talking about this subject.

The old man drank from his glass, set it down on the end table next to his chair, and began to stand. Silas moved forward a step as if to help, but he just waved him away. "Well, Reverend, Mr. Adams and you seem to be good men, and I believe you gentlemen think just as we do here on the plantation. Silas and all these fine people that stayed are, and will always be, part of the family. We will always treat them right and with the respect we want to be treated with. Now you boys go ahead and make yourselves comfortable in the barn. When the workers eat supper, I'm sure they will feed you too. They eat about dark. Your horses should be comfortable as well. We can talk more in the morning."

Silas led the reverend and me to the barn. He showed us a couple stalls we could use for our horses. He pointed out the ladder so we could bunk down in the loft with the hay bails and told us where we could wash up. After making sure we had what we needed, Silas headed back to the fields. We decided to walk on down to the creek so we could let our horses drink some cool water and we could get washed up before we rest.

Resting in that hay was going to be a lot better than the ground I was thinking we were going to be sleeping on.

Later that evening, Silas brought us some stew and some biscuits, which were a sight for sore eyes for two very hungry men who had not eaten a real meal since we had left chattanooga. It was a long ride from there to the plantation. I was leaning against one of the bails, savoring every minute of my food, when the preacher man started talking to Silas.

"Well, Brother Silas, have you ever heard the stories of the Bible and of our Lord Jesus?"

Silas smiled. "Why, yessir, dat's how my mammy taughts me how to read, was from da Bible."

"Brother Silas, do you understand why we need grace and through Christ's death we received that grace? Have you ever asked, why did Jesus have to die on a cross for us?"

Silas set his fork down and answered, "No, sir, I have read da whole Bible, but dey be a lot in dere dat I dun understand, and I dun know why God woulda send His Son ta die for peoples dat are as mean as dey are. I have always believed dat Jesus was God's Son from da time I was a youngun. Mammy always taught us dat God is da builder of dis world and Jesus is His Son. But I never knowd or understood t'all."

The reverend sat up a bit straighter, pointed toward Silas, and asked, "Brother Silas, that bandana you have around your neck, when you're riding on a trail and put it over your face, would you still get dirty even though it helps you to breathe?"

Silas tugged at the bandana around his neck and contemplated what he was saying. "Yessir! Every time I ride, me and my bandanas is completely covered with dirts."

"Brother Silas, that's the reason why we need Jesus. In the Old Testament, the beginning of the Bible, those people made sacrifices to cover their sins, but it could never truly clean them. It would help with the dust like that bandana, but you will still get dirty. That's why we had to have Jesus. When Jesus comes, He is a bandana that will cover you and will never leave you to get dirty again. That's why we need a Savior. That's why He had to make a sacrifice. A perfect sacrifice! Because a temporary covering will never work. We need a wash. Jesus is like soap and water after you take the bandana off. When he cleans you, you're completely clean! That's why we need Jesus. When He sets you free, you're free from this dirty world, indeed!"

Silas's eyes widened. "Mr. Reverend Williams I'z never been explained dat. I'm hapies you finally did. Iz wuzn't sure why mens would need a Jesus wenz wez already had a God. Mammy always said Jesus is God's only Son. He is da only way to get to God our Father. I'z unstan now."

The reverend leaned forward and put a hand on Silas's shoulder. "Brother Silas, I'm glad you do. I hope you make Jesus your true Lord and Savior, and if you haven't, I'm ready to pray with you right now."

Silas nodded. "Yessir, I'z did ask Jesus ta be my God when I'z a youngin and Iz always believed Jesus mine Savior.

'Preciate you so much fur helping me knoz. I 'preciate you fur dat! Never had a white preacher man call me brotha, and I'z 'preciate dat too."

I finished my plate and set it aside. I had never heard a white man of any sort call a black man brother either, and my father was a preacher my whole life. This was more confusing to me than I think it was to Mr. Silas. I had been around the church from the time I was a child, and never had I thought of a picker man as a brother. I turned toward the reverend and decided to clear my mind, but Silas beat me to it.

"Missa Reverend Williams, you no like odder preacha men I'z knows, especially a white preacher mans," said Silas. "Sumpm about youz, Reverend. I can feel da love of God in youz az I'z never felt from any uder mans fore."

Silas wasn't the only one thinking that; I was also. Not sure if God had put all this together, but I was feeling as if this was not quite as random as I had thought when I first met this preacher back in Chattanooga. He spoke as if he saw God inside of even this poor black man. How could this be? That would mean all these people were no different than whites. *This preacher can't be serious.*

Silas shook the reverend's hand. "'Preciate you so much for whas youse duds fur me, Reverend, I'z always memba it. I'z needs da get back in da house and help massa Dratten. He's be looking for me."

The reverend nodded. "We will see Mr. Dratten in the morning before we leave. Have a good night, Brother Silas."

Silas smiled. "Yes em, sir, I wills, Reverend Williams. Mr. Adams. Yous has a good nights. I'z gonna to tell massa what youn did for me taday, and he will 'preciate you in da morning too. 'Preciate you, Reverend. Goods night again, I'z gots to go." Silas grabbed our plates and headed out the barn door.

I sat in silence for a while. "Reverend Williams, I'm confused why a white man would call a black man a brother. How can he be your brother?"

He grabbed his Bible and took a seat next to me on the closest bale. "Mr. Adams, with God, there is no skin color, only man separated by races. In Christ, we are all the same. White, black, oriental, and red men are all the same in God's eyes. We are all the same and are brothers if we all have Christ in our hearts. The same as you or I! I love and will fight for all men because there is no difference in God's kingdom! The Bible says from one bloodline, all races were born. We are all the same!"

"I hear you, Reverend, but I've never thought of it that way nor would I have if you had not told me. I've seen slavery my whole life and never thought about it being right or wrong. I'm tired. I think I will turn in for the night, Reverend. You have a good night."

I wasn't actually tired, just confused about what the reverend had said. I was not sure if I followed his way of thinking when I was taught something different my whole life.

The next morning, we arose right at daylight to a clear but slightly foggy, rather crisp morning. We saddled our horses and rode back by the big house. The reverend wanted to say one last goodbye and to thank Mr. Dratten for his kindness and hospitality.

"God has been kind to us here, Mr. Adams, and I feel we are free to move on from here," the Reverend had said as we rode out of the barn. What exactly did the reverend mean by he feels we could move on from here? *Confused again?* I thought to myself.

We said our goodbyes to Mr. Dratten, and we thanked him for his kindness. Mr. Dratten thanked the reverend for sharing with Mr. Silas. He told us, "If you're ever back in our area again, please feel free to visit any time, gentlemen."

"Thank you, Mr. Dratten," I said with a tip of my hat. The reverend declared that he would be praying for prosperity for this whole plantation and blessings over all who lived on it.

As we rode down the drive from the big house, we were met by Silas, his wife, his daughter and son-in-law, and his two grandchildren He wanted his family to meet the reverend and to thank him for what he had shared with him. The reverend had changed the way Silas looked at our God and Jesus. The words had opened the world up to a much larger place than he had known before. They had also opened up in my world, but I was not quite sure how much it had opened up to me as of yet.

Silas told the reverend how much he thanked him, but he also told us that we were different from the people that lived around them and that we should be truly careful. "Reverend, yous and Missr Adams stays safe on younz journeys 'cause dare ares some bad peoples everywhere. Dey live here, and we should stay clear of any men we might encounter on our way leaving this area!" Silas said excitedly. "Alabamy is still very upset 'cause we'z slaves were freeds by Missa Lincoln. Pleaze keep younselves safe. Dese peoples won'ts take kindly ta younz thinkin' we are brothas, Reverend."

"I assure you Mr. Silas, we will be fine and we have nothing to fear because I have faced many bad men in my time. We have God's protection, and it is more powerful than what the eye can see or an evil mind can create! "Yessir, I'z believe yous good, Reverend!" said Silas. Silas's wife gave us some homemade biscuits she had made that morning and some dried jerky. They were very good people. In my mind, I could not help but wonder why they were so friendly to us after the way the people around them had been treating them for years.

As we rode away, we looked back one last time and saw smiles on all Silas's families faces; that was a sight I would not soon forget.

After leaving the plantation, we rode about half a day's ride. It was nice to get an early start. The day was beautiful with just a few clouds in the sky. The reverend talked about the birds flying in the sky. He talked about how God created all the different trees. He talked about the many kinds of flowers and where he had seen them throughout his journeys in life so far. The reverend seemed to talk nonstop, or he would sing to keep from hearing silence. He told me of the dreams he had of having his own church. Me, I didn't mind his talking. The sound of the horses clomping along was all I really needed. It was soothing to me. His singing wasn't so bad either. By midafternoon, the sun had been beating down on us, and because it had been a while since I'd ridden a good distance, my hind end had fallen asleep. Maybe it was the rougher gait of my fast but not-so-smooth horse that was the problem. So when we came to a large field with plenty of grass for our horses to eat, I figured it was as good a time as any to hop down and take a break. After getting the horses settled, we decided to walk around and stretch our legs a bit.

"You know, Mr. Adams, that I was an assistant pastor at the last church for more than nine years, and I am truly looking forward to being the shepherd of my own flock. God being the head shepherd, of course." The reverend kept looking to the sky like he could see God's plans written up there. We are on our way to make that happen, Reverend. It may take a while to get there, but we will make it soon enough. The reverend turned toward me holding out an apple he plucked off a lone tree on the side of the field.

"If the Holy Spirit guides us on that path," he said. Frustrated, I threw my apple core across the field, asking, "What does that even mean? You said things like that before, about the Spirit leading us and if it's God's will. Are we supposed to go to El Paso or not? I would like to know what we are doing here if not going to El Paso?"

Pausing his steps, the reverend looked at me, answering, "Yes, Mr. Adams, we are, but as the Holy Spirit directed the Apostle Paul, he also directs our paths. Right or left, sometimes it's not the path we would take, but God knows best. If you or I are sensitive to His direction, then our path may differ from time to time."

I stopped to ponder this. "Well, Reverend, I'm not sure I understand, but you are paying the way so you and the Holy Spirit can lead the way. Just make sure it leads me to El Paso!"

"I know God has a better plan for me on the way to El Paso and yours as well, Mr. Adams. Tennessee was a wonderful place of growing, but I believe He has an even better plan for you and myself."

He was so sure of this calling, of growing his ministry, that I was convinced that this is what was supposed to happen. I thought again on how this preacher was different from any other man of God I had ever met. I compared him to my pa, who was a minister. This man had a true power of God in his life. He had a true love for people and not just the people like himself. I've never seen or even heard of a man like this one.

Turning toward some bushes across the field, I yelled, "Reverend, I have got to relieve myself. I'll be right back." As I was kneeling down to relieve myself and do my business, a snake came up from the stream nearby and thought it was a good idea to bite my left foot. The bite just broke the skin through the thick leather of my boot. The cottonmouth just grazed my foot with the edge of his fang. When I came limping back, the reverend insisted on looking at the bite. Once he took the boot off, I remembered the biscuits Silas's wife had given us. I instructed him to take one and put on the bite to suck the poison out. He wrapped it up with the biscuit up in the bandage, then he commenced to pray for me. I don't believe any of the poison got in the small scrape made from its teeth. I figured a little help from God would be welcome just in case.

As I lay there pondering about killing that snake, I decided to ask the reverend to get my Spencer rifle and make short work of that snake if it was still there.

"I have never shot a gun, Mr. Adams, and have no idea how to work a gun. I was the son of a pacifist minister who never owned a gun. My father died at such a young age."

"When I get up from resting a bit, Reverend, I am going to teach you how to shoot a gun because you never know when that skill may come in handy when you least expect it."

The reverend put his hand in mine and pulled to help me up. "I'm not sure, Mr. Adams, if I will need that particular skill."

I pondered his words for a bit and then replied, "It's better to have it and not need it than to need it and not have it, Reverend. Maybe you will need to hunt to survive one day, and that Spirit isn't around to provide."

"My God always provides for my needs, I assure you, but I am willing to learn to shoot just in case there may come a time when that skill may be needed." Placing his hand on his Bible, the reverend declared, "I will only trust the sword of the Spirit when it comes to my protection. God's protection never fails!"

As I started showing the reverend how to shoot, I realized the things I had been taught as a child were not what everyone else may have learned. He was taught about the goodness of the Lord, and I was taught how to take care of myself by learning to use a gun! I explained about the parts of a gun, how to hold it, and demonstrated how to shoot at some targets I set up that were made of some thick tree limbs that were decaying on the ground. The reverend's shooting wasn't as good as it should have been living in the environment we are living in, but he did okay. He was hitting one of three targets we were shooting at. With that task done, we hopped back in our saddles and headed back on our journey.

As we traveled, we crossed a large creek. I was concerned that the reverend was as good on a horse as he was with a gun. It was that thought that led to my concern while crossing this creek. "You alright there, Reverend?" I asked.

The reverend chuckled. "Why, yes, Mr. Adams. God's protection is all around us." I smiled.

"Thank God for that, Reverend, because you need it!" It turned out the reverend had no problems controlling his horse. In fact, he rode like he was born in the saddle.

Once we crossed the river, we came upon a young man who looked like he had been fishing. He had on a pair of overalls and was holding a pole with what looked like a string with a hook on the end. Next to him was sitting a tin cup with dirt and worms that were crawling and looked like they were trying to escape. We both looked at each other for a while before the reverend finally asked him where we were exactly.

The young man looked up and said, "My name is Henry Harrison, and you people are in the great Jefferson County."

I looked at him and patted my horse on the neck. "Do you mean like President Jefferson?"

Harrison nodded. "Why, yes, that's who we named this county after. They founded it in 1819 and named it after President Jefferson to make sure he would help if'n we ever needed help from Washington."

I looked ahead down the road. "Is there anywhere we could find a bite and a place to lay our heads for the night?"

Harrison pointed. "The Florence Motel, you can get a bite and a bed. There's always open rooms at that place. Bill Carpenter owns that place, and he will treat you right. He goes to church with Maw and Paw. We also have a really nice restaurant at the edge of town. Mayor Thompson owns it."

I thought for a moment about another day of not having to eat jerky and rations and finally answered, "We may visit if we can. The reverend and myself are just passing through."

Harrison's eyes widened as he looked toward the reverend. "Reverend? Oh, we have a couple of nice churches that would love for you to visit while you're here. The reverend at our church is saying how all are welcome in the house of God. Except, of course, Indians or pickers."

I was waiting for the reverend to explode on that statement, but he didn't; he held his peace for the moment but explained that he was sure we would be moving on and would not have time to visit this town after all! The young man's head swiveled back and forth between the reverend and me. He lowered his head and said in a confident tone, "Well, if you change your mind, we have a nice town if you want to visit sometime?"

I shook my head. "No, Henry, we'll be moving on. The reverend feels it would be best to continue on for now, but thanks for the offer."

Henry continued on not giving up. "We also have a nice funeral home that is always needing a preacher for those services. Plenty for a preacher to do."

"No," the reverend explained, almost growling at the young guy. "I think it's time we moved along. Thanks for the offer, Henry, but we really must be going."

I remembered a young man that I served with in the war was from Jefferson County. We served together for a few battles. I mentioned to the reverend that I would like to see if I could find him. "I believe he lives in the next town," I said. I could tell the reverend was still pretty upset over the blacks and redskins not being welcomed at the church. But as always, he never spoke out how he really felt about the way people thought. He kept silent after I asked him about finding my friend. "If that Henry kid upset you that much, why did you not say anything to him?"

"There's a place and a time for everything, Mr. Adams, and that kid was not ready for the truth!" We rode in silence once again, but my mind just wouldn't leave it alone.

"The truth is, Reverend, I just think maybe I see things the way these people see them, and it is confusing to me when you called that picker your brother and think that he is the same as us white people!"

Since we were still quite a ways from town, the reverend stopped his horse and looked at me sternly. "Mr. Adams, I would have thought you, being a lawman, would see that all men are created equal, especially in the eyes of God."

I thought for a minute and then huffed out, "Maybe, Reverend, in the eyes of God but not in the eyes of man!"

The reverend turned his horse and began the ride again. "When God formed man, He made them after His image, and all men are made in the image of our Lord God!

Mr. Adams, how can a man be unequal if we all bleed the same blood and breathe the same air?"

Now the reverend started to sound a bit angry. I hurried to catch up to him, as he was moving a little faster now. I thought his horse was reacting to his angry tone. I patted my horse's neck and replied, "Reverend, all horses are not the same. You have just ole work horses and then you have thoroughbreds!"

"Yes, Mr. Adams, you do and you also have kings in Africa and poppers in America, but both are still equal in God's eyes! God will reign over all men, evil or good. If He did not reign over everyone, people who think they are superior to others would receive no consequences at all for their actions. Our Founding Fathers came to this country to escape tyranny, and they brought it with them in the form of slavery! It wasn't right in England, and it is not right in America! Aren't we all slaves to something? When God opened my eyes to the bondage I was in, I realized

I was a slave to Satan and in his control. Now, Brother Adams, the Bible says He whom the Son sets free is free indeed! My chains are gone, and no man or no one can put me back into bondage except myself. You are also in bondage, Mr. Adams. Only you and my Savior can set you free from the way the enemy is keeping you in his custody and unchain you from your bonds!"

As the reverend spoke, I could feel that what he was saying was true. It was a feeling where I felt God's love was so strong I felt like weeping. It felt the same as I did in the jail back in Chattanooga when Jameson made a decision that changed his life over! I was not ready for that...so I changed the subject.

"Like I was saying, Reverend, I have an old friend in the next town and I would like to see if I can find him. If it's alright with you?" I kept my eyes on the road, not wanting to look anywhere else. I could feel the reverend studying me as we continued to ride. Out of the corner of my eye, I saw him lift his head toward the heavens, then slowly lower it back down until he was watching me again. "Mr. Adams, you are a hard man, but the Holy Spirit continues to call on you. Yes, if you would like to visit your friend whom you served with at Chickamauga, we can. Let's go ask around and see if we can find him.

Chapter 3

We continued riding till we came to the small town of Jefferson. We managed to avoid the young man and the church members he had spoken to us about. We rode straight to the local market and began asking about the man I served with, William Morris, and his wife, Arabella. The first person we asked did know them and gave us directions on how to get to where they lived. I knew his wife Arabella's name because he never stopped talking about her and how they both were from here. The entire time we served under Captain Forest in our regiments, that was all he ever talked about.

Their house was located on the outskirts of town. It was a quaint little home with a small white picket fence in the front yard and a vegetable garden out back. When we arrived, we tied our horses at the hitch outside the fence and knocked on the door. When Morris came to the door, I had to remind him of who I was. It didn't take much for him to immediately remember!

"Elijah Adams! How are you doing? It is good to see you, my friend!" I was practically tackled into a bear hug, then he punched me in the arm for good measure. "I had wondered what had happened to you after the war. You salty cus! Looks like both of our sorry hides escaped without injury that the eye could see. A little bit older but intact."

I awkwardly patted him on the back while slightly pushing him away and taking a small step back. "Not much of a hugger there, William."

William laughed. "You were as rough as ole Forest, and I guess you still are there, Adams. But it is still good to see you! He looked the reverend up and down. Who you got with you?" He took a step back. "You look like a preacher."

"Yes," the reverend said as he stepped up to shake William Morris's hand. "Mr. Adams and myself are traveling companions. I'm Reverend John Williams. The reverend gestured with his arm toward the property. You have a beautiful home, sir."

William shook his hand. "You haven't seen beauty until you see my wife, Arabella. Well, if you're a friend of Elijah's, you're welcome here, preacher."

Morris shouted into the house for his wife to come meet an old friend. Once she arrived, she slid in beside her husband, and he slid his arm around her waist. "This is my lovely wife, Arabella, and this little man is Robert William Morris, after my father. Arabella just gave birth to him a few months ago. "Arabella was as pretty as she was sweet. When she walked into the room, it seemed to light up even brighter.

"Very nice to make your acquaintance, ma'am. I am Reverend Williams."

"And I am Elijah Adams." We both spoke up at the same time.

She snuggled closer to William and pulled the baby a bit closer. In a sweet voice, she answered, "Very nice to meet you two gentlemen."

We both tipped our hats. "Thank you, ma'am."

Arabella invited us to stay for supper. "We don't have many opportunities to entertain, especially old friends of Williams. I hope you would consider it?"

The reverend lit up. "Thank you, sister, it isn't that often on our journey that we will have an opportunity for the offer you have extended. As long as it's alright with Mr. Adams…" He turned toward me, and I nodded. "We accept!"

"I have no objections and I would be an idiot to pass on a good meal in the presence of a fine lady like you. I feel like I already know you by the way your husband spoke about you and your beauty the entire time I served with him at Chickamauga."

The reverend and Mrs. Morris were enjoying sharing stories from the Bible. Apparently, she had been a Christian from the time she was a little girl. William and I were not quite as comfortable with those subjects. After supper, we indulged in a very good piece of apple pie, which was my favorite. When Mrs. Morris had come back to the table from laying the baby down for the night, she asked if we would like tea or coffee with our pie. William offered something a little stronger. The reverend and I just accepted the coffee.

After coffee, we sat and talked about local things here in Jefferson.

The reverend asked of the churches in the town. Arabella brightened, "We have attended the Methodist Church from the time I was a girl. The only exception was during the war when the Union Army used it as a command post. Then we met in our bishop's home for a couple of years. We are actually a little worried about a little sect of people that have drawn some weak-minded fools into their fold—a cult, if you ask me, not a church."

Mr. Morris took over. "That preacher, Mr. James, was quite a smooth talker. He got people believing he was the second coming of Jesus. He is very persuasive but also very dangerous. We have Jesus, we don't need another messiah! His ways are making a lot of people around here very upset, and I'm not sure what's going to happen. I hope he's not on the losing end of a rope. Right, Reverend?"

"Yes, sir, Mr. Morris. I do hope they get it resolved peacefully!"

Mrs. Morris asked if the reverend knew how to play the piano. "Yes, ma'am, I do, and I noticed your piano in the sitting area."

"Would you sing and play for us, Reverend?" She jumped up and began to head over to the piano to clear off and pull out the bench.

"Yes, ma'am, I would be honored to praise the Lord with you. Does everyone know 'I'll Fly Away'?" he asked as he sat down to play.

I looked to William and decided to accept something stronger after all. So we retired to the front porch for a cigarette and a drink—with Arabella's permission, of course.

I could hear the reverend and Arabella singing, "I'll fly away, oh glory…" We reminisced of the happenings during the battles we fought and the things that happened since.

After taking a long toke on his cigarette, William began to watch me. "Elijah, who is this reverend, and why are you traveling with him? He is not the kind of person you and I would have chosen to travel with when I knew you before."

I took a toke of my own cigarette and blew it toward the night sky. "I'm not sure if I had anything to do with this partnership. Not sure if it didn't come from higher up than us." I casually leaned up against the doorframe and tried to get comfortable. "Let me ask your opinion about something, William? The reverend thinks that these pickers and redskins are no different than the white man, and he actually calls them brother. He is convinced they were made exactly the same as we are. Have you ever heard of anything like that?"

William slowly shook his head. "No, I can't say I had ever heard that before. Not that it has ever come up in conversation. But in my thinking, I can't believe that! How could we have fought to keep them as slaves! Or at least we were fighting to keep our rights to own slaves."

As I was listening to William speak of how the war was about the slave issue and slaves were no more than animals, something inside of me reared up and made me very angry with this conversation. "I never fought for slavery, for or against! This was an issue of our rights and the government not being able to dictate to us that we should or shouldn't be paying higher taxes. If we didn't pay, we would have our property taken away! Men are men and animals are animals! If that was not so, men could breed with animals and the like! Common sense tells us that!"

William had come out of his relaxed stance and now had his hands up in a "see, I'm safe" gesture. "Okay, Adams, calm down. I was just making an observation. Apparently, you have strong feelings about this issue…"

I took a calming toke of my cigarette and blew it out. "No, I don't. I just… Well, sorry, Morris. I guess that preacher is starting to rub off on me."

William looked inside the house through the front window and watched his wife. "He is having quite an impact on my missus as well. They seem to be having a pretty good ol' time singing those hymns. Do you want to join them?"

"No, let's stay out here and have another drink before his preaching and singing makes me cry or worse! Why don't you show me around your property so we can get away from that singing!"

"Getting to you, Adams?"

"No, I just need a break. I'm just traveling with the preacher back to El Paso because he needed traveling protection, and I need to go back home because my parents still live there. You know, he is different from any man I have ever met in my life." I looked William in the eye and confessed, "Maybe I am the one in need of getting protection?"

"Yes, he is, I could tell that from the first meeting. Well, Adams, I guess we all have our cross to bear."

We walked off the porch and headed off toward the side of the house to start the tour. He pointed out the land he owned and his wife's garden. We kept walking toward the chicken coop and the small barn that housed his two horses and a couple of milking cows. A little farther was his smokehouse. "This preacher needs to learn a lot more about survival than carrying a Bible," I say. "I'm afraid he may learn the hard way. He can't even shoot a gun. I'm trying to teach him, and he's trying to teach me how to pray. He is a strong man of prayer!"

"I hope it all works out for you guys, Elijah. I hope you make it to El Paso with little or no problems. There are a lot of ruffians around these parts and many troubled souls. They may make life tough on the people they don't care for, like the pickers your reverend cares so much for. This and the next county over is known for the ravel that I'm talking about. As you ride on, just be aware of whom you come in contact with or just stay clear of anyone if you can." William paused then continued, "There is a man with a fleabit horse, stay clear of him! He looks for trouble everywhere he goes. He usually travels anywhere from here to the Tuscaloosa area. That's the next county over. Just be careful, my friend."

"I do appreciate it, Morris. I will keep us safe. I was a sheriff in El Paso and a deputy sheriff in Chattanooga. I think I can take care of myself." I was nodding my head, feeling confident in myself and my training.

"We survived the war, and a lot of our friends didn't. But just be safe and cautious, Elijah! I will be praying everything will be fine for the rest of your journey."

I scoffed, "With this preacher, I think we will be better than fine. We will be blessed!"

"I will have my missus to pack you some provisions for on your way," he said.

"Thanks, Morris, but we have about everything we need."

"I have some nice salt back venison wrapped in cheese paper. I killed it last winter around January, and man, it is some really good meat."

"Thanks, Morris, that'll be fine and appreciated!" As we walked back into the house, the reverend was just finishing his last hymn. William walked over to his wife like he hadn't seen her in years. He put his arm around her and kissed the top of her head. Smiling down, he reached out and pulled his son into his arms. "Well, Mrs. Morris, would you mind packing these two gentlemen some of our venison jerky for their trip?"

She smiled at him and then turned toward the kitchen, saying, "I would love to. I will wrap it up in a flower bag for you fine men."

As we turned to leave, William shook our hands, and Arabella also bowed and shook our hands. She said, "Thank you for coming by. We don't get to entertain much, and to be serenaded with your songs was so wonderful. It was very special to have company today."

"I'm sorry but we must be getting along and can't stay any longer. We could have had a regular Bible study if we had just a little more time or a camp meeting!"

"That would have been nice. But your hymns were just what this girl needed."

We said our goodbyes, and the reverend prayed once more for the whole family. As I packed my saddlebag with the meat and made sure my saddle was on tight, I looked over the saddle to take one last look at how a happy family was supposed to look like. The reverend struggled getting on his horse, as he always did because of his stature. When he gained his balance in his mount, we both waved and turned and rode off. Reverend kept looking over his shoulder as if he was continuing to pray for them with every look!

We left the township and made our way onto the trail. The reverend said, "I have a strong feeling about that child and those good people. The child will be a strong man of God someday."

"Never know, Reverend, what life holds for them. General Lee was a baby once! Who would have known he would grow to be one of the greatest generals that he was, or Lincoln to be the tyrant he was? Everyone is a baby at one time, I guess."

As we rode along, the reverend had no problem keeping up the conversation.

We made our way upon the individual Morris warned me about—the man on the fleabit and two others with him. We rode by, and the reverend said, "Good afternoon, gentlemen!" There was no response from the three; they just stared at us. I kept my eyes on them, making sure nothing was going to happen!

We were not sure what was going on with these fools. We continued to ride, and they never moved. We could see them talking among themselves. I kept my hand on my colt just in case! As we rode out of sight of these three men, we rode the way they had just been. Farther down the road, we came upon an Indian girl. She was sitting on the side of the road, crying. She had been roughed up. She had bruises on the side of her face, and her clothes were torn. We climbed off our horses, and the reverend asked, "Are you okay?" She would not speak. The reverend tried to talk to her to find out what happened, but she just sat there staring off into the sky. When he approached her, she stepped back quickly and started to scream! He backed off, still talking with his gentle and kind voice. Eventually, he was able to comfort her with his gentle spirit and kind touch, assuring her he would not hurt her. He prayed for her and wiped her tears away with his bandana very caringly. She was very loud! As we were trying to calm her down, those three men had turned around and rode up.

They knew when we passed them earlier we would be coming upon this young girl. When they got close, the older man of the three that was riding the fleabit climbed off his horse. I noticed he was the biggest of the three. He was over six feet and as heavy as he was tall. He walked straight up to the reverend and pushed him away from the girl.

"What have you to do with this stinking redskin?" The reverend stepped back a foot and I stepped around him and said, "What's it any of your business, mister, what we are doing with her? We should be asking you the same question!"

"Well, I'll tell you," he said as his partners stepped up beside him. All three had slipped off their horses and stood shoulder to shoulder.

The reverend stood in front of the girl, who was shaking now in the presence of these three men. Apparently, they were the ones that had hurt her, so I was squared off against all three. The one thing I've learned is never show fear when you are outnumbered!

We stood about six feet apart, and the other two men looked scrawny but rough and scared. They stood back about a foot behind the bigger, older man. All three looked like they had not had a bath in about a month. The older man had a full black beard with gray on the tips. One young guy looked about twenty or so. The other man looked about thirty and apparently smarter. He was stepping back just slightly. He was the most cautious of the three. I don't think he wanted any trouble. He kept saying, "Let's just go," repeating it to himself a few times. The bigger man thought he could throw his weight around. He stepped forward toward me, causing me to draw my colt rather swiftly. "You step back before someone gets hurt. We are trying to help this girl, and she is scared of you three."

"She's a dirty redskin, a Creek Indian that lives downriver from here. We passed her earlier and she wouldn't talk or get friendly or anything with the boys and myself." He sneered.

"Guess that's why she is shaking in your presence. If you three didn't do anything to her, then why is this little girl so afraid of you right now? You three are the lowest of the low for white men. You look down on Indians, then you try to take advantage of them at the same time. You disgust me! If the reverend can get her to talk, I will take you to jail right now!" I stood my ground and stared them straight in the eyes.

"She won't talk, I've been trying to get her to," said the reverend in a quiet, calm voice. "I think she understands she will be okay with us, Mr. Adams."

"Take us to jail over a dirty Indian. Good luck with that, you carpetbagger!" They climbed back on their horses and said, "This isn't over. I'll see you again and I may be the one holding the gun then! We live here, and I'm not sure who you think you are. You're strangers here, and we have lived here and do whatever we want and to whomever we want. You and that dirty Indian need to be moving on. Not us!"

"I think it's best if you cowboys move on, and there won't be any trouble." Tension was thick in the air. The reverend stepped forward and put his hand in the air. "Peace, gentlemen, we can do this without any trouble."

As the cowboys turned to ride away, he pointed a finger at the young girl. "You keep your mouth shut, little girl, if you know what is good for you!"

I stepped between the reverend and the girl and pointed my finger right at the older cowboy and suggested, "We can settle this here and now, or you trash could ride away, and I mean right now!" He put his hand on his gun, and I stepped forward another foot and pulled my gun up, aiming right at the face of the older man. "I've seen your type my whole life, you're a coward and you think your size allows you to push people around. I'm not to be pushed around by the likes of you. This gun will whittle you down! I'm not afraid of you or your boys! Skin it and let's play. Come on, pull it!"

"I will see you again, and you strangers aren't welcome here! Take your redskin and don't come back, or you'll pay!"

"Just remember, when you're entertaining strangers, you never know who you're messing with! Cowboys!" I yelled. One of the two younger men grabbed the older man by the arm and said, "Let's just go before we can't." And with that, they rode away. Looking back, the older man was truly angry and rode away reluctantly at best. The younger man rode ahead of the other two. The other man stayed right beside the older man to make sure he could control him or at least back him up, if needed.

As they rode away, the young girl began to calm down. The reverend asked if she had family near and if we could take her anywhere. She just pointed to the west. So we rode in the direction she was pointing.

We followed the nearby stream, which led us to the Tuscaloosa area, or so we thought. We came up on a small band of tents and makeshift shelters, where Creek Indians stood looking as we rode into the small encampment.

As we came closer to the Indians, they started speaking their Indian language.

I asked the reverend, "Do you speak Creek?"

"That's Muskegon, I believe," said the reverend. "And I don't have a clue as to what they are saying. I do speak a little Cherokee, but Creek is far different. Not sure why they are here, their reservation is farther south. I will find out why they are here." We dismounted our horses, and the reverend raised his right hand and asked, "Does anyone speak English?"

An older Indian spoke up and said, "Me! Speak white man language! Why does the young girl look hurt?"

"We found her and brought her to you to keep her safe. She won't talk to us, she just points. So we followed her lead here. Maybe she will tell you what happened, she won't talk to us."

He nodded his head and said, "We! Take care of the girl! We were hunting when she got separated from the hunting party! She was by the stream when she was not with us anymore!"

"We found her on the side of the trail, and she was hurt and crying. Three white men were there, but we aren't sure what happened, and she won't talk. These were bad men, and we think they hurt her, but we could not be sure. We are willing to help, if you would like, in some way?"

"We need no help from white man! They have done enough to the Creek nation. We move on now, we traveled to north fort to speak to your great leaders. Now we return home! I no longer need any lies from white men!" He turned and joined the others.

We had no choice but to ride on; the leader of the twelve did not want our help. Besides that, she was in good hands. Twelve is better than one gunman and a preacher, in my opinion, even if there were women and children. They also had a few capable men with them. At least they were headed back to the reservation, and they would be safe there.

As we traveled, I could hear the reverend praying for their safety and the well-being of that little Indian girl. He prayed for the souls of these savages? I was always told savages had no souls. The more he prayed, the more it did seem to me that she was just a little girl who was as scared as any other girl would have been in that situation. Redskin, black, or white—I guess all people do feel the same emotions and must have souls as the reverend believes.

We came upon the town of Tuscaloosa. It seemed to be pretty civil. We could see a church as we rode into town, a nice restaurant, and a motel freshly painted. Most of the people nodded their heads. They seemed friendly to us, people of all colors and persuasions on the streets of dust and mud.

We made our way toward the restaurant to grab a bite to eat. "I need to see the sheriff before we settle down, Reverend. Let's see if he knows anything about those three cowboys that hurt that little girl."

"Yes, I think that would be a good idea, Mr. Adams. Maybe they are wanted, and the sheriff may need help finding them!"

We passed shops and taverns and stores with people moving back and forth. Quite a busy little town. We arrived at the sheriff's office. We tried the handle, and it opened to the sheriff sitting behind his desk with his feet propped up on top of it as he read the local paper. He was a rather large man with gray on the tips of his sideburns and mustache.

"Hello, sheriff. I'm Mr. Adams, and this is my partner, Reverend Williams," I said as we walked in, and we shook hands. "Good to meet you. I'm Sheriff Dempsey. What can I do for you?"

I took a seat in the chair on the other side of his desk and leaned back, and the reverend went to stand beside the window. "We were passing through on the way to El Paso, and we came upon three bad men just on this side of the county line, and they had apparently roughed up a little Indian girl out there. She couldn't have been more than fourteen or fifteen. But she was pretty shaken up when she was in their presence. One man was older, and he had a young guy and a slightly older man with him. The older man was riding a fleabit mare, and he seemed to be in charge."

"Yeah, Mr. Adams, those three are the Gall family. They think they run this town, and it has landed the older man in jail a few times. James Gall, he was mayor here once until he was put out for corruption. The younger man is his son, and the middle-aged man is his nephew. He is usually the nervous kind. I don't think he would do anything like hurt that girl. The Gall family don't like anyone, especially blacks or Indians. But that younger man would do anything his father told him to do, including hurting a girl. Just out of meanness, I'm sure. They are bad people, and you should tumbleweed away from them if you see them again."

"Not to worry about that, sheriff, we can take care of ourselves. I was a sheriff also in El Paso before the war. I've dealt with those kinds before."

"If you come upon them again, just let me know, and I will take care of them, Mr. Adams and Reverend."

"Well, what about what they have already done to the girl?"

"Did she tell you what happened, or did you witness anything? If not, there is nothing I can do about it, right, Mr. Adams?"

"Yes, he is correct, Reverend."

"Did that family of Indians you met say why they were here?"

"The leader said they were there to see someone about a business matter at North Fort. After that, they were hunting on their way back home when she got separated."

"Those Creek Indians were here long before we were. They are completely different than we are, even in the way they speak. In the Muskegon language, the men speak more direct, tougher than the women, and the women speak softer. Some of them stayed around even though they were moved to the reservation in Atwell on the southeast territory. They sometimes travel to see relatives in this area or have business with the Cherokee Nation farther south. Stay clear of them too. The redskins can be true savages even to their own kind. They have their own tribal laws that we could never understand. What we white men have done to them, they do not trust us!"

"Everyone has a right not to like the pickers or the redskins, but no one has the right to abuse them, not while I'm sheriff. But unless I can prove something, I'm not sure what I can do in this situation."

"You're the right sheriff, and since you're a God-fearing man and a good man, I believe you will do your best to bring these men to justice if you can!"

"Thank you, Reverend, I do try to be and fail at it quite a bit. It has nothing to do with being good. It's the law, and this badge says I will keep the peace and the law, and that's exactly what I plan on doing! As long as anyone coming into this region keeps the peace, we can get along, and the citizens of this town will have no issues with them."

"Thank you for that, sheriff, and we will be praying for you."

"Well, as long as you are here, make yourselves at home. Stay as long as you would like, and I wish you Godspeed and good journey to you on your way to El Paso."

"We saw a restaurant as we came into town. Claire's. Pretty good food there?"

"Pretty good, I would say, for this town. Peaceful and quiet most of the time. You should enjoy a good meal there. The cook's name is Sam, tell him your friends of mine, and he will give you the fresh food." He laughed. "Well, Mr. Adams, Reverend Williams, it's been a pleasure to meet you both, but I have business I've got to take care of. Have a good day, gentlemen." He stood up and leaned forward to shake our hands.

"Sheriff Dempsey, thank you for your help, and if we are this way again, we will stop and see you."

"Do that, Mr. Adams, Reverend." He nodded his head, and we headed out the door.

We rode to the restaurant on the other side of town. It wasn't anything fancy, just a few tables and chairs inside and a kitchen. We sat down, and a middle-aged man with a large apron came out of the kitchen. He welcomed us to "Claire's" and told us what was cooking for the day. We ordered the roast beef with a side of corn and potatoes and glasses of sweet tea. Before he left, I asked him if he was Sam. He looked at us and asked, "Who wants to know?" I told him that Sheriff Dempsey sent us over. He paused for a minute and then threw his head back with a belly laugh so hard his whole body shook. He slapped his legs with his hands and headed off toward the kitchen, saying, "I guess I have to serve you the fresh stuff!"

A while later, he brought us our food. It looked and smelled delicious. He set our food down and asked if he could join us. "It's a bit slow today," he said. The reverend and I both nodded and then took our hats off, and he led us in a prayer over the food, the ones who prepared it, and a blessing on the establishment. We introduced ourselves to Sam and began to eat. We told him about our journey so far, and he told us how he and his wife had bought this place from a man who named it after his wife, Claire. Eventually, they decided to retire and go live near their kids, so they sold it to them for almost nothing.

When the meal was finished, Sam asked us if we had a place to stay for the night. He informed us that they rented rooms upstairs, and since it was slow season, they would give them to us at a reduced rate. We accepted the offer, and Sam got up and yelled for his wife. She was a thin woman with dark hair and a smile for Sam that made you wish you had someone looking at you that way.

"I've offered these men a couple rooms for the night. Will you run up and make sure they are ready?" he asked her.

She nodded her head, looked toward us, and headed out of the room, saying, "I am Sarah. Your rooms will be ready shortly. In the morning, breakfast starts at five. It's included in the cost, so just come on down. We thanked them both, and I decided to go outside for a smoke before heading up. So I left the reverend inside, talking to Sam, and headed to put our horses up for the night in the stable out back and enjoy the cool evening with a hand rolled from my pocket. Once I was done, I met the reverend at the bottom of the stairs, and we headed up to our room for the night.

After we checked out early in the morning, just after the sun was peeking, we gathered our horses and rode out. We got about three miles out of town when we heard gunfire. I spurred my horse forward and rode to see what was happening. We rode around a curve in the path and came upon those cowboys we had confrontation with earlier. The Gall family. The older man was standing upright but slumped over with blood running down his neck and his left hand holding a cut on his right arm.

He was cut on the face as well. The two other men were lying on the ground beside him. The youngest man was scalped. The full top of the skull was exposed. It seemed those Indians found them in the night first. The other man was face down and no Indians to be found now! When we arrived, I shouted, "Gall, don't shoot! We are the men you ran into earlier. Can we get you some help? What happened?"

"These savages attacked us while we were asleep. They killed Jed and Jesse, poor Jesse! They scalped him and cut Jed's throat. I thought I saw movement and started shooting just before you showed up." He was shouting now, hysterical with grief and anger, still holding his arm.

"We heard you shooting and came as quickly as we could. What would make the Indians attack you?"

"Jesse hurt that redskin girl yesterday, but Jed and I did nothing but fun with the dirty savage. It was just an Indian. They had no right to kill us like this. For having fun with that dirty savage!"

"I don't think the Creek people saw it as innocent like you did. After all, she was just a little girl. Fourteen or fifteen?" the reverend said with the start of anger in his voice.

"Reverend, you're wrong. She and they are just dirty stinking redskins, and we have a right to beat or even kill them if we see fit to! They are no different than a dog. They shouldn't be here with the white man," the man spit out.

"Well, those so-called dogs apparently bit you and the other two. Guess if you make a dog mad enough, you get bit! They are men, the same as we are, and the white man came and drove them to a reservation. Right or wrong, it's not my place to say. But they were here before we even came to this country! If anyone has rights, it should be them, not us, Gall. They were here hundreds of years before the whites!" the reverend said sternly but with much less anger and a little bit of calmness in his voice.

"Who's going to bring my son or nephew back? Who's going to pay them back for my people?" he yelled in anguish.

"Apparently, if you had left the girl alone this would not have happened!"

"Gall, we need to get you back to the town, and we will help you bury your dead. Your neck and arm are pretty bad, so we need to get you to town to see a doctor." I approached him to help him up as the reverend went to get some shovels so we could bury the dead.

"I am swimmy-headed right now. But I don't need any help from dirty redskin lovers like you two. I will bury my own, and you, too, can burn in Hades along with those savages!"

"Please, Mr. Gall, let us help you to bury them and get you to a doctor!? I would like to give them a proper burial and prayer for the departed," the reverend pleaded.

"Fine, Reverend, if you need to satisfy your God!" he sneered.

From the rain we had had lately, the ground was soft, and the digging didn't take very long. As the reverend began to pray, he said, "Ashes to ashes and dust to dust. Have mercy on their souls. I also ask that you forgive those who trespassed against these two men. Please be with Mr. Gall and help him to find forgiveness in his heart for these people that chose vengeance on these two men. The Indians knew not what they were doing, just acting on their—"

Gall broke in and said, "I won't stand here as you pray forgiveness for them dirty savages! And if you do it again, you will be joining my son in that hole! Hades is not good enough for the likes of those stinking Indians! If I catch them, they will die!" He was so mad his face took on the appearance of hellfire itself.

"Mr. Gall you have to try to find peace in your heart for those whom you hate, or you may never find peace at all."

"Redskins and pickers are all the same and need to be killed, put out of this country, or something to that effect. This is our country now. The only good colored is a dead one!" He was shouting now so angrily I thought with his wounds he might pass out at any moment.

"Mr. Gall, if you call upon Christ, He will help you find forgiveness. He can change your heart."

"This ain't no church service, Reverend, and I don't want to hear your preaching! Now go about your business, and I will do the same!" He stomped over to his horse and painfully pulled himself into the saddle. "I will report this to the sheriff when I get back to town. I know who it was and what the law won't bring back, but I will find them one day, and those dirty savages will pay!" As he rode away, he kept rambling on.

The reverend continued to offer to go with him to get him help. Gall would have nothing to do with it. The reverend was adamant about praying for Gall and him to find it in his heart to forgive those whom he hated. That God would touch his soul and change him.

"You know, Reverend, sometimes men won't change, and there is no hope for some men. I know God can change anyone, or that's what I was always told, but some men are just hard and cold. That Gall is a very hard man. Don't see him changing anytime soon, since the Civil War men's hearts have gotten harder."

The reverend and I finished filling the graves and mounted our horses so we could get back on the trail. As we traveled, the reverend kept praying for the situation and for our journey. "Mr. Adams, people all over this world are hard, but my God is the heart changer! He is a mighty God. He created everything and He can change the hardest of hearts if we just listen and learn from His Word."

Chapter 4

We traveled on until nightfall where we made camp beside a creek. We made sure to keep our eyes open for all comers, friend, or foe. After seeing what had happened to those cowboys, we were not sure if the Creek Indians were all friendly. They may mistakenly think we had something to do with what had taken place. I was keeping a hand on my colt every time I heard a noise, just being precautious. The reverend was starting a fire for the evening meal and singing as he did most of the time, one hymn after another. I started unsaddling our horses as he prepared the meal—biscuits and beans again tonight. The biscuits were kept from Mr. Silas's wife back on the plantation.

Thank God it was a dry night. The rain came a lot, just not tonight! We would lay an old canvas over tree limbs to keep us out of the rain but never dry. We made do with what we had. I learned all this from my dad, who would take me camping when I was a boy.

The reverend kept at me to read the Bible every time we camped. I continued to try to convince him to learn to shoot. The Spencer rifle was ready and accurate. The next night, I shot a rabbit and butchered it as he started cooking, and that made a great main course for our supper. The shot startled the reverend and the horses.

"Well worth the spook," I said as he jumped. "Right, Reverend?"

"You could have warned me, Mr. Adams!"

"No time, it would have run off if I had not shot when I did."

He carried a few spices in his saddlebags. That made the food seem a lot better. After eating I tried to persuade the reverend to learn to shoot. He was pretty adamant not to. I reminded him that there are dangerous animals out there and that if I am on the verge of being attacked by a second bear because the first one was on top of me, he had better know how to aim when the time comes. So just before we lost light, he gave in and tried.

He was able to hit the bean can with the rifle at about twenty-five paces. "Good shooting there, Reverend. Now you are ready to learn the six-shooter?"

"No, sir. Mr. Adams, I'll let you keep that to yourself, and I will stick with the rifle. For protection only."

"Fair enough, Reverend." I pulled my forty-five out and reshot the bean can that was lying on the ground.

"That was fast and accurate, Mr. Adams. How long have you been perfecting that for years?"

"Yes, Reverend, more than twenty to be correct."

The reverend sat down, set the gun aside, and grabbed up his saddlebag. Opening it up, he took out his

Bible and turned to face me, holding it up about shoulder height. "I have this sword. More than twenty years of practice, and I hope mine has the same impact as yours does, Mr. Adams. Both are permanent and can affect a man's afterlife!"

I turned and headed toward where I was going to rest for the night. "I think you may be right, Reverend. "Let's try shooting again in the morning, Reverend? Maybe you can kill our breakfast?"

The next morning, we set a few pinecones upon a boulder and moved out to about fifty paces. It seemed to be more than enough. Three shots at this distance for him to hit the first cone. The second shot he took was a dead hit and the third the same. I set them back up, and we stepped back ten more paces. He also hit everything from there also. We made it up to about a hundred paces. He again hit what he was aiming at. "I think you got it, Reverend, at least to one hundred paces."

"Good because my ears are ringing, and my shoulder is stinging!"

I had to laugh because I had not warned him of the kick of that Spencer. "Sorry, Reverend, I should have warned you about that. Everyone feels that after so many shots, even older shooters like myself! I think you will do alright when or if the time comes."

"Only for food or self-defense in case of animal attacks," the reverend said in a no-nonsense voice.

"I understand, Reverend, that it's hard to save a life if you may one day need to take one."

"God forbid that day ever come, Mr. Adams!" he said with true conviction and passion! A true man of God who prayed over every meal and occasion, he prayed for all the people we had met, including Mr. Gall. Every evening, he would pray for our protection and guidance. Many times I think he spoke more to God than he did to me.

I asked him what he meant by guidance when we knew the path we were already taking.

"Mr. Adams, remember when I could not take the train? It wasn't for any other reason than being led by the Holy Spirit to ride these trails and meet or help those whom we met along the way."

"Did you not think we would meet people on the train?" I asked.

"It was clear we would have, but we would not have met Mr. Silas and his wonderful family. What about the Creek people and how much that little girl needed us when we found her and got her to her people?"

"Yes, Reverend, I can see your point!" I thought to myself, since starting this journey, I had never viewed pickers and redskins as people. My views of things are different now than I had thought of them in the past, especially that little squall having that same look in her eyes as many of the little white girls did in those towns we would come into that had just been raided and burnt by marauders during the war. No difference, just scared!

As we traveled on, the reverend would speak of the moving of the Holy Spirit, the changing of lives, and the healing of the sick. When he would tell these stories or read scripture, I could feel a burning inside of myself. Sometimes, even in the wide open, it would feel like the area was completely full of the presence of God! When I would ask him about that, he would say, "Read Acts two, and I would understand." One of these days, I am going to do that. I believe I had felt that when I was a child in church with my parents. Unless you experience it, you could never know what it feels like or even if it is real.

"Well, Reverend, we will need those prayers. We do have a long trip ahead of us and it won't be easy."

"God has our protection, and I will trust He will keep us safe through this journey we are on.

We traveled through rolling wheat fields and other fields of crops. Some of them were wild and others planted. We stayed on the main trail as much as we could, letting the horses eat while we traveled, and they drank from the waterways when we would cross.

It rained the next day, so we made camp beside a small river. I put up a shelter to help keep our fire going as the reverend unsaddled the horses. We settled down for a wet evening. It was about midnight. This allowed us to get a little more comfortable and sleep a little before daylight peeked over the ridges all around us.

As the reverend and I made our way to the river to clean up the next morning, we came upon some young men fishing. The reverend raised his hand in greeting, asking, "Good morning, boys. How's the fishing this morning?"

They responded that they had caught a few. Trying to find out where we were, we asked, "What would this place be called, son?" The boys looked up, and the one on the left pointed, saying, "Pickens County and Pickensville are just over that rise. This is the Tombigbee River, sir. Not much here except fishing and peoples in the town. All the people get their water from this river and some mighty tasty fishes!"

"You have many beautiful prairies here, son, and many crops also."

"Those are owned by the Yeoman farmers. They have been here for a long time. Even after the slaves left, they still keep on. Once the Union soldiers showed up, they told them slaves if they were mean to them, they could leave and they did just that! My daddy says since President Lincoln was killed, those slaves will be coming back. President Johnson is going to turn it all back the way it was before the war."

"Young man, it is illegal to have slaves now, and they will not be made to return unless they want to. It was never right to keep men in bondage of the flesh or the soul! Slavery will never return to this country. Too many people have died for this cause. Men have fought against slavery for longer than the civil war! President Lincoln was ordained by God to free the slaves." I knew the reverend had to be upset about what was being said, but looking at and listening to him, you wouldn't know it. He spoke in that calm voice of his.

"My daddy says differently! He said everything was the way it should have been. We did alright here in this county till they took our slaves away. Now all we do is struggle. These Yeoman farmers seem to be doing better than most. Daddy says they are thriving, whatever that means. The family has been in this town from the founding of this country, and we are going to leave."

The reverend looking at him asked, "Young man, do you go to church around here?"

"No, sir, we have a church right down the road from us. But my daddy says that church stuff is for people to find something more than what they already have." The man stood tall and proud of what he was saying.

"Your daddy was right in a way, but all men need God just because we all need more than what we have. Look at the water and this land. Even those fish you are holding in your hands, even you and I had to come from somewhere! Nothing just appears from nowhere. Someone or something had to create the world. If we can't put our faith in this world being created, then how can we put our faith in even the ground we stand on?"

"Well, preacher, my daddy says—"

The reverend cut him off. "Young man, have you ever thought that your daddy might be wrong and our God right? Is it better to believe in our parents? People are blinded by our hate for other people. Think of things people truly understand."

The young men looked confused by the talk of this reverend. "Daddy says you don't see God and you see him. How do you know there is a God?"

The reverend looked to heaven and then looked the young man in the eyes and began, "Can you see love, touch it or feel it?"

"Yes, I love my mommy and daddy, so I know there is love."

He put his hand on the young man's shoulder. "Yes, son, you can't see it or touch it, but you know it's there because you feel it deep inside of yourself, correct?"

"That's exactly how I know there is a God, because I feel him all around me."

"See! Just like you can feel love but can't hold it in your hand, you can hold it inside your heart."

The man lowered his head in thought. "Maybe Daddy never thought about that… You could be right, preacher."

"God is as real in your heart as that love you have for your parents! God is like the wind, you can't feel it or touch it, but you see the effects of its power! It may blow on your face or blow you off your feet, but you never see anything.

Wind is all around us. God is also all around us. He is more powerful than any tornado! You can feel him move, or He can move us!"

"Maybe no one ever told my daddy this stuff? He needs to hear this. I thank you for what you told me, and if you want some of my fish, maybe you could cook it up for us? My name is Jimmy Crockston, and this is my brother James. He's shy and doesn't speak. You gentlemen aren't from around here, where are you from?" the young man asked.

"We are from Chattanooga. I am Reverend John Williams, and this is Mr. Adams. We are traveling to Texas. Just passing through this area. Yes, we would love to join you in some of those good-looking fish you caught. Should we accompany you to your house and meet your parents?"

"No, sir, we can just cook them right here. I'll make us a fire. My daddy is gone to the next town over, and Momma, she would be mad if I brought peoples home when Daddy was gone."

"Your father is gone on business, Jimmy?"

"Yes, he is working on rebuilding the courthouse since the Union soldiers burnt it down during the war. He travels sometimes to get supplies from other towns. Pickensville is a nice place, but we needs our courthouse back, and all the peoples come out to help when the building starts. Those Union soldiers tried to make us leave, but no one did. We just waited and scattered until the war was over, then we started rebuilding. When you know this land like we do, you can hide out until the troubles blow over. The Tombigbee River was my hiding place many times. They tried to burn us all out like they did the courthouse. We lost all the records from there and we don't even know whose land belongs to who." He looked very intently as he talked. "We all knew how to hunt, trap, and fish until this war was over, and we younger guys would catch fish for the older peoples and take care of them also. Daddy said it was our duty to do that for them, taking care of us through the good years."

As I listened, I couldn't help but lean toward his father's way of thinking in some of the things he said. I spoke up to interrupt him. "We need to get those fish cleaned if we are going to cook them, so we can get back on the trail."

"It's been an honor meeting you, Jimmy, and all your fascinating stories of you and your daddy."

Jimmy was all smiles when he wasn't talking about the war travesties. He was a rather friendly young man, about eighteen or so. It was funny how when he talked, he would tug at his overalls strap like an older man would. This must be a trait he observed from his father. Then he turned to me after telling the reverend how much he enjoyed meeting him.

"Mister Adams, you don't talk much."

Sort of surprised he asked me that. "Sorry, young man, I was just listening to your conversation. I do that on occasion. I guess from my years as a lawman in Chattanooga. I keep to myself, keeping quiet so others will feel free to speak freely. That's how you find hidden things out sometimes."

"My daddy had a friend that was a sheriff. Pat Garret is my daddy's fishing buddy, and the man would tell some things he went through. He said he knew Billy the kid. I never believed him, but my daddy said you could believe Sheriff Garret. I never liked him. He thought he was a big shot talking on and on. All I know is, Daddy wouldn't let me go fishing when Sheriff Garret was going. He was daddy's oldest friend from the time they was kids. He was a braggart. His stories were interesting, but I didn't believe most of them."

I listened intently because Pat Garret was a very famous lawman. "Your father knew Sheriff Garret?"

"Yes, sir. He and Daddy fish together, drink together, and play poker sometimes. They mostly sit around and talk about them being kids or the war and Sheriff Garret's adventures."

"Looks like the fish is almost done. Let's pray over our food. Dear heavenly Father, I ask that you put your holy blessing on this food we are about to partake of. I ask that you touch Jimmy, I ask that you move in his life and touch his family, bless his mother and daddy. We also ask that you put a special hedge of protection over Sheriff Garret to live a long and prosperous life, in Jesus Christ's mighty name. Amen!"

Jimmy, looking confused, asked me why the reverend did that. He had never heard that before.

"What, prayer?" I asked. "Reverend, you might need to address this."

The reverend, always ready to give an account for his belief, said, "Do your parents not pray over their food?"

Jimmy shook his head.

"Yes, you did say your daddy doesn't believe in religion. We give thanks because the Bible says in Colossians 3:17, 'Whatever you do in word or deed, do all things in the name of the Lord Jesus Christ.' Giving thanks to God the Father through Him. Even Jesus would ask blessings over his food before he would partake of it. So if we want God to bless our food or anything we try to do, we must ask in Jesus Christ's name to bless our endeavors."

Jimmy, looking even more confused, said, "Well, I guess my daddy may have missed everything you know about this God by not going to church."

"Your life and relationship with God is between you and your Savior only. Let me explain why we need Jesus in our lives."

As the reverend kept talking to the young man, I excused myself to head down to the river to eat. About a half an hour later, I could see that young man sobbing and hugging the reverend. I just sat there contemplating why I was even here and if I was the right partner for this preacher to be traveling with. I was scratching my head as Jimmy came over. He told me he was running home to tell his mother what he had done and how Jesus was his new friend!

"Hey, are you not going to eat? It is your fish." I pointed toward the fire and the fish lying beside it.

"No, no, you go right ahead, I got to tell my momma." He ran off, almost skipping, little brother in tow right behind him.

"Well, Reverend, what about you? Are you ready for some supper?"

"Yes, I think so. When I convinced that young man of listening to his heavenly Father over his earthly daddy, the Holy Spirit started working on his heart almost immediately. He repented and accepted Christ into his heart though never even knowing of whom Christ truly is. I gave him an extra Bible so he could start to study and learn of the greatness of the gospel."

"Yes, that boy was too overwhelmed by his father's ways, trying and believing everything his father told him to be true."

"We do the same, Mr. Adams. Most of the time, we believe what we do because of the influences of the people around us whether it be our parents, our teachers, or just those we are around daily. They shape the way we look at this world. Until we move away from man's thoughts and influences in our lives, the Holy One can't be the Lord of our lives. When we experience the true move of God's Spirit in our lives, we can't be the same. It will change every aspect of the way we see life!"

As the reverend spoke, I could feel that burning inside the way I had many times while talking to him. Not sure if God was trying to get my attention or if the reverend was just so full of this Spirit he kept talking about, but I was getting tired of my eyes watering every time it happened! "Well, Reverend." I interrupted him and suggested we move on before it got too late!

As we saddled and mounted our horses, I couldn't help but notice all the rolling pastures as we rode by. The wheat swayed in the winds that blew in our faces and kept us cool. I could smell the water beside us from the Tombigbee River. The reverend paused in his singing, and it became silent for a little while.

"Mr. Adams, do you think we have moved into the state of Mississippi? We seem to be moving right along." I reached behind me to my pack for some jerky and then took a drink from my water canteen.

"Not sure, Reverend. We have traveled quite a ways already, and it has been one adventure after another!" I laughed a little as I said, "I hope it stays this calm for the rest of the journey, but I don't believe that's in the plans for us."

We were trying to travel as late as possible, but we were traveling by moonlight, and the trail was getting rather worn down. We came to a large open stretch of land and decided to stop just for a moment to stretch our legs and let the horses graze. "Should we just set up camp here since it's dark already, and we are still at the Tombigbee River?"

"Sure, Reverend, I'll gather some firewood after I relieve myself." As I made a fire, the reverend offered me some jerky. I looked over to see the reflection of the moon off the water. With the crickets singing and the fireflies lighting up all around, I began to relax and feel at peace. The reverend unsaddled the horses and tied them up so they could graze. He grabbed his roll and sat down and stared toward the water. "We can catch some more fish in the morning for breakfast," he suggested.

"Sounds good, Reverend." I grabbed the pot and raised it toward him and asked, "Would you like some of the coffee I had just made?" He nodded, and we sat there talking and reminiscing about the things that had taken place in the last few days. The reverend looked upset when he talked of those men that had died a few days ago.

"Yeah, but that one that rode off probably deserved to die also."

He shook his head. "All lives are important in God's eyes. He made the good and the bad alike. He allowed the rain to fall on the just and the unjust alike. That's what my Bible teaches. There will always be good and evil men in this world. We can only change ourselves, and God changes the others if it be His will, and they are willing to accept it. We must be the men of God that He has called you and I to be. It isn't my place to pass judgment on any man. It is God's place only. We all need Christ."

I leaned back against my saddle and stared up at the sky. "Not sure what you mean by man of God. I'm no preacher even though I was raised as a Christian. I'm definitely not a Bible-carrying person. Yes, everyone does need Christ, but some men are born evil and need to meet God way before others! I've met men that there is no hope for. I believe those men are beyond redemption!"

He took a sip of his coffee, stared off into the fire, then began again. "Christ died for all men and all have fallen short of the glory of God. We are called to be the leaders of our homes and to lead others to the saving knowledge of Jesus Christ. To love our wives, our children, and our neighbors as ourselves! We are to do everything to help our fellow men. That's what it means to be a man of God."

"Maybe so, Reverend, but this is a hard world we live in. People don't see it the way you look at it, especially after that war hardened men's hearts, drove people into looking at life through broken eyes! Life or death doesn't really mean that much to anyone anymore! Unless it's your own family."

He nodded. "I do agree, Mr. Adams. This has become a hard world, but we still must do our part."

Our conversation was interrupted by a splash coming from the river. I ran to the water, hearing sounds like kids shouting, "Get up! Get up!" The reverend and I ran toward the shouting and found two young picker boys—one in the river and one on the bank. Not sure if the boy in the river could swim, but I jumped in after him.

"Help him, he can't swim!" the one on the bank shouted while he paced back and forth. The reverend ran to comfort him while I was up to my neck in the river, trying to catch the other boy. I swam as hard as I could and finally was able to get my arm around the boy's shoulders so I could pull him toward shore. I climbed out of the water with the smaller of the two boys in my arms and laid him on the bank. I was soaked from head to toe!

Angrily, I asked the boys, "Why are you up at this hour of the night and why were you at the river for Christ's sake?"

The larger boy ran over to the smaller one, dropped down beside him, and pulled him tight to him. He started crying and shaking, pulling the boy even closer and keeping his head down. He pleaded, "We are so sorry, sir. We didn't know this was your land. We didn't know. Please don't hurt us, sir."

The older boy looked very scared and excited at the same time. He said again, "Please don't hurt us, missa."

I looked to the reverend and knelt down next to the boys. "We are not going to hurt you, son," I said in a calm but stern voice. "Would I have saved that other boy if we were going to hurt you? Calm down, son, we are just wondering why you boys are out here."

The reverend put his hand on both boys' shoulders to comfort them and began to explain, "Mr. Adams and myself are just passing through, and we are camping over the hill here. Who are you, young men?"

The boy pointed to his brother and then to himself. "Willy and my name is Samuel. We were out here fishing, trying to catch us some breakfast for the morning. We haven't eat in a day or two, and we are just hungry, sir."

The reverend looked at me with concern in his eyes, then he looked at me and the youngest boy and noticed they were dripping wet. He nodded his head toward us both and asked, "Mr. Adams, why don't you and Will get out of your wet things so we can hang them to dry by the fire." Willy and I stripped down to our underthings. I left them still talking to the reverend and headed back to hang them up on some sticks near the fire. I could still hear the reverend talking to the boys.

"Why are you out here at this hour fishing? Why does your momma allow you out like this and not home in the bed?"

"We can't go home right now, sir." He looked extremely serious as he spoke of the mean white men who wore those white hoods and stuff. "They are scaring us picker peoples. We are all afraid of them. Maw told us to stay away until those white men calms down and got over theirs anger at us."

Why would they need to calm down? What'd been going on to make the pickers so afraid? I turned to look at the boys and was about to ask them that when Samuel started explaining. "Since Mr. Lincoln freed us pickers and the Union soldiers left, the white men have been wearing hoods and burning crosses. Some of them dragged poor Mr. Dupree out of his house one night and killed him right in front of his whole family! His wife and kids watched it all!"

The reverend was almost in tears listening to this. I was as upset as I think I had ever been. "I will go speak to the sheriff about this in the morning! We will have a word with him to see why this is allowed to take place. We will see what we can do and, if we can, put a stop to this." I threw my hands up in the air and then turned to the boys. "Where is the law and justice? Do you know who has done these things?"

They both began to nod their heads vigorously up and down. "Yes, sir, we know all those men. They wear those hoods, but we have lived here and know exactly who they are. They hate us because they are all former slave owners. My maw was owned by one of those men that wore those hoods. We aren't trying to hurt nobody, we just trying to live like free peoples. We don't want any problems. These men are mean and hate us because we are free now. Mr. Dupree was just trying to vote, and he was telling the pickers they had a right to vote too. Maw said that's why they broke his door down and cut his throat right there in the street! They're real mean and evil, always trying to kill some of us. Everyone is scared! We are staying hidden until they stop being so angry. So Willy and me, we going to stay out here at the river so we can catch us some fish until Maw send word for us to come back home."

I looked over to the reverend, who was scowling down at the ground. "Where is the sheriff in all this? Who is the sheriff?" I ask roughly.

"The sheriff is Mr. Sykes. Sheriff Sykes is one of them, sir. He is one of those men that wear those white hoods. If youn go talk to him, it will just make it worse on us all, and they may just kill youns too. I believe 'tis better we just wait it out and stay hidden until this blows over. Mr. Dupree is the only one killed so far, I think. If you cause trouble, it may be more. If the pickers won't try to vote or cause any trouble…there's not been anything happen since then."

I motioned for the reverend and the boys to come on over to our camp. "You're correct, Samuel, but we can't just sit by and let this happen. Mr. Adams and myself will see what we can do for your people. Come on over to the fire here, boys, and warm yourselves, and I will cook you some food," the reverend said as he also sat down to warm himself a bit.

"Thank you for the foods, but please don't say anything to the sheriff because even if sheriff Sykes says he will stop, they won't. They will make it harder on us. Me and Willy will be fine living out here. We knows how to fish and find berries or onions. Been doing it our whole lives, and that's good for us. They may kill us if they find out we said anything to youns. Please forget we said anything, please, sir? Sorry I said anything to youn, sirs. Very sorry. Thought you were one of them hooded men trying to hurt us."

Speaking with compassion, I said, "Son, there are good white men out here that don't look at things the way those men do. We won't go to town and talk to this sheriff or anyone that may try to hurt your people. They have been through enough! We won't cause any problems for you. I'm sure the local authorities will step in eventually, and maybe after the next election, your town can get rid of Sheriff Sykes."

"Mr. Adams is correct that every time there is bad, there are also good things we can't see. God has a way of removing evil, changing lives and hearts. One of these days, all men will see everyone no different. Red, yellow, black, or white, we will all be seen the same just like God does. There will be leaders to step up and change these things! Just like President Lincoln did. God created all men equal, and we all have a God-given right to be free and pursue happiness." The reverend got up and started to gather our food supplies. He looked up and waved the boys over closer to the fire. "Sit by the fire right there by Mr. Adams and warm yourselves while I cook you these beans and biscuits. We have some jerky if you boys would like some? There is also some coffee cooking over the fire. You are welcome to drink coffee if you'd like."

"Reverend Williams, thank youn so much. We do drink coffee, and that there jerky sounds good to Willy and me. We haven't eaten in a day or two." He patted his stomach and watched with longing and relief in his eyes as the reverend poured the coffee into two tin cups and handed out the jerky.

"Will, do you not talk?" I was trying to show the young boy a little kindness.

"He is pretty scared of white men, sir. He probably won't talk to you," Samual explained.

"You boys have nothing to fear from us." I could remember being these boys' age. I remember a time when I was hunting with my father back in El Paso. We came upon a mountain lion, and it scared me to death. That wild cat that my father shot as it jumped toward me to save my life was not as dangerous as the men here that were terrorizing these poor boys. I was beginning to understand that no matter what color a person was, we all had the same emotions and fears. The more I thought about what this sheriff and those men were doing to innocent people, the more angry I became. What gives a man the right to harm another just because of their skin color?

I took a sip of my coffee and asked, maybe with a little too much gruffness in my voice, "Samuel, exactly where are we? What town is near here?"

The boy took a few seconds to finish chewing his mouthful of jerky and answered, "In Monroe, Mississippi, sir. It used to be a good place to live back before the slaves were freed. Es not really big, but there's a lot of us here. Most folks are good peoples, but when some of us freed slaves started to leave, the masses got together and made it hard on us that stayed behind. Since they didn't have the helps they had before, they tried to scare us into helping for almost no money. When we refused, that's when the bad men started putting the hoods on and scaring us! This county was named after President Monroe a long time ago. It was quiet before all this war and mean men took over."

The reverend asked, "Samuel, did you know the Choctaw and Chickasaw people lived here before this became Monroe County? There was peace here for a hundred years before the civil war. I believe someday there will be again!" He leaned over and pulled his old Bible out of his pack. "Have you boys learned how to read?" He held his Bible up to show the boys and asked, "You read the Bible?"

"No, sir, Reverend, we were not allowed to learn to read when we were slaves. Not sure if'en I want to learn or could."

He put his Bible on his lap and opened it, leafing through the pages till he found what he was looking for. "Care if I read you a passage out of the Bible?"

The boy's eyes lit up, and they smiled. "My grand-pappy read, and he would read the Bible every night before we went to bed. He didn't let the massa know. It was our secret that he could read. At night, when all the lights went out at the houses, we would sit around the fire and listen to all those stories in there. We would have so many people listening it was hard to hear if'en you were in the back. Maw used to say it was like Grandpappy had his own church. 'Nothing frees a man like being able to read.' She said, 'Like touching the heart of God when you can read.'"

"Samuel, your grandfather was a wise man. I encourage you to learn how to read and write. Both you and your brother will learn to be even more free by having the knowledge of the Bible and other books. I think I would like to read to you from Psalm 23. Sit here beside me, boys, so you can read along with me." They scooted closer, and he began. "'The Lord is my shelter, I shall not want. He maketh me to lie down in green pastures: He leadeth me beside the still waters. He restoreth my soul...'"

As the reverend read to those boys, their eyes were as big as the moon up above. I adjusted my clothes along with the little ones, moving them just a little closer to the fire so I could get back into them sooner. Willy seemed not to mind sitting there as he leaned on his brother's shoulder while listening to the reverend read. He seemed to be warming on the outside as well as the inside from those words the reverend read. It was a warm night, but I could still feel a slight chill.

After we ate supper and the reverend finished teaching the boys a Bible lesson, he prayed that God would protect them with a special blessing of protection. The reverend insisted they camp with us at night, and we could part ways in the morning. We made them a pallet together beside the fire with the reverend on their right and me to their left. I threw a couple more pieces of wood on the fire and took the first watch. Before the boys fell asleep, the reverend spoke up, asking, "Do you boys pray before you go to sleep? If not, I would like to teach you."

Samuel looked up and answered, "Yessir, we pray with our maw. Me and Willy listen to her pray every night before we fall asleep." He lowered his head and looked at the ground. "We haven't prayed since we have been out here."

"Boys your age should be praying on your own when you can. We all need God's protection. What is your ages anyhow?"

"I'm thirteen, and Willy he's ten."

"As I pray, you boys follow along. Dear heavenly Father in Jesus Christ's holy name, Lord, I ask that you touch these boys. Put your hedge of protection all around us as we sleep tonight. We ask that you put your protecting angels all around us. Lord, if for any reason either of us pass tonight, please forgive our sins and make us heirs of your kingdom. We also pray for this Dupree family. They lost their father in this evil act brought on by corruption. Lord, help this family to forgive those men. Help them not to hold hatred in their hearts but forgiveness and grace. Fill them with Your love and mercy for one another. In Jesus's mighty name! Amen."

I scanned the area and pulled out a piece of wood and a whittling knife. "Good prayer there, Reverend. You three get some sleep. I will wake you up around two for the next watch so I can get some sleep."

"Yes, sir. Mr. Adams, have a good night and thanks for taking the first watch."

As I sat there with my Spencer rifle beside me, enjoying the clear sky, I knew if anything were to happen, I would be ready. Contemplating the events of the day and what these two boys had told us, I felt it was hard to imagine how men could look at others as if they had a right to punish without so much as a trial. Then I remembered that I also held some of those beliefs most of my life.

When I awoke the reverend for his turn at watch, he looked wide-eyed at me, saying, "I dreamt of President Abraham Lincoln. He walked up to the fire and put a log on there from under his arm. He looked at the sleeping boys and said, 'This is why I was willing to die, so they could live.' Then you woke me up."

I stood over the reverend as he got up and informed him, "I fought sleep for the last hour, and no Lincoln came to visit." I chuckled and then continued, "Maybe he will visit me as I visit my eyelids! The horses are behaving, and I am tuckered out. Since the boys have my bedroll. I will borrow yours, if you don't care. Good night to you, Reverend." I lay down and at last I drifted off to sleep.

The next morning, when I awoke, the boys were admiring our horses, and the reverend was preparing food for the morning meal. I walked up to the boys and asked, "Do you like those horses? "This one here is Rose. She was given to me as a wild horse, and no one had time to work with her. I spent a lot of hours just trying to put my hands on her. I put her in a round pen and used a ten-foot pole to touch her from anywhere it was she ran. I worked with her for many days before she realized I wasn't going to hurt her. I would move in a little tighter on that pole until she let me touch her. After that, I could walk right up to her. I slowly eased a saddle on her, standing up and down. She didn't like that much, but she calmed down after about two days. I threw my leg over, and she just stood there. She never gave me much of a hard time and has always been a sweet girl. She is just a little untrusting. She threw me one time in that round pen, thank God no one was there watching." The boys laughed at that. "You think it's funny, but I tell you, I hurt for a week from that fall. I shortened that pen to about ten feet. I taught her how to turn left, right, and stop on command. I've been riding her ever since." I patted Rose on the side of her neck and asked, "You boys want to give her a ride?"

"Yes, sir, Mr. Adams, we sure do!" Sameul said, very excited, and little Willy looked sort of scared.

I tied a rope around the lead of the bridle so I could keep control of the situation. Samuel helped Willy up on Rose, and he rode around me like a child's carousel ride. He only rode for ten minutes or so, and then it was big brother's time. "Have you rode before Samuel?" I asked.

"Yes, sir, but just a few times," he said.

"Okay, I'll take the lead line off, and you just stay right here as you ride." He did very well. "Samuel, you will make a fine horseman soon and you can teach your brother. I picked up Willy and put him on the back of the saddle behind his brother. "Be careful," I told him.

"Well, Mr. Adams, I think you have spoiled those two boys." The reverend walked over to where I was standing and put his hand on my shoulder. I kept watching the boys laugh and holler, "Yeehaw!" as they rode around.

"Yes, Reverend, I think I have. They remind me of the children at the church I went to when I was younger. We would have picnics with all the families of the town."

"That is how the communities were supposed to be."

"You are right, Reverend."

"Amen to that."

After the boys dismounted, I asked, "Well, boys, do you know what you want to be when you grow up? What about you, Willie? Do you know?"

To my surprise, Willie said he was going to train and ride horses just like me. "I want to have a real big black horse and call him Lightning! And shoot all the bad men who hurt us poor picker peoples!" he yelled.

"Sorry you feel the need to hurt anyone at your age, Willie. I hope you can see that all white men are not bad people."

"Yes, Reverend Williams, I know theys bad and good white men just like theys bad and good people like me."

Samuel spoke up abruptly and said, "I'm going to stand up for the weak people and teach them to fight for what is right just like yous two men are doing! No one gonna stop me from telling people they have the right to vote or not to be pushed around by anyone just because they are picker!"

"You're correct, Samuel, you should always stand for what is right even if it may be scary at times." The reverend put his hands on the boy's shoulders.

"I'm not scared!" Samuel shouted. "I just do what my maw tells me to do. That's why wese hiding out here to protect Willie like Maw told me to. I also going to learn to read and tell people about Jesus and God like you do, Reverend!"

The reverend and the boys walked away beside the river toward the south. The reverend said, "Keep praying, boys, and we will see you again soon."

The reverend walked back and started gathering all his things and saddling his horse. "Those will become fine grown men one day if God helps them to stay away from danger and those men with the white hoods!"

I was determined to go to town and confront this sheriff, but the reverend insisted we leave it alone, fearing the boys would be right and it would come back to hurt them. The last thing these people need is retaliation for our actions, he had told me. I finished getting my horse ready and jumped up in the saddle. "This is a beautiful place by the river here, Reverend, but the people make it ugly! Downright ugly!"

We only rode for about an hour or so until we rode into a thriving little business town. They had a bank, a mercantile, a small restaurant with a saloon next door, a barbershop, a stable, and even a boardinghouse. There were a few other businesses mixed in, and in the middle of it all was a sheriff's office. It was its own structure with a large front porch, and it actually had windows up high on the cell walls with bars on them. I was a little impressed. We rode on over to the restaurant whose sign said "Patterson's."

"Reverend, how about a piece of pie or coffee if this place has pie?" Since we had had nothing but beans for days, the reverend readily agreed. As we were walking in, we swung the door open to a small skirmish. A man was being manhandled out the door. He was drunk and causing problems. As he was pushed by us, he shouted, "You don't want to eat here! The food tastes and smells like a bucketful of buttholes. This place has bad food and service."

The man doing the pushing and arm-twisting gruffly informed the man, "I told you not to come back in here when you are drunk. Now, Dwight, you take your business elsewhere and don't come back until you sober up." That was when he promptly pushed him out into the street.

We walked in and were promptly greeted by a medium and stout middle-aged man. He had dark-brown curly hair, a mustache, and was wearing an apron. "Welcome! You two have a seat and pay him no never mind. He was drunk as if you couldn't tell from his odor. Our food is better than some of the other places in this town. It may not be the best in the state, but it's good for Monroe." He directed us over to a small table in the front corner not too far from the window.

"So we are in Monroe? I'm Elijah Adams, and this is Reverend Williams. We are passing through and were hoping you had pie of some sort."

The reverend looked up at him, hopeful. "Yes, sir, Mr. Adams, we sure do. I'm Patterson, Ulysses Gene Patterson. My friends call me Ugene."

"Good to meet you, Ugene. We could use some coffee also if you have some to go with the pie."

"Sir, the missus made some fresh apples earlier this morning, and I will put on that coffee fresh for you. You came at a good time right now. The crowds will show up around lunchtime.

As he served our coffee and pie, a few minutes later, I asked him to join us considering we were his only customers at the time. He grabbed himself a piece of pie and coffee and pulled up a chair "It would be great to talk to you fine gentlemen considering the people that normally come in. Where do you come from?"

I took a bite of the warm apple pie and closed my eyes for a moment. The crust was flaky, the apples were tart, and the filling was sweet, just like my momma used to make it. "From the Chattanooga area traveling to Texas," I answered and then took a swig of my black coffee.

"Glad you came to visit my establishment. You enjoy your pie. There are a few places you could have stopped by for pie, so I am honored you chose my place." The reverend leaned forward, put his fork down, and looked over at Ugene. "You seem like a God-fearing man and keen on doing what is right. Was wondering if you know of anything that has been going on with the pickers in this town?" I leaned forward and nodded my head in agreement. I wanted to know that for myself.

I was surprised the reverend asked since he was holding me back when I wanted to go after who was causing the problems. I knew I could trust what he was doing now, so I just sat there and listened. "Yes, Reverend, the poor colored people are being bullied by some of our very bad men in this town. They seem to think they have a right to control the pickers by hurt and fear. They ride around wearing hoods on horseback, burning crosses in yards, and even killing to prove that the white man is still in charge of the black people. They have brought nothing but fear and death. I have friends here that were former slaves, and they fear for their lives. This town was once a good and decent place to live in before this started. The local sheriff does nothing to stop it, and I believe he is a part of these happenings. I really don't like the way things are turning out around here. I heard a few of those men talking last night here that they are having a meeting tonight to bring someone to justice. No telling what that might mean. Ever since Mr. Dupree was dragged out of his home and killed in front of his family, there is no telling what these men might do tonight. Mr. Dupree did not deserve to be killed for just telling people they had rights! They are freemen now! This isn't right what they are doing! It's not right at all!"

"This makes me very angry. Mr. Patterson, did you happen to catch the names of those men who were talking about these plans tonight and where they are meeting? God forbid they find out you told us who they are," I whispered. "If you choose not to help, we understand."

With a look of frustration on his face, Ugene answered, "No, Mr. Adams, I wish someone could do something to stop this evil. That was James Stevens, Clinton South, and Billy James, and they are meeting at the livery stables tonight at the edge of town. It's the red barn with the large loft on the left as you leave town. That is where they meet just before they move out to cause problems for these poor people. That man I just threw out of here is one of them. I don't think he is one of the men that cause most of the destruction, but he is a part of their group. They dress completely in white from head to toe. Makes me wonder if they even know each other all dressed up like that. Looking like ghosts but all looking alike. Cowards, if you ask me! They meet just after dark and plan all sorts of evil for the evenings. Sorry to talk so much about these things." He looked at us, a little dejected.

"No, we asked, and I thank you for the information. We are asking to help out a couple of friends of ours that live around here. What do we owe you for the pie and coffee?" I said.

"Well, glad I could help, and two bits will take care of your tab. I hope you enjoyed your pie." He stood up and started to clear the table.

"Yes, we did." We stood up and prepared to leave. "Tell your missus that we enjoyed it. It was very refreshing to our deprived souls and our deprived taste buds," I said with a chuckle.

"Just glad to have good people come into my establishment now and then. If you pass through Monroe again, I hope you consider coming again," he said.

"Thank you, Ugene. We will if we ever travel through here again," I said as I shook his hand.

The reverend shook his hand as we walked out of the door and took one look around, and I explained, "This is a nice town if you could keep those instigators under control. You and your missus have a good evening, and may God bless you and your establishment."

As we rode out of town, I rode just a little closer to the reverend and spoke to him in a low tone. "I had a thought, Reverend. Patterson said these men wear those hoods and dress completely alike, and he even wondered if they knew who the other one was. Let's make sure everyone sees us leave town, and I'll tell you my plan."

We rode out of town, and the reverend started singing like he always did. He drew quite a bit of attention with his good voice and his beautiful hymns. After we had gone about a mile out, I spotted a wooded area with a few boulders that had a small game path running around them. I jumped off my horse and led it around the boulder where there was a clearing unseen from the main road and a place where we could tie our horses.

"Reverend, I think we should double-back on foot tonight after dark to the livery stables. I think we can sneak in and knock a couple of these varmints out and dress ourselves in their robes and hoods. They will never know who we are. Let's see if we can put the fear of God into some of these evil men!"

The reverend nodded his head. "That's a great idea, Mr. Adams! They need to fear God once again. Something needs to change here! Yes, let's see what we can do to help with that!"

Later on that night, we snuck up to the livery and began to listen through the cracks in the wall. There were only two men there talking. Their plans was to have a lynching tonight. That man named Clinton had a picker all tied up and ready to be hung! He was all excited that the picker was young and would be a fine example to bring all the blacks into line!

"Thinking they were high and mighty and equal with us because they are free! We are about to show them how free they really are tonight!" he said excitedly.

I looked over and whispered, "Reverend, we have got to put a stop to this. Let's stay right here until they leave. We will follow until we can capture two of them one way or another. Once we put on their clothes, we can blend in until we can make a move. Maybe we won't be seen since it is a very dark night with only a half-moon. Darkness will be on our side instead of theirs tonight!"

"I will follow your lead, Mr. Adams."

"Just stay right with me, Reverend, and be ready for anything!"

About five minutes later, the rest of their little gang arrived. They dressed in their cowards robes and headed out the door, laughing. As we followed close—but not too close behind—I had my Spencer rifle by my side, and the reverend, I insisted, carried my colt! When I had grabbed the guns, the reverend made me promise not to kill anyone. I told him as long as nothing got out of hand. They met up with a couple more cowards in robes and made their way toward the place of the lynching.

When the reverend took the colt from me, he made me promise again not to kill anyone. I promised as long as nothing got out of hand! As soon as they came into an opening in the woods, I decided now was the time to take out the two in the back who stopped to light a cigarette at their own peril. We jumped them, and I was able to knock both men out with the butt of my Spencer! We put their robes on and followed as if we were just more cowards in this small group of ingrates! They didn't even know the others were missing.

We walked with them until we came upon a cabin in the woods where two more men came out with a boy tied. To our surprise, it was Samuel in their clutches, one of the young men we had met by the creek earlier. He was bleeding and had been beaten! The reverend gasped as we saw him. I grabbed him by the arm and whispered, "Keep it together, Reverend! Follow my lead?"

As we walked along with the others, a few more joined in, all hooded and robed up. The leader laughed and said, "He's going to make a fine example tonight. This will put fear into all the hearts of those blackies! I only regret that we have one to sacrifice!" Everyone laughed and cheered.

"Now!" I shouted and I fired my rifle into the air and then I pointed it at the leader and moved the barrel back and forth from one coward to another, daring them to make a move! As cowards do, they all jumped, every one of them. "You men hold it right there and don't even think about moving!" I shouted.

Their leader asked, "Is that you, Tom? What are you doing?" He looked around. "It sounds like Tom," one of the others said nervously. "What are you doing?" he asked again. "We are just having a little fun tonight!"

"No! You bastards are not going to have fun tonight or any other night! You're going to let that boy go! You're going to let him go right now! Or you will be suffering from lead poisoning!"

"You can't shoot us all!" the leader said with a little less confidence in his voice.

"No, I can kill you first and then a few more! Are you ready to die for this little bit of fun? Well, are you? Billy, James, Clinton? And the rest of you? I know every one of you has brought a scourge on this peaceful town of ours, and we are putting a stop to it right now!"

The reverend raised his gun and spoke up, saying, "Whom he doesn't kill, I can get the rest with my six-shooters!" His voice was deeper than I had ever heard it before.

"Tom, who is that with you and what are you doing? We got to keep these pickers under control! This is God's business. This is needed to keep it all under control around here! Keeps them from uprising and thinking they can do whatever they want to!"

"That poor black boy has done nothing to deserve what you cowards are doing to him, and all the others just want to live their lives in peace!" the reverend yelled out again.

Right then, the man holding the rope around Samuel's neck jerked on the rope to make it tighter. Without thinking, I pulled my Spencer rifle up and shot the rope and the thumb of the man holding the rope. The man started yelling, "You shot my finger off! You shot me! You son of a bit—"

I stopped him by shouting, "Shut up!"

This brought everything and everyone to attention, and now they were aware that we were serious! The reverend slowly walked over to Samuel and brought him over beside us. "I have lived in this town my whole life, and you cowards are destroying it!" I lied. "This was a peaceful town until you men thought it was a good idea to start this terror! I know everyone and where you live! If this keeps happening, we have been undercover watching, and we know everyone. Not only will we kill those who keep doing these things, we will also kill your families and burn your houses down around your dead bodies! You cowards lynch one more picker or kidnap one more person and continue to ruin the town I was born and raised in, there will be hell to pay! This town was named after a great president, and you men are destroying it! I should start right now by shooting all of you pieces of human waste! Our horses serve a stronger purpose than you so-called men do! Who wants to be first? Jane and Mary going to miss you or Sue?" As I waved my gun around at all of them, I hoped one of them had women in their lives with that name.

"Yes, she will miss me!" one of them shouted out. "We all have wives and kids. You know we do! If you are Tom, then you know my Mary will miss me!"

"I may be Tom," I said, "or maybe you will never figure out who we are." As their leader started defending their actions, I shouted, "Shut up coward! No more words or I'll start shooting! You will never know who we are or where we are coming from. This stops tonight! No more terrorizing blacks, or you will die in your sins! I will be that hooded man standing right beside you, and there are more than just two of us. This is going to stop in Monroe, or you will pay an eye for an eye!"

The reverend grabbed Samuel by the arm and pulled him over to where I was standing and yelled, "We are taking this boy with us, and if anything happens to him or his family, we will come looking for you, James, Billy, or you, Clinton, or any of you! Get this straight!"

"Please don't kill us or our families!" someone yelled. "Just go and take the picker with you! Please just don't shoot!" another one yelled.

I turned Samuel to look at me, and I think I saw surprise and recognition in his eyes. "Son, you go on and get out of here. These men will not bother you because I will be right here in this town and will hunt them and their families down like dogs if anything happens to you or any of your families!"

As Sameul left, he looked at us and said, "Thank you!" Then he ran off into the night.

"There may be more killings, but it won't just be the blacks only! It will be white also! We will be watching," the reverend shouted. "Are we straight?"

"Yes," the leader shouted. "Just don't kill us or our families. We will officially disband!"

"You tell everyone there is a new sheriff in town, and it's not that cowardly Sykes we have now! Justice will follow me! Monroe is coming back to peace and justice from now on!" the reverend said. "God's judgment is here, and we come with the Lord's blessings! Go home to your families. Stay in your homes for the night. In the morning, ask yourselves, 'Who were they? When will they come for me if I fall out of line?'"

So we backed out slowly and into the night. My Spencer was pointed at the lead coward's head until I could see him no more.

As we walked back to the two men we knocked out, the reverend asked, "Do you think they will follow us?"

"No. They are all cowards and not willing to sacrifice themselves or their families. I should have killed one of them to make sure they know we are serious!" I said.

"You shot that man's finger off, they know you were serious," the reverend replied. "I think their days of scaring, beating, or lynching people are over. They will be trying to figure out who amongst them we are and if we are coming for revenge if they do anything stupid! Nothing is going to bring them to violence again because they do not want it coming back on them. As long as they think we are one of them, then nothing will follow."

We dropped those robes back on top of the two men who were still out. The reverend leaned down and made sure they were still alive. "It's only been about half an hour," I said. "They should be fine."

"Really?" he said, surprised. "It seemed as if that lasted hours."

"It was your adrenaline that did that to you. It can speed up time or slow it down at other times!" I explained.

We made it to the other side of town to our horses without being followed. We mounted up and rode out as fast as we could. A few miles down the road, the reverend started in on his ranting. "I think we accomplished what we came here to do!" he said. "That was a fine idea, Mr. Adams. I was so nervous I thought I may drop your colt. Even when you shot the rifle, it startled me as much as them! I was holding back my liquid that I need to take care of right now before we get back on the trail."

"I pray to God that this works, Reverend," I said as he dismounted.

"God put that idea in your head, and we met Samuel earlier. God's will is that we would get involved in these situations. It will change things! I believe we were led into Mr. Patterson's restaurant. I'll bet all those men may be in church Sunday repenting of their sins. Praying to God holds back his judgment." The reverend mounted his horse, and we headed back out.

I hope to be so, Reverend! I truly hope so.

Chapter 5

The countryside was a peaceful place as we rode on down the trail. Since we were trying to make up the time and distance ourselves from Monroe, we decided to travel through and only stop to eat and sleep for the next few days. The reverend kept up his talking on what happened so far on our journey. He sang his hymns and started praying for our journey ahead and the lives we touched so far. Soon we came upon quite a large trading town with a train depot running into it. The sign said "Aberdean." We admired the beautiful architecture that was being repaired on some of the buildings. A lot of them had quite a bit of damage from the war battles that had come through. There were quite a few people out working together, so I don't believe it will take long for this town to recover.

We rode for miles and passed through one small town after another. When we came upon a field that had a stream running through it, we decided it would be a nice place for us and the horses to take another break. After I washed up a bit to cool down in the creek, I saw there was a small dirt hill with a fallen log in front of it. Looking around, I thought it would be a good idea for the reverend to continue to take a few more practice shots with the Spencer rifle.

"Reverend, you want to take a few more shots with the rifle to see how you are still hitting?" I asked as I set up some pinecones and things to use as targets. I had him go through the gun safety and had him show me how to reload the rifle. When I was satisfied with his knowledge on how to take care of the gun and the proper shooting stances, I had him line up his first few shots. He shot straight as before. He didn't forget a thing and was right as rain as far as the shooting. He was a quick study and proved that every time he squeezed off one shot after another, hitting all targets he aimed at. This aroused a few visitors.

I held my hand up and yelled, "Hold your fire, Reverend. We have some visitors who look like Union soldiers. About nine, I would think."

The reverend lowered the weapon and came to stand by my side. "Let's see what they have on their minds, Mr. Adams. Let's not judge a book by the cover."

"The war has been over for some time now. I fought for the South, but I will keep my head about me. After all, I had a family that fought for the North as well."

They rode up on horseback, and the man in front introduced himself as Captain Farley. "We are assigned to these parts to keep the peace in this province of Mississippi. We heard your shots, so we came to make sure you're not some of the Knight Riders that ride through here from time to time. They are from the south of Mississippi, but they have been known to be all over. Are you men part of or have you come into contact with them?"

"No, sir. We are just resting here for a moment as we travel to Texas. I am Mr. Adams." I tipped my head to my left. "This is Reverend Williams. We're not looking for trouble, only passing through. The reverend here is learning how to shoot, we thought this would be a great place to practice. Those are the shots you heard!"

The captain ordered his second to check our guns. A younger man with a gruff-looking beard slid off his horse and headed our way. As he reached for my rifle, I began to pull back and, looking up to the captain, I protested! "Sir, you will not be taking my Spencer or anything else we possess. Our property is ours, and you will not be take it!" He sat up a bit straighter in his saddle and put his hand over his gun in his holster.

"Sir, we are the army of the United States, and it is our job to keep the peace! Until I determine what you are doing here and if you are keeping the peace, then we will disarm and detain you as we see fit!"

I grabbed my rifle from the reverend and stepped in front of him. "I don't care who you think you are or the reason you think you can touch my rifle. I have owned this rifle since the early sixties. I was a sheriff and I know the laws as well as you all do. You have no right to disarm a citizen unless you suspect a crime. We also have the Constitution now that you must follow. I stand on those principles and will not surrender my rifle!"

The captain motioned for his man to return to his side. He studied me for a moment and then asked, "Are you two traveling from around Chattanooga, Tennessee?"

Surprised, I nodded my head and began to relax a bit. "Yes, we are. How would you know that, Captain Farley?"

He began to dismount from his beautiful palomino horse. It looked to be about fifteen hands and had a light-brown mane. He walked over and held his hand for me to shake. "I exchanged a prisoner once there, and you accompanied the sheriff with the exchange a few years back," he said. "I only put two and two together when you mentioned being a sheriff. I don't recall you being a sheriff but only a deputy."

I clasped his hand tightly and shook, explaining, "I was a deputy in Chattanooga. I was also the sheriff in El Paso before the war! Sorry, I don't remember that prisoner exchange."

"I was a sergeant at that time, so I didn't make the exchange myself, but I do remember you. I never forget a face or the actions of others. I do remember you treating the prisoners we picked up like they were just citizens instead of prisoners. I even heard the prisoners mentioning how well you treated them even though they were deserters from the Union Army. I remember it like it was yesterday. I was based in Chattanooga during the occupation, so I spent many days up on the ridge. It was a great place to relax when I could." Farley walked back over to stand with his men.

I moved over so the reverend was next to me. He still looked a little worried, but I guess since I was used to people in authority, this didn't bother me. "Yes, I guess that's why I stayed after the war was over. It was a very good place to call home for a short while until I got homesick and the good reverend hired me to escort him back to El Paso."

The reverend finally found his voice and confidently began, "Mr. Adams and myself are just passing through here to El Paso. This being the only route through here, with God's grace, we will make it there as uneventful as possible. We didn't mean to cause any issues. Mr. Adams is just trying to teach me how to shoot, and as I always say, practice makes better. So I am taking a few too many shots, I suppose."

Captain Farley laughed. "Good luck on that uneventfulness! That doesn't seem very possible in these parts. You run into these raiders? They bring it with them everywhere they go, and they will take everything you have! Funniest thing about it is, they give it to all the people they think need help. They think they are some kind of Robin Hood and his merrymen, I guess!"

I was quick to explain that we were capable of taking care of ourselves. "As long as they don't touch my Spencer, I'm fine."

Farley laughed once again. "Guess you will need to skin that colt smoke wagon, right, Mr. Adams?" He and his men continued laughing. They grabbed up their reins and prepared to ride out again. "I'm sure you would, Mr. Adams. Well, I don't need to push the issue anymore. Reverend, keep me and my men in your prayers, if you don't mind. We are looked at as the enemy by many people around these areas. We are only here to slow down the activity of these men with the hoods and the actions of some who are trying to hurt the poor pickers and make them slaves again. Not going to happen on my watch. You two keep safe, and we may be seeing you once again if you stay in these parts for any amount of time."

"I'm sure you might, Captain. You have your hands full with these happenings. We are on your side, and we will help in any way the law needs us. I volunteered."

"Mr. Adams is correct, we do not want to see any man done wrong regardless of what color they are. Can I pray for you all right now, Captain?" the reverend asked.

Hearing shots in the distance, they all became alert. "No, sir, Reverend! I am in a hurry right now. You can pray as we ride away. We have business in Aberdeen. If you make it there, I would like to buy you two a drink." Raising his hand, he signaled to his men. "We shall be off!" To us, he yelled, "For now, good day, gentlemen."

"I'll take you up on that if we do see you again! Good day to you also, Captain Farley!" I yelled back.

We watched as the entire troop headed to the west in one quick movement. Looking a little concerned, the reverend remarked, "Well, that was close. Good thing the captain remembered you, Mr. Adams. They tried to take your Spencer rifle…"

We saddled up and rode across the countryside. It was a beautiful country. Apparently, this part of Mississippi has a lot of pines as well as fields ready for harvest this time of the year. The later it got, the more you could hear the whip-poor-will singing. It was a very loud call late in the day. Soon the reverend began to read aloud from the scripture. That would bring back memories of my mother reading out of the Bible to me when I was a child. She would read every night, and my father would preach on Sundays—lots of good memories. The reverend explaining his interpretation of the good book and singing his hymns were all familiar to me. Not having been an active churchgoer for a long time, I really missed it from my childhood. I always heard that if you teach a child, those teachings will never get lost when we grow up. The apple doesn't fall far from the tree. This I know for sure.

My father and mother were both God-fearing people, and I knew what I believed in from their teachings. I became a better man for it! Now, though, I never prayed or thought like I should. I drank too much, overindulged in the cards as well as the women, both decent and not so. The more I was around this preacher, the more my ways were affected by him.

We rode over a large steep hill and started around a bend in the trail when we came upon a small rundown cabin along the roadside. The shutters were falling off, the porch boards needed replacing, and the well house pump looked the worse for wear with rust all over it and cobwebs everywhere. A neglected and sad-looking mule was tied up outside. It looked as if it had been working hard for its entire life. We approached cautiously since we were not sure who lived here. We saw no one and were about to ride on when an older picker lady came running out, exclaiming excitedly, "Praise Jesus! Praise Jesus! He did send you!"

We both looked around, and the reverend asked if I knew her. I shook my head, very confused and maybe a little concerned. "First, I've ever seen her in my life. I do think she is talking about you, Reverend Williams."

She ran up to the reverend and lay her hand on his knee, spooking his horse a little. She wasn't deterred by the horse or the fact that her feet may get stomped. She grabbed him by the hand and shouted, "I dreamed you were coming. God showed me last night in my dreams youens were coming. I have been praying all day that you would come! Almost missed you!"

The reverend and I dismounted from our horses, and I went to tie them up next to the mule while the reverend asked, "What do you mean, Mother? What did God show you in your dreams?" She kept jumping up and down, looked to the reverend and said, "God showed me for the last few nights that He was sending you to heal my husband! You preacher man with that white collar and the black jacket. I couldn't see your face in the dream, but I did see your white collar! God said He was sending a man of God to heal my husband!"

I was so confused and asked the reverend what she was talking about. There is no way she could have known we were going to pass by here today. We didn't even know.

"Not sure, Mr. Adams. You said it just minutes ago, God's ways are not our ways." The reverend slowly reached out and grabbed both of the ladies' hands. He held them gently in front of her, looked her in the eyes, and said, "Mother? Mother? What did I happen to do in this dream you had? Show me what I did in your dream."

She explained last night and the nights before, "I had the same dream! You rode up wearing that hat and that same collar, even the same horse. You followed me into the house and prayed for my husband, who has been sick in bed for months. Three days ago, God spoke in my dreams! I thought he may die! Until the dream!"

"Really, ma'am?" he asked.

"You look and sound just like you did in my dreams," she whispered in awe and excitement.

"Reverend, we better do exactly as God has shown her! This is bigger than what we can see!" She was praising Jesus, crying, waving her arms in the air, and jumping up and down, shouting, "Praise You, Jesus! Praise You, Jesus!" She grabbed my hand and led me in. As we stepped on the porch, it sounded like the boards were not nailed down. It creaked and cracked. The front door squeaked open to reveal a sparsely furnished room. Not much in there but a couple of older handmade rocking chairs, a swept floor with a broom in the corner, and a bed in the back of this cabin. She told us to come on in as she pulled the reverend inside. I was right behind the reverend.

"Mother, what is it I did?" he asked. There was a strong odor in the room where her husband was. It smelled like a mixture of urine and death. Her husband lay there with his eyes closed. He was a very sickly-looking man, around a hundred and twenty-five pounds, if not a few pounds less. He looked very bad, to say the least. We stood there at his bedside, the reverend saying a prayer of guidance under his breath. "Mother," he asked, "What happened to this man?"

She told us she did not know. "He started feeling weak about a few months earlier and has been in bed for many days now. He won't eat or drink anything! He has been losing weight for about a month. He is pretty bad off! Three nights ago, I started dreaming you were coming and had the same dream three days in a row!"

He turned and put a calming hand on her shoulder. "Yes, you have said that, Mother. What exactly did I do in your dreams?"

She looked up then, closed her eyes, and, in a small voice, said, "All I know is you put your hand on his head and the other hand in the air and prayed for him!"

The reverend guided the woman closer to the bed and then said, "Show me what I did, Mother. Show me how I did it."

I watched this little woman lead this preacher by the hand around the bed and take his hand and lay it on her husband's forehead. His head was wet with perspiration. You could see him shivering even though he was sweating. She backed up a few steps and said, "That's exactly how you were in my dreams in your black hat and white collar with your hand on his head, and you lifted the other one up to heaven.

The reverend took his hat off and lay it on the bed. He bowed his head and then started to pray. "Dear heavenly Father in the mighty hands of Jesus, we call on You to command this evil spirit of sickness and death trying to take his life. Depart from this brother. We believe together that by the stripes you bore on Calvary, this man is healed from this infirmary! Move on this brother's life right now!

His wife needs him! By the power of the Holy Spirit in the mighty name of Jesus Christ our Healer, we pray. Amen!"

In amazement, I watched as this poor wretched soul that was on the brink of death regained his color and the perspiration disappeared. I never closed my eyes in fear that I would miss any of the things I was witnessing. I was astounded and speechless for a moment or two. I could feel a strong presence in the room, as if the room had become full of a thick fog!

The little lady just stood there with her eyes closed and the tears flowing down her face. I felt cold chills all over my body as the preacher prayed. I had felt this many times while talking with the reverend but not quite as strong as I had just felt!

A minute later, the old man opened his eyes to see the reverend standing over him. He asked in a steady, strong voice, "Who are you and why are you in my house?" Before he could finish speaking, the little woman fell on him, crying. "Shut up, you old man! This is God's servant. He comes to help you! Oh Lord, thank you so much!" she shouted. "Just like my dream! Thank you, Jesus! I told you days ago, and you wouldn't believe me. God sent these two men here to heal you! God moved and He told me He was going to!"

"Well," the sick man said, "thank you, preacher man, for coming to help us. We don't get many kind white men out here, and when we do, they just look mean and pass by."

The reverend picked up his hat that had slid off the bed when the woman had rushed over. "We would have done the same if your wife had not caught us before we completely passed your home." "God had to have sent you! White men just don't come into our homes unless they are trying to hurt us in some way. Our people are not liked by the whites here in Aberdeen County," the man said.

Brother, God doesn't see color, and neither do I. Now you eat and regain your strength so you can help your missus out on this farm. The reverend walked over to where I was standing. I stepped closer to where the man now sat up in the bed and was introduced to the couple.

"My name is Simun McCall, and this is Ruthie. We are so grateful you are here. I have been sick for so long my poor Ruthie has been taking care of everything since." Ruthie sat down next to her husband and grabbed his hand. "God knew that he was going to heal you, Simun! We just had to have faith that He would. God knows I need him so bad and I couldn't take care of this place by myself! We have been married for thirty years, and he is my partner."

"Mr. and Mrs. McCall, God loves you! He would not have sent us this way if He had other plans for your lives. I can foresee God will give you a lot more years together. The reverend and myself have had quite an adventure, and our path seems to be led by outside forces to help people like yourselves on our way!"

"Mr. Adams is correct," the reverend chimed in. "God's ways are mysterious, and His healing hands are upon you."

"Yes, sir, I believe it, and He is going to move for us now even more! I feel it with all my heart! That old mule out there, we are going to plow that field and bring in the crop this year, and no more sickness will get us!"

I put my hand on the reverend's shoulder and signaled him with a head tilt toward the door. "It is an honor to meet you, but we really need to be moving on," I said.

Mrs. McCall walked out with us as we said our good-byes. As she threw her arms around the reverend's neck, I heard her say, "Here is all the money I have, I want you to have it for what you did for us here. Everything came to pass just like my dream." Then she handed him a coin.

"No, ma'am," the reverend said, "God takes care of us." As he tried to hand the coin back to her, she grabbed his hand and wrapped it around the coin.

She held his hand really tight, shaking it, and said, "Don't you deny me of paying my way and receiving my blessing!"

"Okay, Mother, I will and I will put it to good use." The reverend put in his leather coin pouch and put it in his saddlebag. She made her way to me to hug my neck as well. She told me she wouldn't forget me either since I was the preacher man's protector and friend. After she let me go, the reverend asked if he could have one more hug before we left. Her face lit up even more, and she grabbed him up and squeezed him tight. As I began to head off toward my horse, I saw the reverend slip a paper bill in the pocket of her loose apron she was wearing.

We mounted our horses, waved goodbye, and headed on back down the trail. She continued waving at us until we were out of her sight. When I knew we were far enough so no one would hear, I asked, "I saw you slip that money into her pocket. What was that all about?"

"God put it into my heart to bless her. I try to always follow His leadings. She gave everything she had to God when she gave me her last dollar. The Word says if you give to God, he will return unto us a hundredfold. One of these days, she will be needing a blessing from God, and out of the blue, God will let her find that five dollars. She will know God hears and cares about her prayers! She will start to praise Him. I only wish I could be here to witness her praises to God. It is beautiful to see the joy of the Lord spring forth."

"I've never known a man like you, Reverend. We need to be a blessing to people and treat everyone equally. In God's eyes, there are no differences in the races, it is all the same to Him. That's why we are called Christian because we follow Christ's teachings and strive to be like Him.

"Mr. Adams, when Jesus was here on this earth, He came upon a Samaritan woman sitting at a well. Even though she was from a different race and nation, even though the Jews wouldn't have anything to do with the Samaritan people, Jesus asked if she would give him a drink of water. The woman could not believe that a Jew would ask of her when it is forbidden. The Jews would always snub the Samaritans. The Jews believed they were better than the Samaritans. The Jews believed they were unclean. Jesus loved all people. The woman at the well, being an adulteress, was unclean, but Jesus came to her. He asked her and talked to her, and when she left, he told her of the Father's love and forgiveness."

"I have heard that story before and never realized what it was referring to?" I told the reverend. We rode up a rocky incline, and the horses' hooves were kicking up quite a bit of dust. I took out my handkerchief and wiped the dust and sweat off my face. The reverend was being unusually quiet. I glanced at him to make sure he was doing alright. He had his hand on his Bible, and he seemed to be deep in thought.

Just when I was about to get his attention, he spoke up, saying, "Brother Adams, I promise you this, by the end of this journey with me, you will truly know God's love!"

When we were about ten miles from the McCalls', I heard what sounded like several horses coming in our direction. The reverend and I slowed a bit, and I put my hand on my sidearm just in case. From the other end of the trail up ahead, four men on horseback came charging our way with what looked like two young picker boys tied on the horses. We approached and we asked what these two boys had done and why they were tied up.

The man closest to us answered gruffly, "These two have broken the black codes law! We are taking them into custody. They will be in front of the judge, not that it matters. You need to be minding your own business! We have laws against loitering and them begging and having no jobs. They can't just roam the streets and beg or fish to survive! They need to find jobs, or the judge will give them one! Personally, I think they are just good for nothing, no good, and lazy."

I sat up straighter in my saddle and addressed who looked like the leader of the group. "Gentlemen, my name is Elijah

Adams, and this is Reverend Williams. I believe from what you are saying you caught these boys fishing for their food. If that was all, then that's not illegal. As for loitering, isn't that what you are doing right now?" I looked at them questioningly, but from the look on their faces, they were getting upset.

"Who do you think you are?" he yelled. "We are with the local militia. These boys are breaking the law! We are hired by the local coalition to bring them, and we have them in custody!"

I pulled my six-shooter and pointed it right at his forehead. The reverend started shouting, "Hold on! Hold on there! Just hold on!"

"No, I won't hold on. If any of these cowboys want to start something, I'm ready to finish it!" Two of those cowboys pulled their guns and pointed straight at the reverend and myself! I looked the leader dead in the eye and told him to have his men put their guns up before I put a bullet between his eyes!

The leader started shouting, "Hold on! Put your guns away!" As the tension started to rise, one of the men looked over my head and down the trail. His eyes about bugged out of his head, and he shouted, "It's the Union! We need to go!" They dropped the boys as they turned and rode off, riding as hard as their horses would carry them.

In the distance, we could see Captain Farley and his men coming our way.

Farley and his troop never slowed as they took off after those men. The reverend got off his horse to untie the boys as I rode after the action behind Farley's men! We rode as hard as we could to catch this so-called militia coalition of law keepers. Shots were fired back and forth, including mine. When those cowboys finally stopped, we did also. Shortly after, the reverend arrived and the boys (who looked a bit scared) with him.

Captain Farley recognized me and asked, "Mr. Adams, do you know who these cowboys are?"

I began to shake my head. "No, sir, they were going to put these two boys into custody for loitering and into servitude for not having a job! These boys are too young to be working except on a farm or plantation. All they were doing was fishing and not hurting anyone."

"I know, Mr. Adams, that's all they ever catch these young pickers doing is fishing or even playing when they so-called arrest them. They call themselves The Coalition. They are just terrorists in my book! Creating fear in these innocent young men and women. Harassing and killing black people! They claim to be on the law side the same as a snake that bites you is on the side of walking prevention. They may not have arrested them, maybe just took them out and lynched them. That's what cowards like them do! You just saved those boys' lives." I got off my horse to help the reverend lift the boys from the horse. We all then walked over to the captain to shake his hand in greeting.

"There was about to be a bloodbath if you had not shown up. It was pretty testy for a minute or two. Thank you again for your assistance, Farley!" I said.

"I'm just glad we were in the area, but we have to get on," he answered as he was looking over the boys to assess if they were harmed. We all started saying our goodbyes when the reverend spoke up. "Thank you again for your help. These poor boys were in distress and deserve a better life than what has been happening to them. Will you take the young men back home, or should Mr. Adams and myself take them?"

One of his men dismounted and headed over to stand in front of the boys. He leaned in and began to talk softly to them. When they began nodding their heads, he turned to his leader and nodded. "We will take them home, Reverend. We need more men willing to stand up for what is right as you two have, but we will take it from here." At his words, the lieutenant picked the first boy up and handed him to one of the other riders. He did the same with the other one, and they prepared to head out.

I mounted my horse and said, "Farley, we will be riding on toward Texas. If we can help in any way, you can find us, and we will be at your service."

The reverend asked if he could pray over these soldiers before we departed.

"No time, Reverend. You just say a prayer for us. We have to be moving on to get these boys back home. I'm sure their parents will be worried sick about them." He grabbed the reins and turned swiftly, and they all galloped away.

As we headed on down the trail, I did hear the reverend praying for them. It was a drawn-out prayer that sounded like singing that the danger was not quite over yet. He sometimes got like that when he swore we should travel a certain path because the Holy Spirit was leading us. We came to one of those forks in the path now, and instead of taking the path straight through, the reverend just pointed toward the rocky path that took us the long way around. It was rocky and hilly and everything I wasn't looking forward to.

A mile or two down the road, I was shocked to see up ahead lying in a ditch one of those cowboys whom the soldiers had chased off. He was bleeding from a bullet wound, one he got during the shoot-out I was thinking. As we jumped off our horses and walked closer to investigate if he was still alive, he pulled his gun and ordered us to back up and lay our guns on the ground. He was waving his gun all over the place and then he yelled, "You sorry ambushers hit me. I know what you are here for and I won't be going to jail!"

The reverend looked over to me with his hand palm down, and in that slow calm voice, he said to the man, "Lower the gun, brother. Can we help you? We are here to help if you allow us to. Let us get you to a doctor."

"Back up right now before you meet your maker! I'll blow both of your brains out! I'm not going to jail!" the man yelled as he pointed his gun at the reverend's head and began to steady his grip and take aim.

I raised my own gun, sighted him in, then yelled, "I have you dead in my sights. You drop your gun right now, or I'll shoot!" Then I aimed my gun right at his chest. "You go with us to the doctor, then to jail, or you won't be going anywhere but to hell!"

When I said that, he turned his gun on me and, with a sneer in his face, said, "I'll see you in hell with me!" You could hear both shots crack and then echo through the trees. He fell to the ground with my shot right between the eyes.

The reverend dropped his head into his hands and shouted, "No! We could have worked this out peaceably." I lowered my gun and put it back in the holster and then went to my horse to make sure she was calm and to give the reverend a minute.

"Reverend," I said, "sometimes you can't work it out peacefully." With a heavy heart, he walked over and prayed for that dead man.

After he finished praying, I started walking over. "I guess we should get him loaded up. We will need to take him back to Farley and his troop. He will need to be the witness to what we have here. The reverend and myself draped him over his horse, and we tied him down so he wouldn't fall off. We saddled back up and rode back toward Aberdeen.

We found the troop just on the edge of town. He looked past us to the horse following behind and asked, "Mr. Adams, what do you have over that saddle?"

"One of those cowboys was lying there bleeding on the side of the road when we found him a few miles ahead. He had fallen from his horse, and apparently one of our bullets hit him. When we approached him, he tried to kill the reverend. He took a shot at me but missed in his state.

I can understand why. But my shot was true. These are the results of his actions," I said.

"We could have done things differently!" the reverend tried to interrupt. "We truly could have arrested him without killing him. It is a shame because we will never know the state of his heart and where he stood with his salvation?"

"Reverend?" Farley replied. "From the evil ways of him and his partners, I can assure you he did not make it into heaven! Sometimes this world is better off without men like them in it. I do appreciate you reporting this to me. I will take care of things from here on out. Sorry, Reverend, but these things do happen as long as there are bad people in this world!"

"Let's move on," I said. "Captain Farley, once again, thanks for the help. You and your men be safe. I may see you again sometime?"

"Reverend, you and Mr. Adams stay safe out there," he said with a slight smile and a sarcastic tone to his voice. "You may run into the rest of those cowboys!" As if he knew we may not be done with this encounter for now…

Chapter 6

We rode for quite a while, and the reverend had not said a word to me. He just rode his horse and read his Bible. I tried to make small conversations with him, but he was apparently feeling reclusive and wouldn't say much at all. I think he may have been rattled by me having to kill that cowboy. I told him it was him or us. He just shook his head as if he was saying no, or at least disgusted by the situation. His reaction upset me.

"Reverend, what would you have had me do? Let him shoot you or me? Would it be better that he lived and one of us to die at the hands of his sort?" I asked.

In a conflicting tone, he answered, "Yes, Mr. Adams, it would have been better that I die instead of him. I do know where I would be going when I die, but I don't know about him."

"I'll tell you, Reverend, if he and his posse had hung those two picker boys, what would you think of him now? Would you be thinking God would have killed them?" I asked.

"No, sir, Mr. Adams. It is God's place for vengeance, not ours! It's in His hands, not ours. His place to reap vengeance, not ours!" he replied.

"I tell you what, Reverend, when we get to the next town, we should stay as far away from the people as we can. It is beautiful out here. Wheat fields and potato fields as far as the eye can see. Don't think our horses would mind us staying out here instead." We spotted a great place to rest and relax. I jumped off my horse and ran to relieve myself while the reverend took the horses to a grassy area to graze. I looked out over the fields and said, "Think I will dig a few of those potatoes for our horses."

"We could do that, Mr. Adams." That was all he said. He stayed very melancholy and quiet the rest of the day. Even as we were feeding the potatoes to our horses, he didn't even talk to his horse the way he normally did. They seemed to enjoy this new treat of fresh-cut potatoes. The reverend dug a few more potatoes and put them in the side bag of his mule. "I will make us some potato soup later tonight," the reverend replied.

"Sounds good to me, Reverend," I said.

"Reverend, as long as we have these scalawags and carpetbaggers down here, they will be raising all these issues. That Governor Cord has done nothing to help. Since he has been in office, the black codes and laws aimed toward the picker population keep these poor devils from being free and put back into bondage. I don't know, it might have been better for them to have remained slaves. At least before they knew where they stood. Now they can't be sure where they stand in this society. I remember when I was in Chattanooga reading about a black man being elected in this state. Not sure how long that will last here with the way this radical coalition is doing the poor pickers any way they want to and the locals allowing them to carry out this 'mob rule' justice."

"I'm sure things will be different in the future for our black brothers, here and all over the world. I heard before we left Tennessee that the pickers formed a black and tea convention to fight for their rights as freemen. The black man is starting to stand up for what they believe in!"

I kept walking back and forth, trying to stretch my legs and curb my irritation. "Well, Reverend, I don't weep for that cowboy or feel bad about what happened. Because some things are right and some are wrong. My moral compass never moved over the likes of his shooting."

He turned to me with his calm voice and said, "You shot him, Mr. Adams. You could have done something other than that."

I was in awe at his ignorance. "I offered to turn him over to the authorities. He was given the option to surrender, and he chose the other path, so it was in his hands, and now his dead body is in Farley's hands now!" I said.

"Let's not talk about this any longer. Let's just keep moving toward the west, okay?" the reverend asked as he headed toward his horse.

We mounted back on our horses and rode on. I began to hear music in the breeze. The farther we traveled, the louder it became until we spied a cluster of small shacks with people standing on their porches, playing their instruments. In most locations, the men would either have a shotgun in hand or nearby. I was guessing to make sure we were no trouble. The women and children would always go inside as we passed by their homes. Nothing happened. The reverend wanted to stop and visit, but I suggested we only waved considering we were strangers in a hostile environment.

We enjoyed the sounds as we rode by. We rode until the houses and the sounds were far behind us. We came to a fork at the path. I was going to turn to the right, but the reverend objected to us going that way.

"The Holy Spirit is compelling me to travel the left path," he said. He turned his horse in that direction and continued on. I followed close behind, pondering his words.

"Reverend," I asked, "will you explain to me what you are talking about when you say that?"

He looked back at me and slowed down so we were riding side by side. "When we become born-again believers, we have the Spirit of God living inside us. If we listen, He will lead us and guide our paths. This Holy Spirit is that still small voice that we should listen to when we are seeking God's direction."

I was listening but still not understanding. "How in the world does that happen, Reverend?" I asked.

"Just a few examples," he said. "Do you know when you tell a lie and that feeling of guilt that comes over you? Or when you killed that man earlier? That feeling that made you feel as if you did something irreversible in a bad way?"

I was nodding my head. "Yes, I know that feeling sometimes."

"The Spirit living inside of us leads us on the path God wants us to be on, and if we disobey His leading, we feel bad about our actions. This leading is more prevalent the closer we get to God. Everyone has a conscience, but a believer has a guide! Our comforter is the same as Jesus being right here with us."

"Who am I to dispute what you believe?" I said.

We came upon a few more of those little shacks. The poor blacks lived the best they could in the little abode. Most of them were friendly enough. No one came to greet us or say hi when the reverend would wave at them. The babies would always wave back till the older people would tell them to get in the house.

We rode for quite a while and saw plenty of rabbits, some coyotes, and some deer. I was thinking of killing something for our dinner, but there would be time for that. We were riding in the wide-open countryside. No reason to upset our horses and stop the flow of our travels.

Not sure as to the reason why the reverend felt compelled to travel left instead of right at the fork? Apparently, we made the right move.

We made our way to a peaceful clearing, and we rode upon the old Greensboro cemetery. The sign said "Danson Rabbit Creek 1833." It was a metal gate above the cemetery. There were many interesting tombstones. Judge Edward D. Edwards and his son apparently were killed by a Mary Molly Edwards right there on the tombstone. Hard to believe? John A. Murrell, horse thief and Natchez trace outlaw, killed in Columbus, Mississippi, but buried right here. All was written on another marker.

We rode past the cemetery and came upon the local militia or police of some sort. They were holding a road blockade in which they were looking for alcohol. It was apparently illegal to have it in this county, so they looked through our pack mule and saddlebags. They asked why we had no money and why we had no alcohol. The reverend held up his Bible and said, "This is the only thing of value we possess."

"We don't want your Bible, preacher!"

The reverend asked, "Are you men not Christian?"

The lead policeman responded with anger, "Hell yes! I'm a Christian!" When the reverend heard his response, he asked if he could pray for them. I was laughing at the man's response, but the reverend was not amused. He commenced to pray for them anyhow. "Dear heavenly Father, I ask that You put Your hand of protection upon these fine militia men as they carry out their duties. I ask that You touch their hearts and lead them to a closer walk with You. Amen!" After the completion of the prayer, the leader told us to move along and continue our business. They sat there on the blockade, fighting the good fight of ridding this area of alcohol except what we could smell on their breaths as we talked to them. Fighting crime with crime, I guess. Funny business to me.

We got some distance down the trail and came upon a patch of trees right at dark. We could hear a strange sound of music in the distance. It was a different sound than we were used to hearing, a spiritual soulful sound. We moved closer toward the sound and could see an older cabin that must have been an old picker family playing their music.

We didn't want to disturb them and that soft sound they were playing. We decided to set up camp right here just inside the tree line where we were sure they could not see us and yet we could still hear the beautiful sound. We even started a fire, and because of the trees, no one noticed we were there. The singing and playing made this night a little more special! They sang "I'll Fly away," "Amazing Grace," and some other songs I had not heard before. The last song must have come from maybe a different country. Their soulful voices and music were beautiful and soothing. I think the reverend is still a little bothered by all the killing of the past few days. It was nice to hear him sing along quietly with the songs he knew as he cooked us up those potatoes he had gathered. He then warmed some beans we had left. Potatoes and beans did not sound too bad. We had a pretty good night, and the day wasn't too bad either. We could only hope for the rest of our trip to be the same.

Chapter 7

The next morning, we awoke to a gunshot at the little cabin we had heard singing from the night before. Both of us sprang up, but our wits were not with us yet. No one knew we were just inside the tree line, so we were able to see what was taking place.

Those cowboys, the Union soldiers and ourselves had faced off against a few days earlier, had made the gunshots and were now riding off! They were not alone; they had some of the children from inside the cabin with them. We could hear screaming and crying and the sound of the horses riding away. The reverend said, "Oh my, what do we do? Should we saddle the horses and follow them? We don't have time, we are only a few yards from the house. Let's see if the people in the cabin need help."

The cowboys rode away, and we made our way toward the house. We saw a picker man lying on the ground and his wife on top of him, just crying. She jumped back, startled, and shouted, "Please don't hurt us. He's dying! Please don't hurt us anymore!"

"No, ma'am, we are not with those men that shot your husband!"

"Ma'am, we are here to help! We are not with those men. We are here to help!" the reverend and I answered at the same time.

"They shot him! Why would they shoot him? They took our children! Why would they take our children?" she answered hysterically.

"Not sure, ma'am," I said, "but we have got to get help for your husband! If he is still alive." She had her hand on her husband's chest, and she put her ear near his mouth.

We all were silent, waiting for her answer. "Yes, sir, he is still breathing. He's been shot through the side."

"Looks like he took one just to the left of the heart closer to the shoulder." As I turned the brother over, I could see it had come out on the backside. He was bleeding pretty harshly. "Can you hear me, brother?" I asked.

"Yes, sir, I can hear ya!" the shot man said. "Don't worry about me! Save my children. Please get my children."

"Sir, we have got to get you to a doctor before you bleed to death." His wife started shaking her head with a look of frustration on her face and said, "Greensboro is the closest town about seven miles south of here. No doctor will see him because he's a colored man. Dr. Jones is the doctor, and he won't help the coloreds! He only treats the whites here." She almost spat the last words.

"We will see about that," I said. "Let's get your husband into bed, then I will ride to town and find this doctor." The reverend and I got down on either side of the man, and as we tried to lift him, I asked, "Can you walk, sir?"

"Yes, sir, I will try," he grunted as we put his arms over both mine and the reverend's shoulders. We carried him into the cabin and helped his wife undress him and lay him in the bed. He had to have weighed well over two hundred pounds, standing over six feet. Good thing he was a large and strong man, or he may not have survived his injuries, I thought.

"Why would they take our children? We never hurt anyone. We are just poor farmers," he asked.

"They probably thought they could get away with it. They never counted on us being just outside. We have got to get you some help before you won't be any good for anyone. Greensboro is the name you called that town?"

"Yes, sir, it's seven miles," she repeated. She was crying now and looked completely broken.

"Reverend, you see what you can do to help this man. I will ride hard and find this Dr. Jones and get him here as soon as I can." I ran over to where we had been camping in the woods and saddled Rosie. I rode, leaving the reverend's two animals still tied at our campsite and riding hard with Rosie doing exactly as she was supposed to do as a Quarter Horse. She rode like the wind.

In no time, Rosie and I were in Greensboro. I started asking around at the local stores where I can find Dr. Jones? Pointing fingers led me to his office that was located on the other side of town.

I walked into the doctor's office and saw the doctor sitting behind a desk, writing on some papers. He immediately jumped up when he saw the look on my face. "Dr. Jones, my name is Elijah Adams. I'm a deputy out of Tennessee! We were traveling toward town and found a man that had been shot outside of town, and he needs help right now!"

"Yes, sir, who is the fine gentleman? I may know him, Mr. Adams."

"I didn't catch his name, just that he needs help. Let's go, Doctor!" He looked around the room and headed toward a chair next to a cot on the left side of the room.

"Okay, sir, let me gather my bag and get my horse." I helped him saddle his horse, and we were on our way. I was reluctant to tell him his patient was a black man. If he had known the man was picker, he may not have come. We rode north for a spell, and he started asking questions.

"Where was he shot at and how bad was the wound?" he asked.

"He was shot in the side, and it looked pretty serious. The bullet did exit out his back, but we have to get you to him to get him fixed up!"

"Mr. Adams, does he have a beard? What does the man look like?"

"He's clean chined. He's a rather tall man, big in size."

"Is he a farmer?"

"Yes, Doc, I think he is a farmer."

"In this direction? I don't know any farmers in this direction except for the pickers! I don't treat the blackies, Mr. Adams! I don't know what you would have me do. Those people need to take care of themselves!"

"If you call yourself a doctor, he needs your help! He's a man just like any other you have treated!" He began to slow his horse down, so I rode up next to him and put my hand on my gun.

"The pickers are vagrants, and they can't pay for my services! I have no intention of helping the pickers!" he said as he looked at me.

"When you went to school, you took an oath to help people no matter what color their skin is! Whether you like it or not, the pickers are people that bleed the same blood we bleed. No different than you or me! Right now, he has no color. Just red. If you value not seeing your own blood, you will come with me to help this man! Or I will flog you off that horse and you will walk back to town!"

"You will not sir. I will have the authorities on you as soon as I get back to town!" he said. So I got in behind him, and with my pistol in my hand, I made him take the lead.

"Maybe so if they can find me, or you make it to town to tell them! Fine, Doctor! I told you before that we are just passing through and not stopping. You just keep traveling north ahead of me, and we will get to your patient soon!"

He puffed up his chest and started waving his arms around. "I will not be talked to this way, mister!" he started, but before he could say another word, I interrupted him. "Your daddy should have spanked you and taught you respect for all life, not just whom you think deserves it! That man works hard taking care of his family unlike some of these boys you take care of in this town. Now keep riding! If you turn to the right or the left, I will knock you to the ground, and you will be walking if you can get up. I'll take your horse, and you will find it at the patient's cabin!"

"We will just see about all this, Adams!" he sneered back at me.

When we were almost there, I informed him reluctantly, "I will pay you for your services. Don't worry about that, good doctor."

Nervously yet with a little satisfaction in his voice, he said, "Well, if I am getting paid, I guess I will see what I can do to help this nigga man."

"All you doctors are alike, you only care about yourselves and what you're getting paid! People are no different than animals. Men and women or even children can live or die. It's the same to you as long as you're getting paid, right?" I said.

"I have been treating the fine community here for more than twelve years and I am very well respected in my town, I will have you know!" he said.

"When you only help those whites who can afford it and refuse to help the pickers who are poor because they have always been slaves is no different than the wild Indians who hate every white man just because of the color of our skin! No different! You're worse than them because they have reasons to hate, but you have none! I bet you sit in church every Sunday and justify your actions by the front you put on for the other fakers that sit with you there! Your kind makes me sick!"

"I treated them on the plantation when their masters were paying me to, but now that they are all freedmen, they must pay for their own care. These poor pickers can't afford my services!"

"Keep riding, Doctor! If you open your mouth for any reason except to ask which way, you will be lying on the ground!" After that, all I heard was him clearing his throat and not even looking back.

The good doctor was taking his sweet time riding. Hoping maybe someone he knew would happen to ride by was my guess. I tapped his horse on the backside to get it moving, and the doc fell off. After he remounted, my Rosie continued to push his horse until we arrived at the small shack. The lady was standing on the porch, so I replied, "This is the doctor, he's going to help your husband! Right, Doc?" I gave him a piercing look.

"Yes, of course I am. Where might the patient be?" he asked as he dismounted, pulled his medical bag off the side of his horse, and headed toward the reverend.

I remained in my saddle. "I have got to go find the men who shot him and stole their children. I will pay you when I return if you save him. If he dies, then I will pay you for that also!" I turned my horse to the camp to saddle the reverend's horse while the reverend spoke to the doctor.

"God will repay you for what you do here. He will repay you as you have done to these people. I bless you in the name of Jesus Christ for the good you are doing here!"

The doctor looked dumbfounded. He was one of these people who sit on a church pew every Sunday. Christian in appearance only. An upstanding citizen in that church. He could not but feel embarrassed by what the reverend said. He looked down at his feet. When he looked up, he swallowed hard and replied, "I promise you, Reverend, I will do all I can to save this man. His children will need him when you find them and bring them back home."

"You can expect payment when we return. We have got to find the children before it's too late!"

"What about the children? Who took their children?" he asked.

"Cowboys came and took all three of these people's children and shot the dad when he tried to stop it from happening!"

The mother who was listening was still crying. "Please bring my babies back!"

The doctor grabbed the reverend by the arm. "The Hayes Plantation is where you will find them. The plantation is the place where they take young blacks to work when they are arrested. I never knew they were taking them without cause. We are told the pickers are arrested for different crimes. Just ride east and you will find it about five or six miles from here. Stay on the main route and you will find those children. I don't agree with what they are doing! I don't treat blacks because it is looked down on here in Greensboro. We are being told the blacks are lazy and criminals. I will have no part in this activity any longer. No one has a right to take their children. I hope that will help, Mr. Adams, Reverend. Do your best to find those babies!"

I led the reverend's horse over to him, and he jumped on. We both turned to follow the direction the cowboys had gone. We rode hard, and the reverend informed me what the doctor had said. We followed the tracks east for about five miles or so, and sure enough, we started to see the dust from their horses ahead. They were not traveling that fast, thinking they got away free, was my guess. We were somewhere near a town called Winona. We were staying back enough and out of sight, so they still didn't know we were following. We had to figure out how to get closer and confront them before they made it to the plantation. If they made it there, it may be hard to get the children back.

"Well, Reverend, what do you think we should do? We can't shoot, we may hit the children," I said. I pulled my pistol from its holster and checked to make sure it was fully loaded.

"Not sure what we should do. I am praying for the answer. Also praying for that man back there that was shot. Praying for the Lord to guide the hands of the doctor even though I know he is skilled enough to take care of him. The Lord's guidance is always welcome. Praying God opens up a way for us to help the children to escape."

"The only way the children can escape is if we can help them. More than likely, if they try to get away, they will be shot! If they fight too much, they may get lynched! These men are cowards. Making a living off the blood of others and selling these young black kids are highly immoral! Hard to believe people could be that evil! We need to get them before they go to this Hayes Plantation."

"This brings up hatred toward people, and I don't like the feelings I am having right now. I want to pray but I have these very bad feelings." The reverend closed his eyes and bowed his head. You could see the internal struggle he was having.

"No one likes those feelings of reverence unless you're pure evil! This world is evil, and there are evil people, and sometimes we must fight evil with evil!"

"The Bible says those who live by the sword die by the sword. I chose this sword of the Spirit as my only weapon, and that is the only weapon I will use as my sword! God will take care of this situation if we trust Him." He held up his Bible and had it clutched in his hand tightly.

"God does take care of us, Reverend, but sometimes we must act on our own, and He will bless those efforts!

Maybe He makes us able to shoot straight or fight strong so we can help ourselves. I should have been killed many times over, but God protected me, and here I stand to fight for those children. For this very moment to save those who can't save themselves and you too, Reverend."

"God does have a way of opening doors when we need them the most, Mr. Adams."

"He also has a way of opening wounds for bullets when we need those also, Reverend."

He was steadfast in his beliefs. I had to give him that. He took a deep breath and, as his final request, said, "If at all possible, try not to kill anyone, please, Mr. Adams?"

"I will do my best, but I also won't let these kids be harmed! So let's see what we need to do about this situation."

They had stopped to set up camp. One of the men we could hear complaining. We hid our horses in the woods far enough where they wouldn't be heard and made our way on foot to where we could see the camp. The little girl just kept crying. "Reverend, did you happen to ask how old the kids were? That girl just keeps crying."

"The boys are twelve and thirteen, and the little girl is nine. She must be scared out of her little mind," the reverend said in a sad whisper.

"Why would they want a nine-year-old, good Lord? What could they possibly do with a baby?"

"I can't imagine, Mr. Adams, I really can't! Maybe they are just seeing if they can get anything for them. They can probably make a pretty penny up at that mansion."

We made our way a little bit closer. "I think we will need to work our way around to the front of their camp. We must stay out of sight where they can't see us or hear us! If they do, there is no telling what they might do to those kids."

With my Spencer rifle in hand, we eased closer. We got within seventy yards and stopped for a moment. I saw they were carrying the kids to tie them for the night when the youngest boy started crying. The man dropped him and slapped him. "You shut that bawling up, nigger!" the man said. The older brother tried to console him until he was pushed away from the brother. The little girl just kept crying. I guess they couldn't get her to stop. When they struck her brother, she screamed. We used the noise to make our way to about thirty to forty yards from them. We were still hidden, and I could hear two of the six men arguing. They said they could make enough from the two older boys that they didn't need the girl. She wasn't worth the effort, one of the cowboys had said! They finally decided to just take them all and see what we could get for them.

Night was beginning to fall fast, and the air began to cool. The men took their saddles off their horses and looked like they were in for the night. The leader stood in front of his men and began, "We are only about two or three miles from the plantation. Tomorrow we will drop them off, get our money, and leave the problems there!" The men began to grumble in agreement. "Then we can go find a drink!" That brought a round of loud cheers from his men. "Keep watch! Split up in groups of two and decide which shift you want. The rest of us get some rest. We leave at first light." He turned and headed to use his saddle as a pillow.

"I have two of them within range of my Spencer rifle, Reverend. Should I take them out one by one?" I whispered.

Whispering back, he said, "No, let's wait till they go to sleep. We can sneak in and take the children. The bigger man is gathering firewood and rocks for a fire. Let's hunker down and wait to see what they were up to." They relieved themselves and then started cooking over their fire. We could hear them talking and settling down.

The reverend and myself lay there the whole time until my legs started to fall asleep. I suggested we go back and check on the horses. We inched our way back and found them fine and calm. We retied them at least two hundred yards away where they could not be heard. When the night fell, we had snuck back to where we could watch what was going on.

In the wee hours of the morning, I woke the reverend up. He had fallen asleep about an hour before. "I'm going for the kids. I want you to sneak toward the horses easily so as not to startle them and untie them all at the same time so they have no way of following when we ride off. Hopefully it will distract them when they have to chase their horses. Make your way back to where we are now. After I get the kids, we will ride out of here."

The reverend slowly eased over to the horses. When he was near, I was ready. After untying them, he slapped one on the butt, and they all followed the lead into the dark. I could hear them stampeding, waking one man, who shouted, "The horses have broken free!" They all began to pursue, but the leader shouted to the one in the rear to stay with the camp and watch the brats. So he stayed, and the other cowboys took off after the horses. When they were out of sight, I ran straight up on the man, and before he could see me, I hit him on the side of the head with my colt. When the kids saw this, they started screaming! I quickly knelt down in front of them and said, "Calm down, kids, I'm here to help you! Your mother sent me! I'm taking you back to her!" They were all crying and scared, but they nodded and watched me with fear and hope shining in their eyes.

"Come on, follow me," I said in a loud whisper. I grabbed the little girl up and, with the boys following, headed to the spot where we had lain in wait all night. We lay low, waiting for the reverend to show up. After ten minutes, I started to wonder. After fifteen minutes, nothing! The reverend didn't show up—didn't show at all! My heart began to sink. I was sure they had him! "Okay, kids, we are just going to have to keep moving."

About that time, I heard a gunshot. I still had my Colt in my hand. I heard someone say, "I don't know who is out there, but if you don't bring those kids out right now, this man here is about to be shot! If you want him alive, ease those kids back this way! Now!" I looked up slowly to see what I was dealing with. "Bring those pickers right now! I can hear them crying! I know where you are," he shouted again as he held the reverend in front of him with a gun to the back of his head. "Not only will I kill him, but I will also start shooting in that direction! Everyone with you is going to die if you don't bring them to me." He paused to take a breath. I could see his eyes scan the area we were at and squint as he tried to see our exact location. His eyes were cold, and he was shaking with rage. "One thing is for sure, if you don't bring them to me, this man is going to die now!"

As he spoke, I wasn't sure what to do. Then he said, "I'm counting down from five, and when I make it to zero, this man is shot between the eyes! Bring those coons right now!" Then he counted. "Five!" He pushed the reverend in front of him. "Four!" He spun him around to face him. "Three!" He raised the gun and pointed it right in between the reverend's eyes and then paused. "Two more seconds! If I don't see movement, he's a dead man!"

I leaned down and whispered to the kids, "We have to go back to save the reverend." I stood up so he could see me.

The cowboy shouted, "Drop your gun, mister." I lifted it high so he could see it in the moonlight and dropped it where I would know where it was at. My rifle was lying beside it. I knew if I tried, he would have shot the reverend or one of the kids. There were also five adults and one of me.

I made my way over with the kids. The cowboy said, "Well, glad you could join us! Who are you men?"

"You met us earlier with the bluecoats," I said as one of the other men grabbed the children and brought them over to the tree again. They didn't tie them up, just left them standing to the side with two cowboys, guns trained on them.

"I remember you, Adams. This must be the good reverend. Don't try anything because the boys have their guns on you. What happened to my man that you shot?" he asked.

"He died," I explained. "We took him back to town. Turned him over to the bluecoats captain, and his men took care of him. They buried him close to town."

"Reverend, you go stand by those coons and shut their crying up. I have no use for the likes of you two! I know if we kill a white man, they will not stop looking for us. The pickers I could kill, and no one would care."

The reverend began walking to the children, pleading, "Please do not hurt these babies! Their mother would be heartbroken! She wouldn't want to continue!"

"No one cares about these bunch of pickers," one of the cowboys spat.

"If you must kill anyone, take my life and spare these children! Please!" The reverend pushed the kids closer together and then stepped forward, away from them, so if they decided to shoot him, they wouldn't accidentally be hit.

"You know, Reverend, we can't kill a white man and get by with it!" the cowboy said. With that, he turned his gun right at the little girl and said, "Now you will shut up!" Before he could pull the trigger, the reverend jumped in front of the little girl. He fired and hit the reverend as he leaped in front of her. The reverend fell to the ground on top of the little girl and lay completely still. The gruff murdering cowboy said, "Grab the boys!" Three of the men dragged the crying and startled boys and me away. My heart sank, not knowing if they had killed the reverend and the little girl. One of the cowboys looked over to where the reverend lay and asked, "It was just a little picker. Why would he sacrifice himself for that?"

"Let them die!" the leader shouted. "Let's go!" He waved his arm in a circular motion and began walking to what was left of the camp. We all took off walking toward the east, and by morning, they had rounded up all the horses. I was not a praying man, but as we walked, I asked the dear Lord to be with that little girl if she was still alive. I was almost certain the reverend was dead. Hard to believe that the man who always said the hand of God's protection was upon him had been killed! Tears welled in my eyes, and a lump formed in my throat thinking about it. He tried to save the little girl, and that was his intention. I hope he was successful and she found somewhere safe to go to.

They saddled up all the horses and made me double-up behind one of them. As we traveled, I kept wondering what was to become of that baby left out there under the reverend's dead body.

Chapter 8

We rode for over two miles that morning till we came to what must have been the Hayes Plantation that the doctor had told us about. They kept me on the outskirts. The one I had hit in the head was staying quiet, so maybe he was still groggy from the blow. I was not sure of what was going to happen, but he kept a gun steady on me the whole time. I would ask him what was going on, and he would just tell me, "Shut up! My head is still hurting. I don't want to hear from you!" I could see a small amount of dried blood on the side of his face. I must have hit him pretty hard.

After they made the transaction, they left the two boys there at the plantation and made their way back to where we waited for over an hour. We rode on until we came to a clearing. The leader said, "This will do." I asked the men who they were and what they were going to do with me. He said, "You don't need to know our names. All you need to know is we are a coalition militia that controls the pickers here. We gather the vagrant pickers and put them to useful work here at the plantation! As of now, we have had no problems. Don't you know we have black codes to enforce and we have a right to bring these lazy pickers in?"

I was shaking my head and began to inform them that they had no right to kidnap these people for doing absolutely nothing, and that they had no right to bring them here and sell them back into the same slavery that was before President Lincoln freed them. The one I had hit returned the favor and hit me in the mouth. "I'm tired of hearing from you!" he yelled in my face.

"Give me a gun," I said. "You and I can settle this right now!"

The leader looked out over his men and said, "Should we shoot him?" He looked around and saw a large tree. Nodding toward it, he said, "I have a better idea!" The mean one nodded and said, "You will see soon what's going to happen to you for interfering with the local law! Let's hang him. No one will ever know we did it. He's right here by the plantation. Anyone who finds him will think he was a worker and they hung him for breaking some of their rules! Won't have a clue it was us. We can drag our tracks so no one knows we were here!" He pointed out to a couple of the men on the other side of me. "Get a rope, boys. Let's lynch him! He deserves it for betraying his own kind. Negro lover!"

Angrily, I said, "You know, you men claim to be on the side of the law. You will hang for this. There is a special place in hell for men like you! I pray you men will repent. For now, all you are headed straight for hell!"

"Gag him. I am tired of hearing him," the leader said as he threw his bandana to the man closest to me. I was gagged, tied, and slapped one more time and pushed upon a horse by three men. The other man tied a noose at the end of their rope and put it around my neck.

"You brought this on yourself for not keeping your nose out of other people's business. That reverend deserved what happened to him. We were just controlling these pickers or killing them. No different than controlling a dog or a horse! Why would you care if they are just a tool to be used like a plow horse!" the leader yelled.

One of the cowboys threw the rope over the limb above the horse I was sitting on and pulled the bandana out of my mouth, asking, "Any last words?"

"Yeah, all you men can burn in hell! No matter what you think, those kids that you call animals are still humans no matter how you look at them! They are created in God's image the same as all men are. I've prayed for my salvation, you better worry about your own!"

"Shut his face! Put that gag back in his mouth! We don't want to hear his crap!" the leader said with vile. He then raised his pistol in the air and shot, spooking the horse off. I was hanging and gasping for my last breath!

The gunshot not only spooked the horse but also alerted Captain Farley, who was just around the bend looking for us. They came riding in as fast as they could and scared the cowboys away. As I was hanging there, about to pass out, I saw a familiar face just before I lost consciousness. The reverend was riding with the Union Army. He turned and rode straight for me. He grabbed my leg and pulled me up over his saddle. Of course, I was unconscious while this was happening.

"Need some help here!" the reverend shouted. "Cut him down! Cut him down!" One of the soldiers came over and did just that. I fell off the reverend's saddle and hit the ground.

I did not know how long I was out. When I woke up, all I could see was the good reverend looking down at me. He had his hand on my chest and one in the air, praying and praising God! "Thank you, Lord, for saving this man!"

"Reverend," I said with a croak in my voice, "you got shot. I thought you were dead!"

With tears in his eyes, he answered, "Yes, they shot me. God's Word saved me! The Word of God protected me. The bullet never touched me." He pulled his little Bible from inside his coat pocket. That four-inch-thick Bible stopped that 32-caliber bullet from piercing his body and was still lodged inside. "Looks like you were protected by the Word of God," I said. My voice was a bit raspy and sore from the rope being around my neck.

"The hand of God, Mr. Adams! The hand of God!" He then told me that when he had fallen on the little girl, her breath had been knocked out of her lungs. He was able to whisper to her to lie still and not make a sound. He had taken the little girl back to her mother once the cowboys and I had rode away. When he got there, the Union soldiers had just arrived. When the doctor had made it back to town, he had told Captain Farley everything that had happened. "If we had not arrived here right now and heard that gunshot, we might have never found you! If they had slapped the horse on the butt instead of shooting that gun, you would be dead now! This was all the hand of God! He put it in their mind to shoot that gun and pointed us to exactly where you were at the right moment." The reverend helped me to my feet and led me over to my horse. Rosie, I never thought I would see her again. He had ridden her because he knew she was faster.

"Mr. Adams, ride with these soldiers and find those men!" Captain Farley yelled from the other side of the clearing. "We must go after them now if we hope to catch them. When we return, we will have a word with this Hayes Plantation! We will put a stop to this plantation buying and selling people any longer! Are you up to the task Mr. Adams?"

"I am, Captain. Let's ride!" We rode hard as the reverend started walking back toward the plantation. He was going to stay out of sight and watch to see if he could see the boys. He told us if he didn't see anything, then he would head on back to the cabin to check on the kid's father and wait for news.

We rode for about an hour following their hoof tracks. They rode into a river and appeared to ride out on the other side. Apparently, they had started out on the other side and backtracked back down the river. By the time we figured it out, it was about three hours into the chase. The captain decided that we would turn back before nightfall so we could retrieve the two boys from the plantation before it was too late. When we arrived back at the clearing, he suggested I go find the reverend and head back with him. He assured me he would retrieve the two kids for the plantation. "They will be back home with their family by nightfall. I promise you that," he said.

"Thank you once again, Captain, for what you're doing here and for saving my life. I will be forever grateful to you for saving my life!" I said.

"Mr. Adams, with the help of men like you and the reverend, it's easier to do our jobs." He then led his troops back to the plantation.

I came upon the reverend still walking toward the little cabin. I helped him climb aboard my horse, and we rode. We stopped at the campsite where we had tried to free the children and were surprised to see my guns still lying on the ground. We retrieved them and the rest of our things and headed back to the cabin. It was well into the night when the soldiers arrived with the boys safely. They brought back not only the two boys but also a handful of others. No boy could have been over fifteen years in age. The look of relief, happiness, and pure joy on their parents' faces will be with me forever.

Farley assured us that the Hayes Plantation will not be receiving picker people any longer. A full investigation was going to be conducted on the workers that the plantation has currently. Each soldier riding horseback had a child riding behind them. Farley said this was all they could carry with them. They left some men behind to watch over the rest, and they would be returning with federal agents to shut the slave trade for good! We helped the boys dismount. They looked half-starved and bruised up. The little mother was so grateful to have her sons back home she hugged not only them but also everyone—the soldiers, myself, and the reverend. She bent over and started hugging all the children. "Come on," she said to the other boys, "let's get you youngins fed!" Then she led them inside her home.

Captain Farley took the reverend and me aside and told us he spoke to the plantation manager. He assured me he knew nothing about how those cowboys were capturing these young men. No more would they be receiving the pickers from those characters. I assured him there would be an investigation. They may be shut down soon!" We all turned and looked to the cabin where we could hear little Momma and the boys chattering away and spoons clinking on bowls. She had made a large pot of stew, thinking she might feed the soldiers as a thank-you. Feeding all those boys, I don't think her smile could get any bigger.

"We will be taking all these children to be reunited with their parents at their homes. We will make sure they get there safely. If you two would like to accompany us on this task, you are more than welcome or you can continue toward Texas. I know you are running way behind as it is. Either way, I assure you what needs to be done here will be. How is the father doing? Will he live?" With a slight smile, the reverend said, "He will be fine. He is such a strong man, a fighter. All he kept asking about was the well-being of his children. That doctor did what he said he would do. He patched him up good as new.

"Very good to hear. I would say this family will be needing him to make this farm a family home."

"Captain, how can these fine people be assured that those cowboys don't return here and harass them or something worse?" I asked.

"Now that we are aware these things are happening, my men and I will be patrolling this area. We will be stopping by and checking in now and then to make sure we keep everything in this area square. I will be writing headquarters of these happenings and the Hayes Plantation. I'm having one of my men personally deliver my findings. There will be an investigation. This stuff will not be happening. It ends now!" he said angrily.

"I have confidence in you, Captain." I reached over to him to shake his hand. "I think we will be heading west. We do need to be making our way on to El Paso."

The reverend said his goodbyes and prayers for the family. Prayers and hugs for the other boys that were recovered. Prayers for the soldiers for a safe journey.

We mounted up and headed on the well-worn trail toward the west. I was glad to be leaving one of the closest calls to death I had ever experienced. It was a truly stressful couple of days, to say the least. I may have a scar on my neck forever. I can almost believe what the reverend said of God's hand being upon us. If we had not come this way, those kids would have been lost. The father would have died because the doctor would not have come to treat him. The Hayes Plantation may not be stopped from its evil ways. These things had to be ordained from something bigger than what we could see. I asked the reverend how that Bible stopped a 32-caliber bullet?

"As we were about to go to sleep that night, listening to the singing from the cabin, I felt compelled to put my Bible into my coat pocket. The thickness of the Bible and the money I carried in that Bible were just enough to stop the bullet from penetrating my side. God's hand is behind all of this. He saved my life, the baby girl's life, and yours, Mr. Adams. Not sure why everything happens, but I am assured of His saving power every day! He is always in control, so I trust Him in everything I do. This is why I try to tell everyone of God's loving-kindnesses and grace. He is truly alive and saves lives literally."

"Too bad, Reverend, that more people can't see things the way you see them. This would be a better world full of better people."

"Not sure, Mr. Adams, how people can look at other people as if they are so much lower than themselves just because they are a different color. Willing to shoot that little girl without remorse or respect for human life? Thank you, Lord, for allowing me to step in and take that bullet. That baby has a right to grow up!" he said with tears in his eyes. "She should grow to have a long and meaningful life. Her children may one day be leaders in this country."

"By the way, Reverend, did you happen to get the name of the family so maybe if we ever pass through her again, we can visit them?"

"Yes, sir, Mr. and Mrs. Parks. Not sure of the name of the children, but that mother and father are very brave. True courage in the scary world we live in at the moment. She prayed the whole time for not only her children but our safety as well. When I arrived with that little girl, she fell to the ground face down, praising Jesus for the safe return of that baby." With tears still running down his face, he continued, "When I assured her the two boys were still alive, she reminded me of my mother crying for her children and their safety. Such a beautiful mother!"

"I am so grateful you asked me to come on this journey with you! Not sure why all these things are happening. This has opened my eyes to the supernatural. Seeing God's hand in all the things we are going through is amazing. If I had faith before, I can assure you now it has been reinforced by what has taken place in the last day or so."

As we rode down the trail, I could hear a renewed happiness in the reverend's singing that had been missing for a while. I can't always make out what he was singing, but I could always tell he was happy. God stepped in to help us save so many people so far this journey, including those kids, it looked like. He kept singing and reading from his now torn Bible for around twenty-five or thirty miles. The open field we came upon was wide with thick green grass and large dark green trees that bordered the edges, and behind the trees was a wide clear stream. It was the perfect place where we could camp. I looked over, and he continued to pray even as I dismounted.

"Reverend, praying for anything in particular?"

"Just talking to my Lord, singing his praises. Of His goodness and how great He is. How blessed we are to have such a great savior! How wonderful He is to all His children! Just so thankful that we can reach up at any time, and He is right there for us anytime, loving us through all our weaknesses and faults. His love will never fail or falter! He is always good and faithful!" He walked around with his Bible in his hand and his hands in the air. You could feel the presence of God in this place. The sun was just beginning to set, and its rays were shining through the trees like rays of hope.

"Yes, Reverend, it is a good day. He is a good God!" I walked our horses over to the edge of the water and went about finding wood for our fire. "I'll have this fire started if you want to bring out the beans."

"Mr. Adams, we still have some jerky. God always provides what we need. Maybe not what we want or anything to make us comfortable but what we need he provides! We will be fine. I think I would like to try to find us some cheese when we get to another bigger town. See if there may be a dry goods store, we could sure use a large piece we can carry in our saddlebags. We need to replenish many of our supplies."

Sounds like a plan, Reverend!" It ended up being a clear night with a full moon. I put a large log on the fire and said good night to the reverend. Just before I started to fall asleep, I felt the need to quietly say a little prayer of thanksgiving. As I closed my eyes, I lay back, and hearing the reverend humming softly had me remembering the singing from the little cabin as we did a few nights before. Bringing back those memories, I was able to fall into a restful sleep.

Chapter 9

Before we left Captain Farley, he had told us we would be headed southwest toward Vicksburg. We had traveled a day or so uneventfully, which was a good change from all the excitement of the last week! We traveled with singing and prayer. The reverend would read his Bible out loud a lot. I can't say I didn't need it or that it got on my nerves because it did. I let him do what he needed to do.

"Mr. Adams, can I ask you a question?" he asked me one morning.

Nodding, I looked over at him and answered, "Of course, Reverend, what's on your mind?"

"I know you do not agree with slavery or treating others differently, so why would you have fought with the

South instead of the North during the war efforts? That was the only reason the picker people are free now?"

"Well, the misconception by many is that the Civil War was about freeing the slaves, but it was not. It was about the government trying to regulate commerce unfairly from the South. The farmers and ranchers were so successful that the North was trying to tell the South they had to pay more in taxes than the Northerners! Jefferson Davis, President Lincoln, the Republicans, and all the Southern states believed that no more states would have new slaves. The South decided to secede from the United States due to not wanting to give away all of its wealth unfairly to the North. America is a great place until the government gets out of control and tries to enforce its will on people who need to be left alone, especially when those people had done nothing but be successful in the ways they did business."

"If the war was about slavery, why was it almost two years after the war started that the emancipation proclamation was not proclaimed? The war started in 1861 due to the Southern states seceding from the Union. The emancipation proclamation was in 1863. This is why I fought with the South because the government over-stepped the bounds of our Constitution. Nothing good came out of this war, only death and destruction. Turning men's hearts toward the thoughts of killing and tearing down instead of building up is not my idea of freeing any-one! We freed the slaves but bound all that participated in the godforsaken war! No one ever wins when good men have to die!"

"Never heard it explained quite that way, Mr. Adams. That does bring to light what was behind America's worst nightmare. Too many lost their lives for a cause that could have been solved with negotiations instead of bloodshed."

We rode without talking much after this conversation. I think we both were remembering things from the war that would not leave our memories for quite a while—

nightmares, for me, from the battles I was in. The reverend helped with the sick and injured from the battles around Chattanooga and Rossville.

"Mr. Adams, I think when we arrive at the next large town, let's take a break from this traveling. Sleeping on a real bed would be a good change. Washing in a warm bath would do us some good. The cold creek baths we have been taking would clean you but never refresh the spirit. I also would like to change into my other suit. This one has a hole in it now." He slid his finger through the hole the bullet had gone in.

"Sounds good to me, Reverend. It would be nice to clean up with a shave and a clean change of clothes."

"I am seeing some buildings ahead. That must be Vicksburg. It looks quite large from here. I had heard the war destroyed most of the large buildings, but it looks like the people have rebuilt it. Not seeing much activity on the streets from here. Let's ride on in and say hi to the good people. What do you say, Reverend?" I prodded my horse to move faster and started praying for this to be an uneventful visit.

We rode closer and slowed to a walk. The reverend assured me he had been praying and that God's hand was upon us and He would protect us.

"God has shown up many times on this trip. I have no doubt about that, Reverend."

We came riding into town through Main Street. I scanned some of the signs to see what kind of businesses were in sight. There was a restaurant, a motel, and a dry goods store. I think we are in the right place, Reverend. We rode down the street to the motel that had a sign that read "The Silver Dollar"—a good name considering that was all I had in my pockets, a few silver dollars.

We decided to go in and see if they had room for a couple of dirty travelers. We dismounted and tied our horses in front of the motel, and I grabbed my rifle. Walking into the motel's front door, we saw the hotel clerk behind a small desk. The reverend walked up and asked, "Sir, do you have any rooms available?"

He smiled up at the reverend, nodding his head, pulled a key from his pocket, and unlocked the top drawer of the desk. "Yes, my friend, I have got two rooms at the top of the stairs, no problem. Fresh linens only slept on a few times. That will be a dollar a night," the hotel clerk replied as he pulled out two keys and held them up.

"We will take it," I replied to him.

The clerk turned the registration book around to the reverend and said, "Sign here and that will be a dollar per room in advance, please?"

I started to step back toward the counter, but the reverend pulled his Bible out and paid for both rooms. "I can pay for my own, Reverend!" I protested.

"No, sir, Mr. Adams, you pay for the care of the horses, and I will take care of the rooms."

The clerk looked at us as if we were true out-of-towners. "You gentlemen are from Texas with those accents?" he asked.

The reverend told the clerk that he was from Tennessee, and I was from Texas. We are traveling back to Texas and will only be staying one night to clean up and get a good night's sleep. The reverend then asked if he had a bath available.

"Yes to that also," he answered excitedly as he rounded the stairs on his way to the back room. "That is two bits for that! It's open right now. If you would like, I can have the girl heat you some water right now. If you would like the girl to wash you, that would be extra."

The reverend spoke up quickly to reject the help. "Yes, we will take the bath, but no to any help!" The reverend began to follow the clerk but stopped to look back to where I was still standing.

"You go ahead, Reverend. I will take care of our horses." Then thinking I might need to know, I asked the clerk, "Could you tell me where the local livery is at? Also, this restaurant beside us, is it a good place to eat?"

The clerk came walking back in the room, saying, "Ms. Louisa owns one of the best restaurants in the area and is a very good cook. She will take care of you, fine gentleman. Tell her I sent you there." He walked over and handed the reverend a towel and then turned back to me. "You can stable your horses at the end of town with Mel Samson. He owns the livery." He walked me to the door and pointed me in the right direction.

The reverend headed up to his room, and I took the horses to the stables. Sure, they would enjoy a night of sweet feed and soft hay to rest in the same way as we will enjoy a night in a bed with something other than dirt to make us comfortable.

The sign said "Mel's Livery" in a handwritten bill above the barn doors. I walked into the yard to find Mel at the anvil hammering on a horseshoe. He waved and asked what else I needed. He looked over the horses. "This paint has a loose shoe. Want me to fix that too?" he asked.

"Yes," I replied. "If you have room, my horses need stalls, some sweet feed, hay, and some rest. I'll be back by noon tomorrow to retrieve them."

"Want me to shine those saddles and bathe your horses as well?" Mel asked.

"No, sir, we just need the shoes checked and the horses stabled so they can get a break for the night."

For a big man, he was soft-spoken with a Russian or German accent. He said, "Yes, I have three open stalls in the back. You can pay me when you pick the beasts up in the morning." He told me a price that included fixing the shoe, and I agreed that would be fair. I thanked him and immediately started thinking about finding a drink and a bath in that order.

I grabbed my change of clothes from Rose's saddlebag before I left her. I went around the back of the hotel where the reverend was walking out of the bath area. "I had her draw you some water for a bath as well. She is filling it right now. It may be ready now." He still looked wet, but he looked clean and relaxed.

"Thanks, Reverend. I will knock on your door when I finish so we can get a bite to eat after."

"I will be in my room reading when you're ready," he said as he headed up the stairs to his room. After I bathed, I retrieved the reverend. He suggested we get a shave before we ate. That sounded like a good idea to me. The barber was a very tall, slim man with yellow teeth. Even though he smelled like a freshly smoked cigar, he did a pretty good job.

Stepping into the restaurant, we looked around for a place to sit. What do you know? We saw a familiar face. The reverend stopped, suddenly saying, "Mr. Adams, look over there. That's Mr. Patterson from Marion, Mississippi. Wonder what he is doing here and with a beautiful woman." She was a well-proportioned blonde with blue eyes and thick lips.

"Let's say hi to the couple," I said.

"Yes, sir. Mr. Adams, we should." We walked over and stood right in front of the table, and the reverend said, "Mr. Patterson, fancy meeting you here?"

Patterson, surprised to see us, said, "Mr. Adams, Reverend, what are you doing here?" He stood to shake both our hands. "Good to see you both. Are you staying here in Vicksburg?" He sat back down and took a sip of his drink. "We just arrived yesterday. Oh, by the way, gentlemen, this is my wife, Jennifer." The reverend and I both tipped our hats to the lady. He took his wife's hand and turned toward us. "This is Mr. Adams and the good Reverend Williams. We met in Marion when they came into the restaurant to eat," he said.

"Very good to meet you, fine gentleman," she said.

"These are the two men I told you about a few weeks ago. I met them on the night when everything changed in Marion."

"Really, then it is a real pleasure to meet great men as yourselves. Thank you so much for everything you did to help save our town that night," she said.

Mr. Patterson waved a worker over and had them add two chairs to the table. "Have a seat, Mr. Adams, Reverend. Will you join us for supper? While we are eating, I would like to share with you the happenings in Marion lately."

"Thank you, Ugene. We would love to eat with you and your beautiful wife."

Before Jennifer Patterson or Ugene could answer, a little black waitress asked what we would like to eat. I ordered eggs, bacon, and coffee. She replied, "We don't have bacon, but we do have fine cured country ham if that will do for you, sir?"

"Yes, ma'am, that ham sounds really good," I answered her.

"Biscuits, sir?" she asked. She seemed a bit shy and kept playing with the hem of her apron.

"Yes, ma'am, biscuits would be fine."

She turned to the reverend and asked, "For you, sir, what would you like?"

The reverend said, "I will have the same as he." He tipped his hat and started to stand, tipping his hat to the waitress as well as Mrs. Patterson.

"I will be right back with your coffee, sirs," she said, looking confused that the reverend would tip his hat at her as well as stand.

She was only gone for a minute when she brought two cups and a pot of coffee. She set them on the table, poured the coffee, and walked away.

"Mr. Patterson, or should I call you Ugene?" I asked.

"You can call me whatever you want to as long as you call me at suppertime." We all laughed. "You can call me Ugene, that would be fine."

"Call me Elijah if you insist on first names. Patterson... sorry, Ugene, I think we can consider each other friends now?" We sipped our coffee, and Ugene filled us in on why he was here. "We are visiting my wife's relatives who are from this area. We met just before the war broke out when I came to visit with our pastor at a revival our church held here. We courted off and on for over a year until her father agreed to let me marry this beautiful woman." He picked up her hand and caressed it as he looked at her with love in his eyes. "Then we moved back to take care of my family's restaurant. Since my family is in Marion and her family is here, we come back here and visit as often as we can.

We took our time eating the wonderful-tasting food once it arrived. Ugene kept looking at his wife and then at us, like he was anxious to tell us something. They both seemed to radiate excitement. Finally, when I was about to say something about it, he put down his fork and began excitedly, "I need to share something with you two gentlemen about that night I met you in my restaurant. Something happened. We talked some that night of the

Klan activity in Marion." He began speaking with his voice slightly lowered, and his eyes kept looking around the room. "After that night, when we spoke…apparently, two men were wearing Klan attire. They threatened to kill all the Klan members one by one if anyone continued to terrorize and harm the colored folk."

The reverend, keeping his attention on the two, looked at me out of the corner of his eye. Then, with a look of curiosity on his face, asked, "Really, Mr. Patterson? You don't say."

"Yes, sir. Reverend, it appears that they threatened not only the perpetrators but their families as well. The men making these threats were holding a Spencer rifle. It just so happens more than fifty men that happen to be in our little group of good citizens own a Spencer rifle. No one is sure of who those two men were. Just that they are local and know all the men and their wives from that group of hooded citizens that threaten everyone else. All those activities have ceased. Our little town has become very quiet and peaceful again. Things may act up again, but no one is sure who these men are and what would happen if they started their evil activities again!" Ugene sat back and kept looking back and forth between the reverend and me.

I just sat back in my chair with a knowing glint in my eye and a straight face, saying, "It is good to hear. Sounds to me that someone did a good thing for those people in that town. Don't you think, Reverend?" He leaned forward and took another sip of his coffee. Nodding his head in my direction he said, "Yes, it does, Mr. Adams. I think God directed those men, whoever they may be, to act as counselors of peace." The reverend signaled the waitress over, and we all ordered a piece of homemade pie. When she made it out of earshot, the reverend continued, "Mr. Ugene Patterson, I am truly glad we bumped into you here. Mrs. Patterson it has been a pleasure to have met such a lovely lady and to hear the good news you have brought to us here."

"It made life easier for the people in our little town, didn't it, Jennifer? Especially for the coloreds. Life was truly a nightmare for those devils."

"Don't know about calling them devils, Ugene. Seems to me God has moved on their behalf. There are a good number of believers in those people."

"You're right, Reverend, just a poor choice of words on my part. I will tell you. Jenny and I are so grateful for what you two did back in Marion that night."

The reverend and I both tensed. "Hold on there, Ugene. We did nothing and we need to keep it that way, right? I am, however, happy that someone had the grit to stand up for what is right and do something to put a stop to what we all know is straight out of the pits of hell!"

"You will never have to worry about Ulysses or myself telling anyone of what happened that night because we don't know what happened. Just thankful it did. A real god-send for peace! However, we have been praying for whoever it was that helped out to receive a blessing and protection from the Father above."

"Funny how we happened to be here at the same time as you. One hour later and we would have never bumped into one another," Jennifer said.

"God's hand is never shortened to work things out for His greater purpose. It does mine and Mr. Adams' hearts good to hear when God's work has paid off for the good to those who love Him."

"I'm not sure what God's plan is here, but it seems to have worked out so far. You keep saying to be led by the Spirit, and it sort of seems like that's what is happening here."

We were interrupted by our little waitress with our pie. The reverend stood again and tipped his hat to the friendly Negro lady.

"Now stop that standing, youse gentleman, and eat yourn pie before it gets cold." She laughed slightly, then walked away. We were all chuckling as we continued to talk as we drank our coffee and ate our pie for about an hour or so.

When we stood to shake hands and say our goodbyes, I noticed something unusual. "Ugene, I just noticed you have a six-shooter on your side. He put his hand on his gun as if to make sure it was still there, then looked at his wife. "I always do when I travel. Never know what trouble we may run into. I feel it would be better to have it and not need it than to need it and not have it. Even though we traveled by carriage, you can't be too careful. If anything happened to Jennifer... A gun can sometimes stop bad things from happening when words can't. I don't think I could live with myself for not being prepared."

"I agree with you completely, Ugene," I said. "Well, Reverend, I think it's time to take a siesta. Sleeping under the moonlight is fine for a short period until you roll on the wrong rock or, God forbid, a snake." I chuckled and took a step back while the reverend shook Ugene's hand and said a short prayer over the couple.

"Thank you, Reverend, for the blessings and thank you both for the conversation." Ugene and his wife sat back down. "I will be keeping you in my prayers." We both turned and headed to the door.

Walking out of the restaurant, I scanned the area and caught sight of the saloon over to my left. "Sounds like people are having a good time in there. I think we need to have a drink. What do you say, Reverend?" I looked at him, but he was shaking his head, and his eyes looked a bit droopy. "I think I will retire for the evening, Mr. Adams. If you need me for anything, you know where to find me. I'll be in my room reading or sleeping. You have a good time. I am looking forward to a soft bed."

"I think I will make my way over there for a beer or two. I will be up shortly. After hearing their story on what happened, after we left, my brain went into full gallop. I think I will be able to sleep much better after a couple to calm my nerves.”

Making my way into the tavern, I scanned the room and saw maybe a handful of people. There were a few gamblers in the corner indulging in a game, but not much more was happening. I approached the bar where a medium-sized man with rich black hair and a thin pencil mustache was wiping up the counter in front of him and then asked, “What will it be, sir?”

I leaned my hip on the counter so I could still see what was going on in the room and answered, “Beer, cold one if you have it.”

He reached around for a glass while saying loudly, “Yes, sir, coldest in town. He filled the glass and then set it on the counter in front of me.

I looked over and, at the other end of the bar, saw two older gentlemen. One leaned over to the other and slurred, “I think I had one too many! Who don’t know if I can ride home." He began to sway back and forth. His speech was also a little hard to understand. The other man put his arm around his shoulder and said, "If you want to ride back with me, I can give you a ride back to your place. I'm good and going that way. I'm not drunk!" He was slurring his words as well.

"Ize think I'd take you up on that. Don't think I can make it on horse by myself. Not sure I can hang on. You may have to hold me there." The first one began to walk around the other man and head toward the front door.

"You know my horse, the bay with the star. Go ahead, get up on her. I'm right behind you. I'll get you home!" He gestured to the door where a horse was tethered right outside in plain view. "I'll be out there shortly after I settle my tab."

The first man bumped into me and everyone else as he stumbled out the door. No one paid him any mind. No one made a big deal of him bumping into them.

His partner paid his tab and walked to the door, shaking his head and shouting, "You plain idiot, what are you doing?" He stepped outside, drawing mine and everyone else's attention. We all stood and ran to the front window or out the door to watch the spectacle. I ended up in the back of the crowd and heard nothing but laughter. I stepped out on the walkway after making my way through the crowd to see the first older man (who I later found out was named Sam) had mounted the horse backward, facing the back of the horse, and had both hands on the butt and was looking at the tail questioningly. The other older man (who I found out was named Jed) was shaking his head and yelled, "You're my friend, but I'm not riding facing you! Da gummit, Sam! You're going to have to turn around, or you're going to have to walk." Sam began to rub the horses but then leaned down to put his arms around it as if he was going to hug it. "Aw, come on up here and take me home. Your horse is broke, so maybe we need to take mine. Her head fell off!"

"Sam, you idiot, you're turned around the wrong way. If you're gonna ride like that, slide on toward the rear! I'm not riding facing you."

Everyone stood around, laughing at these two drunks trying to help each other climb upon that horse. Sam was already mounted, and Jed was trying to get his leg over Sam's head so he could ride correctly. Believe it or not, Jed was able to get mounted and get his feet in the stirrups. His partner was still facing the backside of the horse as they rode off that way. We could hear them arguing as they headed out of town. "You better hold on, Sam. I'm in no shape to hold an old drunk in the saddle while I'm struggling to hang on myself."

"Now, Jed, you know I'm an excellent horseman, so leave me alone and find this horse's head!"

After the excitement ended, I walked back inside and drank my beer. The bar attendant asked, "Have you had enough?"

I looked around for a moment and began to feel my eyes were a little heavy. "I think I'm done," I said as I lay a bit on the counter.

He picked up the bit and said, "That was two bits, sir."

I laid another in front of him, turned, and headed for the door. *I believe it is time to see how comfortable those sheets in my room really are.* I walked to the hotel, undressed, and finally lay down. This bed felt a lot better than what I had been sleeping on for the last few weeks. I put my gun belt and my hat over the bed rails above my head. You know, I don't really remember lying down—just the fact that I slept like a newborn babe.

I awoke the next morning to someone knocking on my door. I rolled out of bed and went to open the door. It was Reverend Williams. "Why, good morning to you!" he said in an all-too-cheerful voice for this early in the morning. "Mr. Adams, are you about ready to mount up and ride?"

"Yes, sir, Reverend. Let me get washed up and dressed, and I'll be ready to go. After we get us some coffee, of course. We can retrieve the horses and mule after the coffee and be on our way," I said.

"Sounds good. I'll be waiting for you downstairs." I shut the door and hurried to get dressed and slipped my boots on. I poured some water from the vase into the basin so I could wash my face. Putting my gun and hat back on, I made my way to the door. I took one last look around the room, making sure I haven't forgotten anything, grabbed the key, and walked downstairs.

There was coffee in the lobby of the hotel, so we grabbed some mugs and drank some as we checked out. The reverend thanked the clerk for a nice room and bed to rest our heads on.

We made our ways toward the stables. Once we saddled up the horses and tethered the mule, we mounted up and rode over to the local dry goods store. Tying the horses in front of the store, we walked in to replenish some much-needed supplies for the journey. Beans, coffee, and jerky were at the top of my list. The clerk was busy when we first walked in. I guess this being a busy town, they did a good business. I looked around at some of the things he had displayed while I waited my turn. There were shelves of canned goods lining the shelves to the right of me and a barrel of pickles on the floor to the left of the counter. To the left was a little of this and that you might need in a home, cooking things like pots and pans, spoons and spatulas, cheese graders, and the like. Behind the counter were large barrels and sacks of things like flour, sugar, lard, and salt. Each barrel or bag had a scoop in it, and there were sacks stacked to the side next to a scale for measuring the amount asked for. It didn't take long for my turn to come.

After handing him my list, I asked, "Would you happen to have any cheese?"

Still measuring my beans and coffee, he replied, "We just received a fresh batch yesterday from the Amish. Happened to come in fresh on the stage."

"Must have been the same stage the Pattersons arrived on," I muttered, but it must have been a bit too loud because the store clerk looked confused and said he didn't know the Pattersons, but the cheese had arrived on time.

The reverend came up beside me and announced, "I'll take a large cut of that cheese, son. Do you need anything, Mr. Adams?" he asked me. I looked over to the left and up front at a display of guns and ammo stacked about. "Yeah, I could use a box of forty-five shells if you have any? I've used a few in the last couple of weeks. Hate to run short just when I may need them most."

After our supplies were stacked on the counter, the reverend began to count out the payment to the man. (He never would let me pay for anything.)

"Let me have the supplies, Reverend. I'll take them out while you settle up here," I said as I began to gather them in my arms.

He paid quickly, and we ended up carrying them out together. We walked down the stairs toward the mule. My foot bumped something, so I shifted the supplies up and to the side so I could see what it was. A piece of old board that must have fallen off something was my guess. When I looked up again, the reverend was already standing behind the mule, stuffing the saddlebags. I remembered the rifle shells laying on the counter, so I asked the reverend if he would put the rest away while I went to retrieve them. I walked across the boardwalk and began putting some of the supplies in my bag when I heard someone shout.

Later, the reverend told me, out of the corner of his eye, he saw those two cowboys that had tried to hang me walking out of the restaurant. From the other side of the hotel, he saw the mean one still had a large bruise on the side of his head. They were walking toward me, he had said. Everything started moving as if it was in slow motion! His partner was trying to grab him by the arm, saying, "Forget it, let go!" The big mean cowboy started running toward me, fighting to put his six-shooter out of the belly belt it was tucked into.

The reverend screamed at me as he reached over the mule, trying to get the rifle from my horse. Before he could get to the Spencer rifle, he heard a gunshot. Looking completely devastated, he had closed his eyes, saying, "Dear God! No!"

He said I had drawn my gun but had not raised it up. In the street, the mean cowboy was falling to the ground as if still in slow motion. His partner threw his hands in the air, shouting, "I don't have a gun, don't shoot… I don't have a gun!" He was staring at the boardwalk.

What do you know? Ugene Patterson and his six-shooters saved my life. Standing on the boardwalk, pistol still smoking, his wife beside him with her hands over her mouth looking white as a ghost and startled. He was apparently a pretty good shot to take that cowboy out from fifty feet.

I ran over to the cowboy now lying in the street in a puddle of blood, pointing his gun back and forth from the one on the ground and the cowboy with his hands in the air, shaking. "Patterson, you just saved my life. This scoundrel tried to shoot me in the back!" He put his gun back in the holster and took his wife's hand to try to comfort her, it seemed. "Elijah, are you alright?" he asked.

"I am now, thanks to you, Patterson!" I answered. We turned back toward the other cowboy. He was still hysterically yelling, "Please don't shoot me. I tried to stop him from this play he made. He wouldn't listen to me."

"Yes, but you didn't stop this!" I pulled the collar of my shirt to reveal the hangman's mark from around my throat. "This scar I will carry for the rest of my life because of you two and the rest of your gang. You son of a bit…"

I was interrupted by the reverend, shouting, "Thank you, Mr. Patterson, for saving Brother Adams!"

He turned to me and, grabbing my arm a little too tight, said, "God has performed another miracle by saving your life, Mr. Adams."

Right then, the sheriff came running up from around the building. Immediately, the sheriff recognized Mr. Patterson. "Ugene, what's happening here?" he said.

"Sheriff Cooke, this man lying on the ground tried to shoot this gentleman right here! Jenny and myself happened upon this as we were walking on the boardwalk. I had to shoot him before he could shoot Mr. Adams in the back," Ugene answered.

"Who are these people?" the sheriff asked angrily.

"I am Elijah Adams, a deputy sheriff in the Chattanooga area, also a former sheriff in El Paso. This is Reverend Williams, also from that area. I am escorting him to Texas. We were just passing through when we bumped into Ugene

Patterson and his lovely missus. He happened to be walking by as we were buying and loading supplies for our journey when this scalawag tried to hang me a few days back!" I pulled the bandana from around my neck to reveal the scar on my neck. "They tried to hang me! If not for me being saved by the reverend and a Captain Farley with the Union security scouts, I would have been hung. That happened just above Greensboro." I pointed down to the bleeding man at my feet. "If he happens to survive this bullet, he needs to go to jail! His partner is here too!" I swept my hand to point at the other man, who looked a little shaken. The sheriff was looking at the two men and the reverend like he was absorbing all the information. He looked at the shaking cowboy. "What do you have to say?"

The other cowboy started saying, "I don't know what he is talking about. We are the local militia from the Greensboro area. We go around catching runaway fugitives. We saw these two men who set some of our captives free, so my partner was going to confront them when he was murdered by these men."

Patterson spoke up. "I don't know who that man is, but I will vouch for these two men here. They are friends of mine from Marion. Good men and I think if you check everyone's story out, you will find the truth with Mr. Adams and the reverend. I think those two cowboys need to be jailed for both trying to hang and then shoot Mr. Adams in the back."

Sheriff Cooke was bent over the man on the ground to see if he had a pulse. "This one is dead, but that cowboy is going to jail for attempted murder on Mr. Adams."

The still alive cowboy was holding his hands above his head. He started saying, "I did nothing. I don't know what they are talking about, and this man did this on his own. I had nothing to do with shooting Mr. Adams."

The reverend spoke up then and explained everything that had happened to us for the past few days until now. When he told them about himself being shot, he pulled his small Bible from the inside pocket of his jacket and held it out to the sheriff. The book had a bullet hole right through the middle, and the bullet was still stuck in it. The sheriff listened to the whole tale, his face never changing. At the end, he looked at my neck then the Bible still held out in the reverend's hand. "I believe with the witnesses today and the evidence presented, there is proof enough for me there to put him in prison for a long time." Sheriff Cooke grabbed the cowboy by the arm and led him toward the jail. "Reverend, Mr. Adams, I need you two to come to the jail for a statement." Halfway to the jail, he yelled back, "You as well, Mr. Patterson! When this varmint goes to trial, we will need everyone's statements for evidence! Think about ten years in prison waiting on him once this is said and done." He waved down a young boy that was running past to go fetch the doc and the undertaker. "Have the doc do a death report and tell the coroner to haul off this scum out of my street," he said. We all followed the sheriff down the street that was slowly filling with townspeople.

Keeping my voice low, I thanked Ugene again and asked if I could buy him and his wife their next meal. As they were thinking about my offer, I glanced to see the reverend seeming to be in thought. The reverend looked at me and said, "I can tell you it was God's appointed timing! That we were all here at this exact time was not a coincidence. Mr. and Mrs. Patterson, God has sent you here to help us out at this time."

Ugene looked to his wife, squeezed her hand, and answered, "Well, Reverend, thank you both so much. We would request that you please pray that God help us to conceive so we can start with our family. We have been trying for quite a while."

The reverend walked over and took Jennifer Patterson's hand in his and said, "God is about to move in your life.

Right now, I would like to pray over you." We all stopped outside the sheriff's office, removed our hats, and bowed our heads. Even the cowboy took his hat off as the reverend began to pray.

"Dear heavenly Father, I ask that you open the womb of this sister, help her to conceive, and bring a healthy child to this beautiful couple. Lord, if it be your glorious will for their lives, give them more than one child. In Jesus Christ's mighty name, we pray. Please put a special blessing and protection upon them. Amen!"

Mrs. Patterson, with tears in her eyes, hugged the preacher's neck. "Thank you, Reverend. We have been trying for two years. Nothing has happened yet." Smiling, he looked at the couple, saying, "Write to me in El Paso when you have the baby. I will be interested to know what you name your firstborn. If I ever get back to this area or Monroe, I will be stopping by to visit you wonderful folks."

While the reverend had been explaining to the sheriff, the Pattersons had helped pick up all the supplies that the reverend and I had dropped on the ground. The Pattersons were following the sheriff into the office to make out a statement. The reverend and I tied off our horses and mule outside and then made our way in as well.

"Sheriff Cooke, what do I need to fill out?" I looked back behind me for the reverend. He was nowhere to be found. I looked out the door to see him with the under-taker and the doc. He was helping the undertaker and oth-ers pick the dead cowboy's body up and load it on a wagon. Before he left the body, he prayed over the deceased man. A true minister till the very end—cares for that poor devil even though he is more than likely burning in hell as he prayed! Maybe the reverend is praying for the man's family. No telling what goes on in the reverend's mind.

I turned back toward the sheriff and explained to him that the reverend would be here shortly so I could go ahead and make my statement. Soon after, we all made our statements, said our last goodbyes, and departed toward a ferry the sheriff had told us about that was headed over the Mississippi River.

Chapter 10

When we made it to the ferry, I noticed there was a small crowd of mixed company waiting to depart. Some were cowboys, and a few were broken-looking men still wearing their federal soldier uniform shirts. One Union officer was still in full uniform. They were not standing near each other. One picker family was standing on the far end of the ferry, trying to keep their distance from everyone.

The reverend and I boarded the ferry with our horses and mule. Tying them up to the railing, we waited as they began to pull the ropes that would carry us over the Mississippi River. I was enjoying the peaceful ride over the calm river, and I started talking to the reverend when I noticed he did not answer. When I turned to look, the reverend was making his way toward the picker family. *He definitely has a heart to help those whom he feels need of him the most. Always tends to lean toward the hurting.* While he made his way to the little family, I made my way over to talk to the cowboys. I happened to bump into the deputy sheriff of the St. Josephs Parish area. He was a friendly fellow, saying howdy before I could introduce myself.

"Where are you headed to, sir?" he asked. He turned to me, and I could see his badge on his lapel.

"We are just passing through, heading to El Paso. The gentleman talking to the little family over there is my traveling partner. I'm Adams, and he is Reverend Williams."

"I am Anderson Snieder, the deputy sheriff of the town of St. Josephs. Do you two want to tag along with me as we make our way to town?" he asked. I looked again toward the small family. "I will run it by the good reverend. I believe he will approve, and you could maybe show us around a little. We will be looking for something to eat and maybe a place to sleep. Good that I met you here, sir."

"Good to meet you, Adams. It is good to meet those who fought for the cause," he said.

"Yes, sir. I fought with the federals. Even though we didn't win, we still kicked a little butt, didn't we, sir?"

As we talked, Deputy Sneider happened to mention he had been here the entire time during the war. "Didn't have much fighting to do. We surrendered—we surrendered big-time. We just threw down our arms and let them ol' Union boys take over. They're all over the place now. I hear there's a big establishment over there in Alexandria. A big Union holdup right now, helping out the pickers and all. Keeping the good ol' white boys under control."

"Yeah, from what we've seen, they need to be kept under control."

"You don't say," said the deputy as he leaned up against the rail.

"Yeah, you see this scar on my neck right here? That's from one of those 'good ol' boys.' Well, needless to say, that good ol' boy is no longer with us."

"Really? Well, at least he didn't get you before you got him."

No, no, sir, he didn't. But I think hell gained one hell of a man, and he's burning right now."

"Well, I'll tell you, Mr. Adams. There are a lot of bad people. Seems like the war brought out the worst in 'em."

"You're right, deputy."

"Well, it was good meeting you, sir. I'm gonna make my way over to the reverend and see what he's got going on with these picker people down here."

I walked my way across the ferry and came up to the reverend.

"Reverend, how you doin'? Who are these fine people?" I said as I patted the reverend on the back and then turned to face the family.

"Well, I tell you, Mister Adams, this right here is the Harris family. This is George and June and their children—Sasha, Anna, William, and Tulley. They are heading to Alexandria."

"Oh, really? That deputy sheriff told me that there's a big Union outfit there that is helping the colored people there. Helping them stand against the meanness, standing against the whites that are going around terrorizing these fine people."

"Yeah, that's what they were saying."

"Well, I tell you, it's good to meet you, fine folks," I said.

"Good to meet you, Mister Adams. I've heard a lot of good things about you from the reverend here. You seem to be a good man. We don't mean to cause any problems. We headin' over here to Alexandria, and the reverend said you gentlemen might ride with us to help us make it there." George said.

"Well, we'll take you as far as we can. Unless our paths part, I don't see a problem with us travelin' together. That might not be a bad idea. That way we can help protect your children." George and his wife were nodding their heads and looking a little more relieved.

"Yes, sir, I do appreciate that," he said. "Ever since this freed stuff happened, the abolitionists have come by, but they don't stick with us. They get scared off as soon as these mean men come on, they change their minds, and they move on."

I turned to the reverend, looked toward the deputy, and said to the family, "Well, I can assure you this, we don't throw in. We'll fight to the very end if the cause is right."

When we departed from the ferry, Deputy Sneider and I rode up front, and the reverend tied his mule to the back of the wagon where the children rode as their parents drove the team. The reverend rode beside them. I leaned closer to the deputy, saying, "I guarantee he's back there right now sharing the Gospel all he can with the kids. Those children need to hear that. They also need to know that all white people aren't bad. If they didn't know it, they will by the time we part ways." I leaned back in my saddle, took a look around, and, in a louder voice, said, "Well, Deputy Sneider, I do appreciate you showing us around as we go down through here. Oh wow! Look! Over there is a nice, big plantation." I was startled and surprised by the size of the operation.

The deputy glanced over and shrugged. "It is. I mean it's one of the nicer ones. It's a Felicity Plantation. It's still active. Eh, we don't have any slaves there anymore, but still some of the ex-slaves stuck around. The Klan is so active here right now—"

"*Klan*?" I interrupted. "What do you mean by *klan*?"

"You know, the white men that put on the white hoods and ride around, causing fear into the black people. They wanna make sure they stay on top of 'em and keep 'em under control. Just because they are free doesn't make them equal with us now."

I just sat quietly, listening to him speak. I didn't have the same opinion as he did anymore. I could tell he still wasn't over the fact that Lincoln had freed these people and that we fought a war and lost. I just let him keep talking and explain to me how the Felicity Plantation used to produce more cotton and sweet potatoes than any other plantation around here. One of the most profitable in the area.

We rode on up a ways, and the deputy said, "If you look up in the distance, you'll notice there's another plantation. It's closed down now. That was the Kemp Plantation. Apparently, they used to be mean to all their slaves and lost all of them. As soon as the Emancipation happened, every picker in there rebelled. They hurt one of the slave owners and took off in the night. That was one of the reasons we had an uprising in the Klan in this area. They started to hang one young man. That picker didn't even do anything. They just accused him of hurtin' a lady. She took off running when she thought he was going to do something to her. She just slipped and hit her head on the table. He even helped her up and took her to the doctor, yet they still accused him of doing something wrong. I disagree with that one completely."

"Well, deputy, there are many, many things that've happened here after the war that I truly disagree with, but what do you expect? With such bloody battles where you've killed your own neighbor or had them die right in front of you, there are no kind hearts anymore, people just don't have them. They've seen too much bloodshed, harbored too much hatred. That's what America has become about right now. So what do you expect?"

"Yeah, I guess you're right." He paused, taking a deep breath. "You are right. Well, you'll find a little bit of both in St. Josephs. If you decide to stay, I'll show you around. If you don't, well, at least you gave me some company and some good conversation. By the way, what's the weather like in Chattanooga?" he asked.

I began to laugh at his abrupt change of topic. "Actually, it's about the same, except not as humid. It does get humid back home in Chattanooga but only for midsummer and certain times of year. It's pretty humid over here."

He smiled. "Yeah, it does get that way. It gets pretty bad, but it's good for the potatoes. Helps them grow. By the way, have you been to any of our swamps here?"

"Matter of fact, I have. Back when my troop was moving toward Tennessee, we came right through here. A lot of snake- and gator-infested waters. It was not my cup of tea."

"Well, I was raised around here, so it doesn't bother me much. I used to hunt gators. Matter of fact, gator tails is one of my favorite things to eat. That and boudin."

"Boudin? I don't know what boudin is," I said, picturing some of the weirdest foods I have eaten.

"It's a Louisiana Creole sausage. If you like sausage, you'd like boudin. I can get you some in St. Josephs, if we happen to be there, or some crawfish pie! You'd really enjoy that too. Or a little bit of gumbo. Louisiana is famous for our gumbo."

"Well, that all sounds good, but it'll be up to the reverend or these fine people if they wanna come in there and eat." I pointed behind us to all who followed.

Abruptly and urgently, he began shaking his head and exclaimed, "Oh no no no, sir, Mr. Adams. No no. You and the reverend can come, but the pickers have to stay on the outskirts of town. They'll get hurt if they come in there."

"Oh, really?" I answered as I looked over to him.

"Yeah yeah. Pickers are not allowed in our establishments. I mean, if they need something from the store, they have to stand on the porch and submit the list of what they need to the store owner, and he'll go get it for them and bring it back to them. As long as they got cash."

"Well, I'll have to ride back to the reverend and tell him what you told me. We'll see what happens." I slowly did ease on back to where the reverend and the Harris family were. Reluctantly, I began, "Uh, Reverend?" He was smiling and looked so happy I really didn't want to be the one to change that.

"Hey, Mr. Adams! We're just riding along, teaching these kids a little bit about the love of Jesus and how God created the heavens and the earth. It's just sweet they had their own little Bibles someone gave them. They said they don't hear a lot of reading, their mom and dad can't read. June and George here, they never learned how to read. Their master would never let them learn how to read. They never had it explained to them exactly why God chose certain people to be his chosen people. I'm just explaining it to them. All the children here, they really enjoy it. They're free now, but I don't know if I have time to teach them how to read. I would really like to."

"That'd be good, Reverend. That'd be good." I pulled him a little bit closer to me and said, "The deputy there, Deputy Sneider, told me that they don't allow pickers in town in St. Josephs. Not right now anyhow, so they will have to stay out in the outskirts. While you and I, we can ride in town. He's told me about some really good restaurants. They got some really good food there. We can even bring these really fine people some food back too!" he said sarcastically.

"Well, Mr. Adams, I've got to say, these are God's children right there, and if they're not welcome, I don't think I'm welcome there either. I wonder, Mr. Adams, if Jesus Christ was to show up, would they allow him in there with his sandals, long hair, his beard, being darker-skinned, and being from the Middle East? Nah, Mr. Adams, you go right ahead if you want to. I'll stay right out here with the Harris family. If you want us to, we'll wait on you right outside of town. But I don't think I'll leave these fine people. They ride along with us because they want God's protection, and I swore to them that God would protect us, so I'm not gonna leave them."

Nodding my head in understanding, I faced the reverend. "You know what? I agree. You folks, we'll just keep riding on by, we won't even stop in St. Josephs. You have plenty of food, right?" I asked Mr. Harris.

"Yes, sir, we do," George said. "And the missus, she'll cook some up right tonight for us. We don't have any meat, but if one of you fine gentlemen comes up with a rabbit or some sort like that, we'll cook it up. We've even eaten snake a time or two if we had to. So you come up with some meat, my missus, she'll make you a right fine meal. She's got a whole bushel of cornbread in here and biscuits, and we got beans and we got carrots. She could even make a stew! We got onions. It's just green onions, but they still make a right fine stew. My missus will cook us up right tonight."

"Well, thank you, thank you so much, Mr. Harris. I think the reverend and myself will take you up on that. And yeah, we'll find some kind of meat. Whether it be rabbit or some of the sort, we'll find something."

"Alright, sounds good to me, Mr. Adams, Mr. and Mrs. Harris. It'll be good now. I'm gonna continue teaching these little children how much our Lord Jesus Christ loves and died for them."

"Okay, Reverend, you do that. I'm gonna ride back up here with the deputy. He seems to be a good-enough kind of man. His heart may not be right, I don't even know if mine is, but you know what? I think he'll do what he's supposed to when the time comes."

I rode up with Deputy Sneider until, off in the distance, we could see St. Josephs. I could see where the road forked up ahead too. I already told the deputy I wasn't gonna ride in. I explained how we were just gonna keep on moving, and he understood. We shook hands, and he rode back and shook the hands of the reverend, Mr. Harris, and tipped his hat at the missus and the children. He rode on after he told me which way to go. That there was another fork in the road and told me where they both led to. He said if we just continued on, there'd be no issues. He said there was a lot of Klan activity but that they didn't really come out until nighttime. We still had three or four hours before that happened, so we just kept on moving. Finally, we lost sight of St. Josephs on our backside, and we kept traveling about three or four hours from there and came upon a creek. We got down in there and started fishing. It just so happened we had a little bit of twine and a hook. The boy got down and dug us up some worms, and it wasn't long before we caught a few fish.

"I think we are gonna have stew tonight. Mmm, can't wait. If she cooks as good as her husband says…Mrs. June then looked up from where she was looking through her supplies, pulling out various items. "I guarantee you, I'll be truly appreciative. I guarantee the reverend will eat his fill."

I noticed when we first met this family, they were very standoffish. With the love of God in his heart and the way he touches people, I knew the reverend would have them feeling like part of the family in no time at all. Eh, I'm just not that way. I don't have to be. Sometimes it's a little lonely, but it also gets the job done when it has to. I noticed that Mrs. Harris, she liked to keep them kiddos behind her, them being so young and all. I guess she didn't know what we would do.

We unsaddled our horses and set up camp for the night. We cleaned the fish, and Mrs. Harris started her stew. We made our way down to the creek to clean up a bit. The reverend stayed up teaching the children. Mr. Harris and myself started talking about the things he had seen and how grateful he was that Mr. Lincoln had freed them. He'd heard that there'd been a Freedman Bureau where everybody gathered together to help each other, helping black people establish land and farming, seed, and so forth. He heard there was even a school starting over in New Orleans, so black people could get an education. About the time we reached the river, Mr. Harris took his shirt off. All over his back were welts. I could see he'd been struck quite a few times.

I'd seen it done a few times in my life and didn't like it. I never could understand why you would have to beat a man into submission. Treat a man right, usually he'll do whatever you need him to. But sometimes, slaves, when they don't do what they're supposed to, you'd get a little rough with them.

Realizing I had been lost in thought, I stripped myself, washed up, and put on a change of clothes. When Goerge was finished, we headed back so we could listen to the reverend sing praises. "I think you'll like the reverend when you hear him pray over your food. He makes you feel like you're truly gonna be blessed. Even if it was just a desert chicken and you were eating it and didn't taste very well, by the time he was through blessing it, it would taste like a Thanksgiving turkey!" We were both laughing when we approached the fire.

"Well, I tell you, Mr. Adams, I'm just thankful you fine gentlemen come along with us," George said. "I just like having good company. I've known a few good white men in my life but not a lot. My massa was kinda mean to me, kinda mean to all of us. I noticed you looking at these welts on my back. Well, my missus, she has the same on hers. She really didn't deserve it. If you'll notice, that oldest child out there, how she's just a little lighter skin than the others? That's from the massa. He used to like to force her even though she's married to me. I rose up one day and put a stop to it, so I got these welts all over my back. Once she saw me getting beat, she decided she wasn't gonna put up with it any longer either. So we carry scars. We call 'em scars of love."

"Mr. Harris, I'm sorry you both had to go through that, you and the missus. There are cruel people in this world. There's also decent people. You know, when I was a kid, the reverend would tell you this too. You know, Jesus, he took stripes for us. And the word says, 'By His stripes we are healed.' You know what? All these things you went through in your lifetime, I'm thinking all these stripes you got, it healed you guys. And maybe God will move in your lives, help you start with a new one," I said.

"Yeah, I'm prayin' when we get to Alexandria, God will move for us. He'll change things. With the Union Army being there, maybe we'll have a little protection. We'll obtain some kind of land. I've got some money that I've saved over the years. I was gonna buy me and the missus freedom with it. But since we are free now, I can use that money to purchase a farm or some land or start something. We got our hopes!"

"Yeah, I'm hoping so, brother. George, don't give up hope, buddy. We're gonna get you to Alexandria, and we'll see what we can make happen. Just so happens we are traveling in that same direction, and like you said, it's good to have company. Now let's see how good a cook your wife really is."

George laughed. "You won't be disappointed, sir, you won't be disappointed."

As we came back closer to the camp, we noticed the reverend had babies all over him. There was a child on each leg, and the other two were on his shoulders, pretending to read along to the Bible he had opened. I think they were truly involved in this story he was telling them. Funny thing was, he was reading from psalms, the very same psalm I just quoted to George.

"Mr. Harris, I got to say, this smells awful good."

Mrs. Harris smiled. "It'll be done in just a little bit, so you settle yo'self down, and I'll spoon you up some and bring it to you."

"Thank you, ma'am. Thank you so much."

She went to hand a plate to the reverend, and the reverend shook his head as he was pulling the children off him. "No, ma'am," he said. "Feed the children first."

She looked at him funny. Mr. Harris looked over at his wife and gave her a small smile of reassurance and then spoke up and said, "Sorry, Reverend, we used to feedin' the massa first before we ate, she just doin' this outta habit."

The reverend looked up at Mrs. Harris. "Well, ma'am, you go right ahead and give it to the children first, but before you give any food out, let me say the blessing if you don't care."

"Yessir, yessir! We do need a blessing. God's already blessed us with your companionship, and we thank God you're going with us. Children love you, Reverend, they love your stories."

The reverend smiled and looked around at each of the children. "I love them too." He smiled at each of the children.

"I've never known such good white mens. Never known mens like you before. I'm kinda glad my children are seeing that all white mens aren't bad." She served all the children first, us men second, then herself. No one ate a bite as we waited for the reverend to say the blessing. "No, no, not all white men are bad," the reverend said. "But there are bad men out there."

The reverend took his hat off, and we did too. He began to pray, "Dear heavenly Father, we ask that You bless this food we are about to receive. Ask that You give true nourishment to these fine people. I thank You so much for allowing them to come into our lives. Lord, I know You put us together, I know that You ordain every step of a righteous man. I know that Mr. and Mrs. Harris are righteous people. So, Lord, I thank You once again for bringing us together and giving us true friendship in Jesus Christ's mighty name. Oh, and bless these babies as they consume. In Jesus's name, again I say amen."

We all began to eat. The children were especially engrossed in their meal. Not even a sound could be heard except for spoons hitting bowls. "Well, Mrs. Harris, this might be the finest stew I've had in months! Matter of fact, maybe since my mom made something like this when I was younger. This is some really good stew. What do you think, Reverend?"

"Mrs. Harris from the way you can see that I've been eating, I'm really enjoying this! This is a blessing, a true blessing!"

"Thank you so much, gentlemen. I'm glad you're enjoying it." I believe her cheeks were turning a little red. I tucked back into my stew, and she began to pass around some biscuits.

"And these biscuits, is that buttermilk I taste?" He was smiling and staring at them like he hadn't seen them in forever.

She beamed. "Yes, sir, it is buttermilk. It was readily available to us. We hardly had milk that wasn't buttermilk."

"Well, all I know is, this is some of the best food I've ever eaten. Thank you so much, ma'am." I spoke up.

"Well, you eat up. There's not much left, but I think the children had their fill. Me and George have had ours. So you, Mr. Adams, you and the reverend eat all you want."

"Thank you so much, ma'am. I think one helping is enough for me. I think I will have just a tad more coffee, though. Reverend, you want a little more coffee there? What about you, Mr. Harris?"

George shook his head. "Yeah, I'll have a spot more, that'll be good."

"No, I'm good," said the reverend and kept on eating. He took his biscuit and rubbed the bottom of his plate. I was beginning to wonder if he was gonna bite a finger trying to eat that last biscuit. It was some good stew.

We all finished eating, and Mrs. Harris gathered up all the dishes and headed down toward the creek. Mr. Harris stood up and said, "I'm coming with you, I got me a little torch right here. I'll follow you down there."

The reverend said, "I've got the babies, you go right ahead. Me and Mr. Adams are right here."

So they made their way down to the creek. The kids and I sat right there, and I taught them a little prayer to pray before they went to bed at night.

"Dear God, bless us as we lay down to sleep. Put a blessing upon my mom and dad. And I ask that we sleep tight and wake up early and feel refreshed in Jesus's name." And all the children prayed for it.

"Well, Reverend, when the Harrises get back, I think I'll turn in."

"You go right ahead, Mr. Adams, I'll stay up with the kids."

I took off my hat and rubbed my head. "Maybe one of us should watch while the others sleep."

"Well, Mr. Adams, I'll take first watch tonight. I feel good. I'll wake you up in a few hours and let you take a second watch. We'll wake up Mr. Harris for the last watch."

"Sounds good to me. I'm gonna go crawl up under my blanket and call it a night."

So I did. The reverend stoked the fire with another log. All the children crawled in the back of the wagon, and Mr. and Mrs. Harris made them a pallet under the wagon. And we were all gathered around the fire. I could slowly hear the reverend singing. "What could wash away my sins? Nothing but the blood of Jesus."

He was singing so quietly to himself, but it was kind of soothing. I truly felt we did have the blessings and protection of God, helping me sleep good.

About four hours later, the reverend woke me up and said, "Mr. Adams." When he said that, I sprang up with my hand on my six-shooter.

"No no no. Calm down there, it's your time, your watch. I just put another log on the fire, so I think you're good on the fire."

I wiped my eyes. "Okay, Reverend. Thank you."

"The coffee that was left, I set it back on the fire, so if you want some, it'll be a little stale, but it'll still be hot. Maybe just enough to keep you awake."

"Alright, Reverend, thank you, I appreciate it. Everything alright?"

"Yeah, the children are sleeping like babies in the back of the wagon. Mr. and Mrs. Harris are under there snuggled up."

As the night went on, the reverend fell asleep. The humidity was on us, and it started to get chilly. I walked over and picked up my blanket, brought it over next to the fire, and lay on another log and wrapped my blan-ket around me. As I was sitting there, I stayed awake for a while, dozed off for a second or two, stayed awake for a while, dozed off again, and woke up again. After a few hours, I thought about waking up Mr. Harris. But then I thought, *Nah, I'll let him sleep. He can watch the next night.* It had been a good night. Fine meal, good people, good sleep. I slept pretty well for four hours. That was enough to get me by the next day. *Tomorrow brings a new day, we'll see what happens*, I thought.

Once we got up in the morning, we all decided we were gonna ride a little south from St. Josephs. We traveled along the river, following it south until it took us right by Harrisonburg. We tried to avoid Harrisonburg because we weren't sure what we would find there. Riding with the Harrises, we weren't sure what kind of people we would find or run into, especially since the deputy sheriff told us that this family wouldn't be welcome there. So we keep moving south. I knew that this river runs into the main branch of the Mississippi if we kept following it. This path would take us straight to Alexandria, which is exactly where we need to be going. It was a rough ride, especially since we had the kids in there. The reverend liked to get off his horse, tie it up to the side of their wagon, climb in there, and read Bible stories to the kids. I think he was having a good ol' time.

As we traveled along, we would try to avoid people unless they came up on us or we were passing them. If we came upon black folk, they would wave at the black people we were with. If it was white folk, they would sort of look funny at us. They wouldn't wave, wouldn't say anything to us. They would look at us mean, like we were doing something wrong. We rode on by them, not caring what they thought.

We settled down that evening where there was a large part of the river, a big flat area we could make a fire at. Mr.

Harris and I walked away looking for firewood, while the reverend stayed there with Mrs. Harris and the children. We finally gathered enough wood to build a nice fire, and Mrs. Harris cooked up some good food again. I actually got some rabbit, and she made stew with it. This woman really knew how to cook.

The next few days were pretty uneventful other than the few mean looks we'd get from the people that we'd come in contact with. We finally came to the river where we needed to cross, and we had to take the horses and the wagon through and got a little stuck in the higher water. We had to get mine and the reverend's horses hooked up to the wagon and pulled the wagon across the twenty-five-foot spread of water we had to get through. The kids were scared to death, as only natural. Mrs. Harris set back in there and kept them calm. It was a little rough, but we survived.

There was nothing but wilderness after we got away from the river, but we kept heading south. We weren't sure how far we'd go until we came down to Alexandria. We just kind of figured we were going the right way. On the fourth night, after we had crossed the river, we were awakened by some sort of noise. I looked over at the reverend and Mr. Harris, and we all agreed that Mr. Harris and I should go investigate it. The reverend stayed back to watch over Mrs. Harris and the children. As we made our way over, I kept remembering the prayer the reverend said every night before we'd go to sleep. That God would put a hedge of protection around us and that he would camouflage us from the enemy, that no one would be able to see us when it comes to danger. To protect this family, to give us his loving hand and his loving guidance. I would continually listen to the reverend as he prayed this prayer because the whole time we were coming this way, the reverend kept telling us, "No, I think the Holy Spirit wants us to go this way." And I was listening because with the things that had happened on this trip, I thought I should be listening. I had not been steered wrong so far.

We came up on a little rising on the other side of the pasture we'd been riding through. We eased up on this little knoll, and on the other side was a valley. And in this valley, there were all kinds of men wearing sheets on their heads. We knew, looking down at these men, that it was a Klan. They had a cross out there, and it was on fire. I'd never seen anything like this before. I looked at Mr. Harris and asked, "You know what this is?"

He shook his head. "Yessir, I know what this is. They're gonna hurt some black folk."

There was a large crowd gathered around. We could see a silhouette behind this cross; there was a tree, and right under that tree was a black man that was hung. His feet were dangling. It was terrible. I pointed down to the cross and looked at Mr. Harris. "Look there, Mr. Harris, look behind the cross."

He nodded his head. "Yeah, I see it."

I put my hand on his shoulder. "You know what, we don't need to do anything about this, we can't endanger your family. We've got to let this go. We need to steer clear of all these people. Let's head on back and gather up everything and let's get on out of here. We'll ride by the moonlight."

"Yessir, yessir, Mr. Adams, I think you're right. Let's head on out of here and get the reverend, the missus, and the children and let's please head on."

We snuck out of there and got back to camp and headed over to the reverend, who had already kicked the fire out. We tied our horses off and moved in closer. About that time, we heard some riders off in the distance. So we got the kids and Mrs. Harris down under the wagon, along with Mr. Harris. We took all of our blankets and threw them under there and said, "Keep the kids completely still! We don't need them seeing you!"

Sure enough, the riders came up to our camp. Four men rode up to us, and one of them asked, "What are you doing here? Why don't you have a fire built?" the leader of the men asked.

"Well, we already cooked and were about to lie down in our wagon, we don't need no fire."

The same man spoke up again and said, "Well, someone needs to start a fire. You gonna sleep here overnight without a fire? What about the coyotes? What about the snakes? How are you gonna keep them away?"

"We don't need any of that," said the reverend. "We got the good Lord taking care of us!"

"Really, you don't say, where are you men going? Why do you need a mule, two horses plus a lead for your wagon? Why do you need so many?"

I spoke up and said, "You know what? That's none of your business. We need all this, and that's the only thing important. When we get to town, we're gonna sell this other horse. It doesn't matter what we do with our property."

"Where are you going, you think?" he asked.

"That's none of your business either. We're just traveling. We stopped here for the night just to get a little sleep. Once we get rested, we'll be about our business."

The man responded, "Well, we were just curious. We don't mean no harm. We're just traveling around, making sure everything is good. We're the local militia."

"Yeah, we saw you local militia down the ridge down there. We don't want anything to do with what you people do. We don't care. We just wanna be about our business," I responded to him.

"That's fine. We're gonna let you people go. We have no conflict with you, especially you, Reverend. We're gonna make sure that nobody causes any problems around here, that's all. We'll be patrolling these areas. Make sure we don't have any kind of people we don't need around here, ya know, like pickers. We don't hold kindly to their kind around this area. You know it wasn't long ago we had to kill a bunch of them pickers."

"Really? Were you men a part of that?" the reverend asked.

"No, sir, I wasn't. But many, many people around here were. We don't put up with no uppity-pickers. Killed about three hundred of them that night."

The reverend shook his head. "That is not godly. That is pure evil!"

"Reverend, what do you know about being godly? Walk around high and mighty, carrying your Bible, thumping people with it. You know what? God sometimes causes people to be killed. God sometimes calls his people to be slaves. Abraham Lincoln thinks he can come around and tell us that we don't deserve slaves, taking away our rights and acting like we've done something wrong. They turn these pickers loose to be their own people. I don't know who he thinks he is, but he got what was coming to him, didn't he?"

"Sorry you said that, sir. I prayed for Mrs. Lincoln when that happened. I pray for all these poor picker people that's still being done wrong by the likes of people that don't think they deserve freedom. They're God's people the same as you are."

"You listen to me, Reverend, you listen closely. They're no better than a horse or a dog. The bunch of animals we brought from Africa over here to help them out by giving them a place to work, a place to live, we fed 'em every day. Now they can't even take care of themselves. So that's why we have to put 'em in jail and have to put them back on the plantations. They don't even have an idea on how to take care of themselves because we been taking care of 'em for all these years. Now Abe Lincoln thinks he can make humans out of 'em. They ain't no better than an ape."

I could see the reverend was fired up when he said that. The reverend pointed his finger right at him and said, "I rebuke you in the name of Jesus Christ, and I command that evil spirit to depart." And the man that was doing the most talking fell back and almost fell off his horse. His eyes got real big, and he said, "Boys, let's leave these guys alone. Let's leave 'em alone, let's get out of here. I don't, we don't wanna mess with this."

I could see the fear of God come up on him. Something about what the reverend said put the real fear of God into him. The reverend spoke up and said, "The wages of sin is death. From one bloodline, all races were born. Not you or anyone on this earth has a right to call any of God's children anything less than that! I rebuke you! I rebuke all of this in the name of Jesus Christ! This is pure evil, and we will not have it! I stand on the right hand of the Father! Jesus Christ said, 'In my Father's house there are many mansions!' That's for anyone and everyone that accepts his will! White, black, it doesn't matter! They're all God's children!"

The main cowboy said, "Let's get out of here, men, before we cause the fires of heaven to rain down on us!" They turned and rode away quickly. The reverend was still shouting at their backs.

I was also afraid that the reverend would cause the fires of heaven to rain down on them. Brimstone, I was sure it was about to fall. I've never seen the reverend this mad. He was really mad!

After they rode away, we gave it about five minutes, and I told the Harrises, "Get on out from under the wagon. They're gone. You and the children get in the wagon. Let's get going." They hurried out from under the wagon, loaded, and the whole family hid in the back of the wagon with the reverend driving.

We drove all night and through the next morning, and I kept my hand on my gun and kept scanning our surroundings. I was listening for any sound of pursuit or looking for signs of an ambush. I could hear the reverend switching between praying and singing of the goodness of the Lord. We couldn't have gone far. We must have gone twenty miles from the time we left till we arrived at the outskirts of Alexandria.

Chapter 11

The reverend stopped at the outskirts of Alexandria, and the closer we had gotten, the more nervous Mr. Harris and his missus had become. Mr. Harris looked over at me, his face sick with worry. "Maybe we should hang out here on the outskirts until you two fine gentlemen go in there and investigate whether we're gonna be welcome there or not."

I nodded. "You know, the reverend wants that to. Make sure your family is safe."

So we found them a spot that would hide the wagon and a place where Goerge could hide so he could see the town but keep out of sight. It was a little spooky leaving them there since it was starting to get a little dark. It was a big town with lots of old, beautiful buildings. The reverend and I discussed that if it wouldn't be safe, we didn't feel like we should leave the Harris family here, since there was a lot of Klan activity in neighboring towns and the lynching of that poor man. I just didn't know if it'd do any good to tell the local authority about that. That was a good ways back, and I didn't know how connected the sheriff would be with that kind of activity. It is a little worrisome for myself and definitely for the reverend.

I looked over at the reverend. "Reverend, I was meaning to ask you, back when that cowboy was about to shoot me, you know, the big mean one, was it just me or did I see you in the corner of my eye pulling my old Spencer out of that saddle?"

The reverend rubbed his hand across his head. "Well, at that point, I wasn't sure what to do. It was without thinking. I just grabbed the gun. I didn't know what I would do at all at that moment. Most of the time I don't."

I chuckled. "Well, if you would have used the power that you used back there to drive off those Klansmen, I don't think we would have needed a gun. I think we would have survived if that power would have shown up then."

The reverend nodded. "Yeah, Mr. Adams, it happens that way sometimes. That's the same power that raised Jesus from the grave and gave Samson power to push down that temple to kill all of those Philistines. You know, there is no reason whatsoever in this world you could not know that power too, Mr. Adams."

I looked down and shook my head. "I don't know about that, Reverend. I believe but I've never been that close. It would take a real man of God for those things to happen. Just like yourself. Never seen babies take a liking to a man like they have you, especially you being a white man and them being pickers. I would have never believed that in my life, especially what all that family has been through with white people."

The reverend sighed. "Yeah, they have been through a lot. That's true, Mr. Adams."

"Well, let's see if we can find some Union soldiers here. Maybe someone can tell us where the fortress is that they have been talking about."

We didn't get far into town when we first spotted some black people. There were quite a few. We came up on some Union soldiers, one of them a lieutenant. We got down off our horses and walked up to the soldiers. I tipped my hat. "Lieutenant, this is Reverend Williams, and I'm Elijah Adams. We happen to be coming here from a long distance, and on the way, we met a black family, and they were told that you had a fortress here and that you would be patrolling this area."

You could tell the lieutenant had seen some battles in his lifetime. He had some scars on his face and was missing a finger on his left hand.

The lieutenant tipped his hat back. "Well, yes, sir, it's good to meet you, Mr. Adams and Reverend Williams, did you say? It is good to meet you. We do actually have a fortress, Fort Randall, ten miles from here. We do patrol, but I can't guarantee the safety of no one. There are still a lot of hard feelings after the war. We do everything we can to do what's right around here. You know, actually, there is a colony of black people that live on the other side of town that I've heard quite a bit about. You might wanna find a black person here and ask them about this colony. They actually have about twenty blocks of black families that live there. They have their own community. They police themselves. They have their own stores that they buy and sell from. Matter of fact, I believe they come from Haiti. They've been here for well over a hundred years, so I don't think they'll have a problem at all." He looked over at one of the black men passing through. "Matter of fact, there is Mr. Johnson right there. He is a friendly sort, and I think he is sort of the big wig in that community, so you might want to talk to him." The lieutenant raised his hand and his voice, shouting, "Mr. Johnson! Mr. Johnson! Do you have time to talk to us for a moment?"

Mr. Johnson walked over to us. "Well, yes, sir, lieutenant, yes, sir."

The lieutenant introduced us to Mr. Johnson. "Mr. Johnson, this here is Elijah Adams and Reverend Williams. Now, gentlemen, if you don't care, talk to Mr. Johnson here. He might be the man you want to talk to."

Mr. Johnson clapped his hands together and gave us a big toothy grin. "Well, sirs, what might I do for you, gentlemen?"

"Well, I tell you, the reverend has become acquainted with a picker couple that has been trying to flee from Mississippi because of all the bad white activity over there. They were coming here to Alexandria because they heard there was a fortress here, a fort that would protect them from such activity for freedmen. Is this true, Mr. Johnson?"

Mr. Johnson nodded. His grin was getting bigger. "Why, yes, sir, it is! There's been freed black folks here for quite a while. We've been here since the 1700s. My family has. I guess you could call me the mayor of that community. Me and a bunch of the elders sort of control what happens there. We have our own laws, our own rules."

The reverend spoke up. "I just want to make sure that this family will be taken care of and no Klan activity will harm any of these people. They have four beautiful children that not only need protection but also need to learn how to read and write. Is that something that your community can help with?" The reverend looked him right in the eye when he spoke.

Mr. Johnson laid his hand on the reverend's shoulder. "Well, yes, sir, we do have a teacher that works with the children. Reverend Simms is our pastor and schoolteacher. Although he has been away for a few weeks. We are trying to educate ourselves and help all survivors that make their way here for a new start. I've heard that in Washington, we have senators and congressmen and representatives of the picker persuasion to fight for our rights as a freed people."

"Yes, sir, and you have a lot of white people doing that. We had a lot of white brothers of mine die in that war. Some are fighting for President Lincoln, and some are fighting against him."

"Well, Mr. Adams, we do appreciate everybody's sacrifice for what's happened. But you know, this would have never happened if all of these men had to follow God's guidance in the beginning. Do you agree, Reverend?"

The reverend's eyes lit up. "I truly do! All men are created equal and should be given the same rights bestowed upon us from our creator. He created all black, white, yellow, red. We're all the same. We all bleed the same color."

"Yes, sir, Reverend Williams, yes, sir. I think your family would be more than welcome here. Not only do we have our little community, but we also have the fort, Fort Randall, outside of town here. I do believe they would be more comfortable coming over to Fort Ward, which is what we call our place. We have a place called colored Rosemont. I think I have a room available for them there right now. Until they can start their own little farm, I think that would be good for them."

I smile at the prospect. "Okay, Mr. Johnson, how do we get there?"

"I tell you what, I'll send my grandson up here. He'll meet you two gentlemen here in an hour exactly where we are standing. He'll lead you where you need to be. Just northeast of the town is where the fort is at. You bring them up here. You look for Tenth Street. We are just past there. You'll know it. When you come into our community, there will be people of my color, and you'll know exactly where you're at. You'll smell some mighty fine cooking. I promise you, you gentlemen will be welcomed along with this family. What did you say their name was?"

"It's the Harris family," said the reverend.

"You tell these fine people to come on over. What were their full names?"

"George and June Harris and their kids—Sosa, Anna, William, and Tulley."

"Well, you tell these fine people they are more than welcome in our community. We will treat them like family as soon as they get here, and we will give them protection the best we can. I can't promise you there's not some activity we have to deal with, but we keep to ourselves. We deal mainly with the Union soldiers when they come through. They buy some of our goods also. We got some of the local restaurants that come and buy some of our goods. We have some of the best hog meat. They make the best bacon you'll ever eat."

My mouth started to water. "Mr. Johnson, you don't even realize how long it's been since I've had bacon."

Mr. Johnson threw back his head and laughed. "Well, Mr. Adams, I promise you'll have bacon tonight! You are more than welcome to come and join us!"

I stretched out my hand. "Mr. Johnson, let me shake your hand. Very honored to meet you."

"Honored to meet you too, Mr. Adams. You fine gentlemen seem like good people. We need more and more people like you. Reverend, I cannot wait to meet this family."

"Well, Mr. Johnson, by God's grace, I think he has led us to you people, and I am so thankful to have found you."

As we began our walk back to retrieve the Harris family, I looked over at the reverend who had a huge smile on his face. "It kind of seems like this fine family has found them a place to go."

"Yes, it does, Mr. Adams. I think God's hand was upon us this whole trip. I think we were supposed to be there for this family. Who knows if they would have made it here without us, especially with what happened the other night."

"Men's hearts are full of hate. They just hate people for no reason. Just because they may have had a successful plantation that they think they have a right to keep people captive and do them any way they want to. Yeah, Reverend, it doesn't seem right, but you know slavery has been in the world for a long time."

The reverend sighed. "Yes, I know, Mr. Adams. I know."

"Well, there's the wagon just a stone's throw from here. I think this family will be delighted when they hear what Mr. Johnson told us."

As we rode closer, I called out, "Mr. Harris, Mrs. Harris!"

The reverend called out, "Children, children!" They were nowhere to be found. The whole family was vacant. The horse was there, the mule was there, the wagon was there, but the family was gone.

The reverend took off his hat and clutched it in his hands. "Dear Jesus, I wonder what happened. Do you think the Klan wandered by?"

"Maybe so, Reverend."

We climbed off our horses and started looking around for any signs of foul play or any kind of raid or any blood-stains. Didn't see any new bullet holes in the wagon. I couldn't understand it.

"Let's spread out. Reverend, you go to the left, and I'll go to the right. We'll walk down this Red River, and we'll see what we can see."

We walked on slowly, lightly saying, "Mr. Harris, Mrs. Harris." I could hear the reverend. "Children! Children! William! Anna! Are you here?" About that time, the reverend said, "Mr. Adams!"

I made my way over to the reverend as quickly as I could.

"Look there." The reverend pointed across the river.

Mr. Harris was teaching the children how to fish, and Mrs. Harris was braiding her baby's hair. They were more than a stone's throw away from where we were at, not to mention the moving water from the river, so they couldn't hear us.

The reverend said, "Thank God. Thank you, Lord, for keeping your hand of protection on this family."

I patted the reverend on the shoulder. "Yeah, Reverend, let's go retrieve them and get them into town."

As we walked closer, Mr. Harris jumped up. "Oh, oh, it's you two gentlemen. Thank God. Well, lookee here!" he exclaimed, pulling up about seven fish that he had caught. "Well, you two gentlemen have been gone for a little while, so we decided to go fishing! We've been very lucky at it. The children, William and Anna and Tuley, did great! They caught all kinds of fish. Suse is over there with Mrs. Harris getting her hair done. She doesn't want anything to do with the 'slimy fish.' She's all girl."

"Well, Mr. Harris, we've got some great news!" the reverend announced with a grin as wide as Texas. Mr. Harris was hopeful but cautiously asked, "Really, what did you find out?"

"We met a Mr. Johnson in town, and he is from Haiti. Apparently, there is a Haitian community right outside of town. They call it…what did they call it there, Mr. Adams?"

"They call it Fort Ward, Reverend. The reverend was so excited he began talking and waving his hands around. "Yes, sir, Mr. Harris. This Mr. Johnson apparently leads this community. They said it's about fifteen or twenty blocks right outside of town. Not only do you have that, they have a schoolteacher to teach the children to read and write. They can also put you up in a room until you could start your own little farm right outside of their community. They also sell goods amongst themselves and they protect each other, so I think it's going to be a good place for you."

I spoke up. "Also, there's a Fort Randall about ten miles outside of Alexandria, so the Union soldiers patrol it. I think you're going to be fine. It's sort of like when you heard about this Union fort. It was not actually the fort you were thinking of, it was a fort where all these people live. It's where you will be welcomed as family is what they told us!"

"They said they were going to feed us all tonight!" the reverend said. "They've invited Mr. Adams and myself to stay and eat with you, and we are truly looking forward to it!"

Mr. Harris shook our hands. "Thank you so much! Thank you so much for what you've done for us!" He looked back toward Mrs. Harris. "Did you hear that? Mama, did you hear that?! We're finally gonna be safe, the children are gonna be safe!"

With tears in her eyes, she reached over and hugged the reverend's neck, and he started crying too. She released him and ran toward me and reached over one of the children who was now standing in front of me to hug my neck. I chuckled slightly. "I'm not one to cry."

"Oh, Elijah Adams, I know you won't, but I may cry all over you!" she said.

She gave me such a strong hug, and as she pulled away, she gave me a kiss on the cheek. It sort of felt like when my grandmother would kiss me on the cheek. What a sweet lady.

We loaded up the children, packed up everything, and made our way to town. The reverend didn't climb aboard with the children, but he did ride beside them. He was explaining to them about the teacher and how they were going to read and write! You should have seen the smile on Mr. Harris's face. It was a good day. As we rode closer, I rode in the front to make sure that nothing was going to interfere with this moment. We got a few strange looks as we came into town. But sure enough, as I led the wagon down the street, there stood a lone young black man, the grandson of Mr. Johnson.

"Are you Mr. Adams?" he asked. He had the same large grin across his face that he inherited from his grandfather.

"Yes, sir. Young man."

"Grandpappy, he told me to bring you people into the fort with me."

"Yes, sir, what's your name?" I asked.

"I'm Timmy! Timmy Johnson!"

"Well, Timmy, it's good to meet you! I'm Mr. Adams, and this is Mr. and Mrs. Harris, and the children right there, I think one of them might be your age. And right there is Reverend Williams."

The reverend rode closer. "It's good to see you. You want to climb up on the wagon?" he asked.

"Yes, sir! I'd love to ride up on that wagon!" So he climbed on up and pointed the way, and we followed. I still kept my eye peeled just in case something might go wrong. Timmy looked over at me and saw the worry on my face. "You don't have to worry, Mr. Adams. We are almost on our side of town. Nothing hardly ever happens over there, unless you talk about some of the neighbors getting in arguments, but we try to keep to ourselves." He looked over at the reverend and smiled. "You know, Reverend, our Reverend Simms, he doesn't look like you. He doesn't have that funny-looking collar that you got. He just wears overalls, but he teaches us. I know all about Jesus. He said he didn't believe that Jesus is a white man. He believes he is a darker-skinned man. Is that what you believe, Reverend?"

"Well, we won't know until we get to heaven. As what I understand, he's sort of a little bit lighter than what the Indians look like, so he's not black, he's not white, he's sort of olive color is what I've been told."

Timmy laughed. "That's funny. I'll have to tell my reverend about that!"

"Yes, sir, Timmy, it's good to meet you." Reverend reached over and patted him on the leg as he was riding right beside him on the horse next to the wagon.

Timmy pointed ahead. "Well, right up there we are!"

I shook my head. "Yeah, right there it is, I saw Tenth Street just like Mr. Johnson said. And what do you know, we came up on nothing but dark-skinned people. Every house, all I saw was dark-skinned people. They all looked at us awfully funny as we rode into town. Mr. Johnson came walking out of his house, saying in a loud booming voice so all around us could hear, "This is a new family coming to move in with us. They're going to be a new part of our community! Come on out and meet these fine folks!" He turned toward us and held his hand out. "Mr. Harris, Mrs. Harris, these two fine gentlemen right here told me about you and your plight. Told me that you came here to get away from all the trouble that you've been facing. Come on down here and let me shake your hand!" Mr. Harris stepped down off the wagon and shook his hand.

Mr. Johnson gave him that huge grin and said, "Son, welcome home. You'll be welcome in our community. Nobody is gonna do you wrong from now on."

"Thank you so much, Mr. Johnson! Thank you so much! I am George, this is June, and we are the Harrises."

Mrs. Harris spoke up and said, "These are my babies right here. This is Susie, William, Anna, and Tulley! Thank you so much. We heard there was a fort over here where we would be safe, and little did we know this is what it would be."

"Yes, ma'am," Mr. Johnson said. "We've been here over a hundred years. We come from Haiti. My grandfather was from Haiti. We came over here to make a better life here. No one in this community had ever been slaves. We're freedmen. We've got some former slaves here now, but the original founders were never slaves. We've been freemen since we've come to America. You and your family are more than welcome."

"Well, it's good to know that," said the reverend. "There is hope. Apparently, there is a beam of light from heaven in this community, even over a hundred years ago."

"Do you know why my grandfather left Haiti? Because our own people were trying to put us people in the slave industry, bringing us over here and selling us. That's why my family, along with about four or five other families, escaped. We came to America, and we've been freemen ever since." Mr. Johnson led us to his house. "Come on in! My missus has almost got supper made, and we're gonna have a fine meal. Mr. Adams, she made a big batch of bacon just for you!"

I chuckled. "Thank you so much, Mr. Johnson. That smells so good I can smell it from right here."

Mr. Johnson laughed. "Well, I don't know if you can smell it, but maybe the thought of it brought the smell to your nostrils. Let's make our way over there."

He took us into the house. It was him and his wife, daughter, son-in-law, and grandkids. They all welcomed us there with open arms, even the reverend and myself. We all sat down and had a fine meal. We told them about our adventures. We had a really good time with this fine family. After supper, Mr. Johnson walked the Harrises over to the colored area, and he showed them the room they would be staying in. "Eh. It's not big enough for your big family, but it'll do for right now."

"Yes, sir, Mr. Johnson, we are very thankful for it."

Mr. Johnson points down the street to the livery stable. "You can take your horse down there and your wagon after you unload it. My nephew runs that stable, you can just tell him I sent you down there."

"Well, Mr. Adams, Reverend, I can find you a place to sleep, or you can go back over to Alexandria. There's a few fine motels if you wanna get a room over there." He gestured around. "I could always make you a pallet on the floor."

"No, sir, Mr. Johnson. I sure appreciate your hospitality. I'm gonna make my way back to town, is that fine with you, Reverend? I'd like to sleep in a bed tonight."

"Yes, sir, that'd be fine. That'd be fine," he said.

"Well, I think we'll say our goodbyes. Mr. Johnson, Mrs. Johnson, thank you so much for the fine food." Mr. and Mrs. Johnson shook our hands and welcomed us to come back anytime we wanted to.

"If you keep serving bacon like that, I may come back more than you think. If I'm ever in this area, I'm gonna be knocking on your door," I told them.

Mr. Johnson laughed. "If Mrs. Johnson was white, she'd be red right now! She'd be blushing! She loves when people brag about her cooking."

"Well, that was some of the best. Thank you so much again for having us."

The reverend turned to the Harrises. "I can help you unload your wagon."

"No, no, sir. You and Mr. Adams have done quite enough for us. You just don't know how much easier you made this trip for my family, and we really appreciate what you've done for us. Thank you so much, Mr. Adams, Reverend." He reached over to shake my hand, so I patted him on the shoulder and shook his hand.

I said, "Remember, Mr. Harrison, you have a friend in us. I hope one day I will see you again."

The reverend spoke up. "If not on this side of glory, we'll see you on the other side of glory!"

The reverend squatted down and said goodbye to the children. They swarmed him like flies. Every one of them had tears in their eyes. "Please don't go!" said Tule, her being the youngest.

The reverend said, "Well, you've got a new home here. They're gonna teach you how to read, write, and all sorts of new things."

"Who's gonna tell us about Jesus?" She looked up at him, her bottom lip puckered.

The reverend patted her on the head. "They've got a reverend here, they have a church here. They'll teach you about Jesus. Little Timmy said that he goes to church. They also teach about Jesus here."

All of the children swarmed all around the reverend, kissing and hugging him, just crying. The reverend was crying too. And here comes Mrs. Harris crying once again. She knelt down and threw her arms around all the children and the reverend. I thought it was never gonna end. They had to have hugged for two or three minutes. Children crying, momma crying. I think every one of us had tears in our eyes. I walked over and patted all the kids on their heads. Then I grabbed the reverend around the arm and sort of picked him up.

"Come on, Reverend. We've got to go. Kids, hopefully one day I will see you again. I'm just glad you've found a place to live, a place to call home."

"Yes, sir, I think we have. Once again, thank you so much," said Mr. Harris.

The reverend spoke up. "No, thank you so much Mr. Harris, Mrs. Harris. I've enjoyed being with your children so much, and I cannot wait to get into my church, and I can minister to families just like yours."

Mrs. Harris took the reverend by the hand. "Reverend, you're exactly what these communities need."

The reverend looked around at the Harris family. "Do you mind if I pray one more time over your family?"

"No, sir, you go right ahead," Mr. Harris said, nodding his head.

We all pulled our hats off, and the reverend bowed his head and laid his hands on top of the children's heads. "Dear heavenly Father, in Jesus's holy name, please pour

Your spirit of protection upon these babies. Allow them to receive a full education. Allow them to become doctors, lawyers, senators, congressmen, maybe even presidents. Put your hand of blessing upon these fine, fine kids. Also, the parents. I ask that you bless them, give them a special blessing, Lord. Put your holy hand upon them. Mr. Harris is a true man of God and a true protector. Mrs. Harris is a true mother hen. She will do everything she can for these babies. And, Lord, I ask that you put a hedge of protection on the Johnson household. These are fine people. Lord, as you made a way for the children of Israel to come out of bondage, thank you so much for making a way for the Harrises. In Jesus Christ's mighty name…children, what do we say?" And everyone said, "Amen!"

We said our goodbyes, and the reverend and I turned around and walked out. We untied the mule from the wagon, climbed aboard the horses, and made our way toward Alexandria, which was just right up the road. As we were riding out, I thought the reverend was going to ride backward. He just kept staring at the kids.

"Reverend, I know you're going to miss them. There'll be more kids."

The reverend nodded. "Yes, I know, Mr. Adams. There's just something special about that family."

"Yes, there is. You're right, Reverend. Now let's go get us a hotel room and maybe a beer!" The reverend let out a laugh. "Mr. Adams."

"C'mon, Reverend, you can have a beer."

"Yeah, I suppose I could, but I choose not to. I want to indulge in God's wine. I don't need that kind of stuff. I got everything I need right here." He held his Bible out toward me.

"By the way, Reverend, every time they search you, they find no money. They find no money on me 'cause I don't have much. But what I do have, I keep some in my boot. So where are you keeping your money? In your boot?"

As he rolled back the back cover of his Bible, he opened it up, and what do you know, his money was right there inside the Bible.

"Well, Reverend, I guess when you said this was the most valuable thing you have, you meant that in more ways than one!"

"Yeah, that money means nothing. It's just a means of getting us from here to there. This Word right here will last forever. It's the only thing that means anything in this world."

"The way that everything starts falling into place, Reverend, I'm beginning to believe that!"

Chapter 12

When we arrived at the hotel, we dismounted and inquired about some rooms. The Sapphire hotel was a pretty nice place. Beautiful front room with Queen Anne furniture throughout. The clerk, although he was an older man, was very kept up. I looked at the reverend and told him, "I'm not sure if we'd be able to afford this place."

"Ah, never mind that. It'll be fine."

As we checked in, we asked the clerk if there was a bathhouse that we could use. Same as always, it was in the back. He said, "I'll inform the girl that you gentlemen want a bath."

"No, Reverend, you go right ahead. I think I'll get one in the morning. I think I'm gonna have me a beer or two and play some cards."

The reverend nodded. "Well, if that's what you wanna do, Mr. Adams, you go right ahead."

"You go ahead and turn in. I'll take the horses down to the stable."

The reverend spoke up. "No, no, Mr. Adams, you go ahead. I'll take the horses down to the stable and take the bags up to the rooms too. It'll be fine."

"Well, actually, we don't have clean clothes." I looked over at the clerk and asked him if there was a laundry service around here.

"Yes, there is, sir. There is a Chinaman's laundry just right down the street here. If you go down the street here and visit them, they'll take care of you."

"If you wanna take care of that, Reverend, I'm gonna go over here to the saloon. You come on over if you wanna hang out with me a little bit. I'll buy you a beer."

"You go right ahead, Mr. Adams."

The reverend took the horses and the mule to a local stable, and he checked our horses in, and the stableman unsaddled them. The reverend, with our clothes up under his arm, went to the laundry place where they told him they would have it done in the morning.

"I guess I won't be getting a bath until the morning," he said and headed for the door. Right before exiting, he turned and said, "I'll check with you in the morning, sir."

The reverend made his way back to the hotel. As he started to go up the stairs, he noticed there was a picture on the wall of Abraham Lincoln. He asked the clerk, "Really? You keep a picture of the president on your wall?"

"Well, it's just to remind us who the president is, even though he's not the president any longer since his assassination."

"Yes, it's pretty sad about that, I'd say."

"Yeah, I'd say also. By the way, Reverend, what's your name?"

"Reverend John Williams. Good to meet you, sir, what's your name?"

"My name is Donnie Sapphire. I own this establishment. This is the Sapphire Hotel."

"Oh! Very nice!"

"Well, Reverend, I'm glad to have you here, you and Mr. Adams. I'm sorry you couldn't get your laundry done tonight, but I can still arrange you a bath if you want, or you can take one in the morning."

"Yeah, I guess we'll take one in the morning, sir. But I sure do appreciate it. I think I will make my way over to the saloon and see what Mr. Adams is up to. I'll see you in the morning, sir."

The reverend carried our things up to our rooms and made his way over to the saloon. As soon as he walked out the door of the hotel, he noticed a horse in front of the saloon. It was a stallion—a beautiful horse.

"That is one beautiful horse," he said.

The gentleman standing beside him looked him dead in the eyes and said, "Does your horse know that you lust over other horses?"

The reverend took a step back and said, "Excuse me?"

The man repeated, "Does your horse know that you lust over other horses? Uh-huh. Stop looking at something that you can't have."

"Okay, brother, if you say so." He started laughing as he continued walking to the saloon.

What kind of establishment am I about to walk into? he thought.

As the reverend walked into the Sunshine Saloon, he noticed that I had got myself into a card game. I waved at the reverend as he walked up to the barkeep. "How about a glass of milk?" he said.

"Well, Reverend, we don't have any fresh milk. I can give you some water."

"What about some coffee?"

"Oh yeah, we got some coffee. I'll make you a pot right now. Give it about five minutes, I'll have it brewed up for you."

"Thank you so much, sir. This sure is a beautiful tavern." The reverend looked around the bar. There was a huge mirror above the bar and glasses of liquor around the mirror, deer head on both sides of the room, dance hall girls all over the place—plenty of entertainment. There were cards on one side of the room and cards on the other. Apparently, these people were having a good time. The reverend thought to himself, *This isn't too bad while I have a cup of coffee and take in the entertainment.* He happened to notice there was a piano in the corner, and there was no one playing it. The barkeep brought him his coffee, and the reverend took a sip. "Would it be alright if I played your piano?"

The barkeep looked confused. "Are you a minister?"

The reverend smiled and nodded. "Yes, sir, I am."

"What are you doing in a bar, Minister?"

"I'm just visiting your fine town, so I just figured I would come in for a cup of coffee and see how things are in this nice little town."

The barkeep cocked his head to one side. "Well, you're more than welcome to play the piano but none of that church stuff. That's not what this place is about."

"Okay, I think I can think of something to play without playing church music." He made his way over to the piano from the bar. He sat his cup of coffee on top of the piano and sat down to play. He slowly started to play a tune, and I looked over at him and smiled. The reverend thought that I might have thought he was going to start playing "Amazing Grace." The reverend started singing "You Are My Sunshine." Apparently, it was a hit. Everybody liked it. A couple of cowboys who apparently drank a little bit too much started shouting, "Play another one! Play another one!" So the reverend obliged. He even snuck in a few

Christian tunes. It seemed no one recognized what he was playing, which was a good thing. There was silence over the room while he was playing. I was still having a good time playing my cards. Some old drunkard slid up beside the reverend. "Play something I can sing there, sir!" The man smelled horrible. "Ah, you a preacher?" the man slurred.

"Why, yes, I am, brother," the reverend answered without taking his eyes off the keys.

"Play us good song there, preacher," he asked.

The reverend played "The Yellow Rose of Texas," and the drunkard started singing. When the song was over, the reverend paused for a moment with his head bowed, then started to play "Holy, Holy Holy! Lord God Almighty."

One of the saloon girls remembered it from her church days and started to sing along. He continued to play while she started to sing, "Holy holy holy! Lord God almighty." It wasn't long until half the bar was singing, including the bartender! After a little while, he realized that no one was buying beer and spoke up to put a stop to it. "Preacher, that's enough of that. I think it's time we call it quits with the piano."

It was too late. The drunkard sitting beside the reverend was in tears, and so was the saloon girl that was singing. Apparently, the power of God is more powerful than any bartender. No matter what he wanted, it didn't matter. God's got his own way.

He continued to play, and the barkeep walked over and put his hand on the reverend's shoulder. "We've got to stop this. This is a bar, not a church. You've got to take this outside, you've got to take this somewhere else."

The reverend abruptly stood up, hugged the bartender, and whispered something in his ear. The bartender bowed his head, walked behind the bar, and squatted down behind it. I wasn't sure what the reverend had said to the bartender, but I was worried he might be getting a shotgun. So I stood up and excused myself from the game. I walked cautiously over to the bar and looked behind it. The bartender was sitting on the ground with his face in his hands, weeping. Relieved but a little confused, I turned to leave but stopped upon hearing the piano begin again, and the reverend started singing, "Amazing Grace." There was a calmness that I began to feel and then an eruption of an overwhelming feeling of the presence of God. It was the way I felt when I was a kid in the meetings when the preacher would be so on fire preaching a message that just touched everyone in the room. It was not only the girl who was singing but also half the bar!

Suddenly, the reverend stopped playing, turned around immediately, and said, "In all my years of preaching, this is the first time I remember seeing Jesus show up in the back of a bar, and now He's walking right toward me!"

At this point, all the men either ran out the door or ran forward crying like babies, falling to their knees with their faces to the ground and repenting right before the piano stool! This was such an amazing event to witness. I began to feel a bit of fear and turned to walk toward the door. I got about two steps and felt myself squat down on my knees, repent of my sins, and call upon my Jesus. I couldn't believe how strong this was. The little bit of beer I had drunk I could no longer feel it in my body. I felt such a clarity, and my heart was breaking for the man that I had been. That's just what happens when Jesus steps into the room. He makes every one of us feel unclean because of His purity. This was the strongest move of the Holy Spirit that I'd ever felt or seen. As I lifted my head up, I could see the reverend walking around, kneeling with each and every individual. He was praying with them and talking to them. He was leading them to Christ right here in this bar. Cards and chips spread across the floor and on the tables that were dripping with turned-over drinks. Some of the chairs were turned over, and hats and coats of those who fled in haste were lying about. It was such an amazing event to witness. I remained kneeling for about ten minutes. As I got up, I felt that my life was completely changed. I knew it in my heart for sure. Not looking back, I made my way out of the bar, leaving the reverend praying with the people, tears running down my cheeks.

I walked into the hotel. The clerk looked at me with amazement, not believing what he was seeing. I went past him and walked up the stairs to my room. I got in my room and continually prayed. I walked over to the wash-basin and washed my face and my tears away. I took my clothes off and lay down. My heart was clear. No longer did I have that feeling of heaviness like I had felt every night since I was a young man. It was such an uplifting feeling. I wasn't sure what I should say or do. Quietly I closed my eyes and said, "Dear God, thank You for what You've done. In Jesus's mighty name, I pray." I reached down and pulled the covers up. I fell asleep and slept so, so well. I dreamed about a time when I was a child. My father pushed me in a swing in the backyard. My mother called me in for supper. I dreamed about the dog running around my feet as my older brother took me fishing. My older sister helped my mom do the dishes. My father sang "Amazing Grace," and Mom would join in as we sat in the living room. It was so clear in my dream. All of a sudden, I could see my dad's face. He looked older than I remembered him being. He looked right at me and said, "I love you, son. I truly love you." I was about to say, "I love you too, Dad," when my eyes popped open, and it was morning.

I walked out of my room and knocked on the reverend's door, but there was no answer. I checked the door, and it was open. As I pushed the door open, I saw his bag on the bed, but I didn't see the reverend around. So I made my way downstairs and asked the clerk if he'd seen him.

"I saw him about an hour and a half ago as he woke up very early and headed out. All he said was, 'Bless you, brother.' He hasn't returned."

"Well, what about that bath? Also, where did you say that place was to get our clothes?"

"I think I saw the reverend take your clothes, and he's up to his room. If you'd like, I'll retrieve them for you. There's a bath waiting out back. The reverend told us last night he was going to bathe in the morning, so we warmed him up some water. You can use his bath, and we'll warm him up with another one when he returns."

"Thank you, sir, I'll take you up on that."

I went out back to the bathhouse and slipped into the tub. Just as I began to relax in the hot water, the clerk knocked on the door. "Come on in!" I said.

He walked in with my clothes and said, "Enjoy your bath, sir. Here are your clothes." He laid them on the chair by the door.

When I had finished bathing, I walked back into the hotel and asked the clerk if there was anywhere I could get a bite to eat.

"Yes, sir. Three doors down is one of the best restaurants in town called Flo's. Good black lady. She used to be a slave cook for one of the plantations. Now she owns her own restaurant, believe it or not. Our black community helped her obtain that."

"That sounds good to me. I think I'll go over there and have a bite to eat."

When I arrived at Flo's, I grabbed a table and placed my order. The waitress, who had dark skin and kind eyes, brought me my food. It looked so delicious. That clerk was not mistaken when he told me they had some really fine food. They got some of the best biscuits and gravy I'd ever eaten in my life. Before I could finish eating, here came the reverend. He walked in and spotted my table right away. When he arrived at my table, he pulled out a chair and sat. "Elijah, good morning to you! How are you feeling there after last night?" he said.

"Well, I'll tell you, Reverend, you disturbed my card game and my beer, but I couldn't be happier for it. I felt such a change, such a relief last night. It was very good. I don't think I've been in a situation like that. There had to be ten people kneeling on that floor and the bartender behind the bar crying. It was unique."

"Yes, sir, Mr. Adams, it was. The Lord Jesus Christ stepped in, and when he does, he changes lives. You can't be the same when you experience Jesus Christ."

"No, sir, Reverend, I believe you're right. I definitely feel a difference in my life this morning. I've never had such good sleep and such sweet dreams as I had last night."

"That's good to hear, Mr. Adams! I'm thankful!"

"Well, Reverend, I'll go down here and retrieve our horses and the mule. I'll resaddle them and get us ready to go. We can take off after you eat breakfast if you'd like. You weren't planning to eat breakfast with me, were you?"

"Actually, I had food earlier with Mr. Johnson."

"Down at Fort Ward? That Mr. Johnson?"

The reverend paused as if trying to gather his thoughts and say something hard to hear. "Yes, sir. I don't believe I'll be going with you, Mr. Adams. I think my path stops right here in Alexandria."

"Really?" I answered slowly as I sat back in my seat.

The reverend folded his hands, set them on the table, and sat forward. "Yes," he answered. "When I woke this morning, I was saying my morning prayers and I had word from the Lord about my journey being over. I pondered this all the way to picking up our clothes. As I was walking back to the hotel, I saw Mr. Johnson was heading toward me. A calmness settled over me, and I asked him if I could help him with anything. He asked if I could meet him at the restaurant after I dropped off my clothes in my room first. When I returned and sat down, he told me that after we left his house last night, he received a message. It seems their Reverend Simms was off visiting a family to pray for a sick family member. On his way back, his horse got spooked by something and threw him. The poor man's head landed on a rock, and he died instantly. The reverend that passed away was also the schoolteacher. I've been talking to Mr. Johnson, and I asked him if it would be alright with his community if I could step in and be the reverend and be their minister and also the children's schoolteacher. You know what Mr. Johnson told me, Mr. Adams?"

"What's that, Reverend?"

"That they had been praying that God would lay it upon my heart to take over where the other minister had left off. I believe that the strong movement of the Holy Spirit at the bar last night was God's way of telling me this is where I'm supposed to be."

"Well, I can see that, Reverend. I can see the love you had in your eyes for those children. I'll say it once again, I've never met a man like you. You have absolutely no regard to skin color and to love people as much as you love them. You don't even know these people. I know that those are good people, the Harris family have great children. Seeing you become as close and attached as you have, so quick. Never known a man like you, brother, never known a man."

As we were speaking, Ms. Flo came out from the back, walked over to the reverend, reached down, and hugged his neck. "Reverend, welcome to our community! Preacher, whatever you want to eat is always on me. You come here for every meal if you want. My grandchildren were needin' a schoolteacher so bad. Thank you so much for putting us in your life and allowing us to be a part of it. Thank you for being a part of our community!" She was very sad about their loss yet so excited she couldn't stand still.

"Thank you, ma'am. How do you know me?" he asked as he stood to pull out a chair at our table.

"Mr. Johnson is my brother. He came to see me just a little while ago."

"Oh, really? He must have come to see you as I was taking a bath."

"I'm so happy to have you here." She looked down, just then realizing the chair was there.

"And your name, ma'am?" I asked.

"My name is Flo, Flo Kindred. My husband died a while back. It just so happened he saved up enough money along with the community to   help me buy this restaurant. It was just an old shutdown building when I bought it. Everyone pitched in and helped me turn it into what it is right now."

I looked up at Ms. Flo and said, "We'll, ma'am, you make the best biscuits and gravy I've ever eaten in my life. Your food is mighty fine, ma'am."

"And who might you be, sir?"

"I'm Elijah Adams, I'm a friend of the reverend here."

"Well, sir, good friend of the reverend, that meal right there is on me also. I thank you so much for bringing this fine man to our community. We were all praying to God all night that he might stay. Didn't know God would provide a white man when we needed a preacher, but God knows what he's doing. Hallelujah, praise God! Reverend, how about a piece of pie? I made a nice apple pie, and I'd like to see you have a piece and a cup of coffee!"

"Yes, ma'am, that would be great!"

"I believe I'll have one there too, ma'am. But I insist, I'm paying for my meal."

"Well, if you insist." She smiled as she walked back to the kitchen.

It wasn't long until we received our pie. The pie was so good we were quiet for a while. When we were almost finished, we sat back to relax.

"Well, Mr. Adams, what are you planning on doing?" he asked me.

"I'll tell you, Reverend. I'm gonna head to El Paso. I think we're gonna take a train over there. I'm going to buy a train ticket, load up Rosie, and take the train the rest of the way. I know you said you thought God wanted us to be riding across to El Paso, but I still have a long way to go, and I am missing my family, my mom and dad, awfully bad. So I do think I'm gonna load up and get there as soon as possible. I think a train is the way I should go. I believe I've had enough adventure with you on this trip, Reverend, to last me for quite a while. So I think I will get on a train tomorrow and get out of here."

"Well, Mr. Adams, I do appreciate you bringing me this far, and I will be corresponding with you."

"Yes, sir, Reverend. I'll check on that church that you're supposed to be going to. By the way, what is the name of that church?"

"The First United Christian Assembly right outside of El Paso."

"The First United Christian Assembly?"

"Yes, yes, sir, that's it, Mr. Adams."

"I can't believe I haven't asked you that before. That's my father's church. He's been the pastor there for fourteen years now, I would say." I sat up straight. I was beginning to get a bad feeling in my chest. The reverend just kept on talking, not realizing the impact his next words would have on me.

"Really? Well, I was asked to go there and pastor that church because the previous minister there had passed away. Only right before we left had I received that letter."

I sat in silence for a little bit, just thinking about what that meant. Sorrow filled me. Then a feeling of peace settled in my heart. I knew where my father ended up. He was rejoicing in glory. "Well, Reverend, I guess my mother truly needs me now. We must have left before I received the letter about my father from her."

"I wonder why she didn't wire you, Mr. Adams?"

"Not sure. She might have been too distraught. After all, they'd been married for fifty-four years."

"Well, I'll be praying for your mother and your safe journey, Mr. Adams."

"Reverend, I would appreciate that. I thank you so much for what you've done for me too. I don't know if I've kept you safe, or the power of God in your life has kept us safe. Not completely sure. But I'll tell you this, I'm your friend, Reverend John Williams. And when you get to El Paso, you come and see me. If I ever get back to Alexandria, Louisiana, I'll definitely come and see you." We both stood, laid some money to cover our meal, and headed for the door.

Once we stepped outside, the reverend stopped me by putting a hand on my arm.

"I wish you'd stay and go to at least one church meeting."

I looked around and contemplated what I had to do before leaving. "Let me check on a train ticket. Maybe I will." He nodded his head and gave it one last try. "Tomorrow is Sunday, and I'm not sure if the train runs tomorrow or not. You're welcome to come to service at ten o'clock in the morning. It'll be my first time ministering to these fine people. I believe they are going to have me put Reverend Simms to rest in the evening."

"I think I will be there in the morning, Reverend, I think I will."

Realizing I ate more than I should have, I looked at the reverend. "I think I'm gonna have to go find an outhouse."

The reverend laughed. "One's right there behind the hotel, actually, if you wanna run back there and visit it. I'll see you inside the hotel."

As I headed to the back of the hotel, I did see at the end of the road there was a train depot. Once I came out and washed my hands, I headed inside the hotel and asked the clerk, "Does the train run on Sundays around here?"

"No, sir. It runs on Monday morning."

"I guess we'll be spending two more nights here, the reverend and myself. I'll be checking out on Monday morning. What'll I owe you?" The clerk was looking uncomfortable. "Eh, the reverend has already taken care of all your bills. He said that everything that you owe, just put it on his account."

"I'll be sure to thank him. Thank you so much for your help, Mr. Sapphire. I do appreciate you giving me a room. Your beds are mighty comfortable." A smile spread across his face. "Thank you so much, sir. You're welcome to stay here anytime."

"Thank you so much. I'm gonna make my way up and find the reverend."

"Yeah, I saw him go up earlier, I think he is in his room."

When I got to the top of the stairs, I knocked on his door. The reverend opened it up. I looked past him and saw his Bible lying on his bed. I could tell he had been kneeling, praying, and reading it.

"Reverend, I won't keep you but I will be joining your church service in the morning. Mr. Sapphire just informed me that the train won't be running until Monday morning, so I will be at church in the morning. I think we'll enjoy ourselves."

"Well, Mr. Adams, I want to thank you again for bringing me this far and keeping me safe. I know that God has brought us together, and I know that everything that has happened in this entire journey was God's hand. I know without a doubt that your path and my path will cross again someday. Your mother will be more than blessed to have you there. Be sure to tell her I send my condolences, and one day, I will meet your father on the other side. Hopefully, one day, I'll meet your mother on this side."

"That would be good, Reverend. That truly would be good."

The reverend reached out his hand to me. "Here you go, Elijah. Here's your pay."

"Uh, Reverend, that looks like a lot more than we agreed to."

"Well, considering they have a parish there at the church, I won't need much money. And Flo offered to feed me, and I'm sure the families will offer to pitch in and help out, not to mention all I have to do is wire Mr. Siskin's foundation, and he'll send me whatever I need. So you go on, take this money just to get you home and get you started again. Help your mother out, I'm sure she needs the help now."

"I'm sure she does, Reverend, and I do appreciate it. And, Reverend, you got a true friend right here in me any-time you need me for anything."

I spent a little time in my room, cleaned up, and cleaned my gun. I happened to read a little bit of the Bible that they had in the room drawer. I had a really good time and was feeling better that day than I had in a long time. I decided I'd go walk around town for a spell just to see what I could run into. I made my way down to the depot, and as I looked around, I saw quite a few sights. This was a fairly large city. There was even a clothing shop across the street. Maybe I should look around for a barber, get cleaned up, and buy a new outfit. Sure enough, a few buildings down is a barbershop on the corner called Bill's Barber Shop. I walked in and asked the shopkeeper, "Sir you got time for a shave and a haircut?"

"Yes, sir! You come on in and take a seat. I'm just finishing up with this gentleman."

We nodded at each other as the gentleman gave the barber a coin and walked on out. I sat down and the barber asked, "What'll it be?"

"Just trim a little off the sides, shave my neck, and shave off a little bit of these whiskers."

"What about your mustache, sir?"

"No, sir. You leave that mustache. Just a shave, just take off the beard, I'll be fine."

"Yes, sir, it looks like you haven't shaved in about a week…or two."

"Yeah, I've gotta get rid of that. Think I'll be going to church in the morning."

"Reverend Williams?"

"Yes, sir."

"I happened to hear what happened at the bar last night. If it's true what they say about him, may we all need to be going to that church, but I heard he is down at the picker fort. Is that true?"

"Yes, sir. He's gonna be their new reverend and their new schoolteacher."

"You don't say," he said as he took off a little bit of the whiskers on my face. "Well, I guess those people are entitled to some preaching, too, and a little bit of schooling. I know their last preacher was a pretty good man. For an older man, he was awfully friendly every time you'd see him in town. I've even bought some vegetables from them from time to time. Actually, down at Flo's, she got the best pie I think I've ever eaten. The best biscuits also."

I laughed. "Yes, sir, Mr. Bill, she does. I told her that this morning after I had eaten."

"Well, I appreciate you coming in here and conversing with me. We could always use a new customer. Hopefully you stick around, sir."

"No, no, I'll be on the train Monday heading toward El Paso."

"Well, sir, you enjoy yourself and have a safe trip!" I stood up ran my hand through my hair and over my face and chin, feeling how soft and smooth they both were. "Oh, by the way, would you happen to know what time the train runs?" I asked.

"It runs at eight thirty, I'd like to say sharp, but nope, never sharp. Sometimes late, sometimes a little early."

"Thank you, sir."

"Would you like a little bit of cologne?"

"Yes, sir, I think I will. I'm about to walk over here and buy me a new suit. That would be good."

He squirted a little bit in my hands, and I rubbed it on my jaw. "This smells really good. Thank you, Mr. Bill. What do I owe you?"

"Two bits."

So I paid him and turned to walk away. Just so happened across the street was a brothel, and one of the prettiest redheads I think I've ever seen in my life was standing right there at the door. I turned back to Mr. Bill and asked, "Mr. Bill, who is that pretty thing standing over there?"

"That is Betty Jo. Don't get near her. She'll tangle you up in a web that you won't be able to escape from. I visited her a couple of times myself. Shh. Don't tell the missus! I'm telling you what, there are some mighty fine women over there."

"Well, I'm gonna have to go over there and visit. Think I'll step over and get my new suit first."

"Yes, sir, yes, sir. You come back and see me, okay?"

I walked on down to the clothing shop and stepped inside, and the gentlemen inside said, "What can I do for you, sir?"

"I think I'm gonna get myself a new suit. This one's kind of worn out, my other one is a little bit worn out also." I grabbed the edge of my vest and ran my finger along the frayed edges. The shopkeeper looked me over. "What's that, thirty-six long?" He looked me up and down. "Yes, sir, that's exactly my size." He walked toward me.

"Well, stand right here, I've got a perfect one for you. Are you looking for black and a jacket? Would you like a vest, or are you going to keep the one you've got?" he asked.

"What do you got as far as a vest goes, sir?" He walked over to a table, moved a few vests aside, picked one up, and headed back to where I was still standing.

"This one right here is a nice red one with the black collar. It has inlaid pockets for your watch and even has a wallet pocket right here. Inside the jacket's a small pocket for a derringer if you want it." I took it from his hand and inspected the seams. "Sounds good to me, sir. Sounds good to me."

After I bought my outfit, he bagged up my old clothes, and I made my way over to the brothel. I slid my gun back behind my jacket and walked in there, and sure enough, there stood that pretty redhead. I walked up to her—she was standing beside the bar. I leaned against the stool at the bar, turned, and yelled, "Barkeep," since he was at the other end talking to a couple gentlemen there.

"Yeah, what'll it be, sir?" He was wiping his hands with a towel as he walked over.

"How about a shot of whiskey."

"Yes, sir." He laid it down on the counter and said, "That'll be one bit."

I laid him a coin down, looked over at the pretty redhead, and said, "Betty Jo, I presume?"

"Well, yes, why, yes, I am. So you've heard about me?"

"Well, I've heard a little. I've just noticed how pretty you were standing in the doorway, so I figured I'd come visit."

"You're more than welcome. Would you like to go upstairs?"

I chuckled. I looked her up and down. Very pretty. I reached over, grabbed my glass, and took a swig of that liquor. It turned my stomach immediately before it could even hit my belly, I do believe. I had never felt so nauseous. I coughed.

Betty Jo grabbed my arm. "Are you alright, cowboy?"

"Yes, yes, I'm fine."

"Are you ready to go upstairs?"

"Yeah, yeah, let's go."

So we started walking. She put her arm in my arm when we got to the stairs, and as she grabbed onto the rail of the stairs and started to make her way up, something inside told me I couldn't go. I couldn't do this. I was not the man I used to be.

"What's wrong, sugar? I got a nice room upstairs, you'll like it. Also got a little bit more whiskey up there if you need a little bit more of that." She came back down the steps and rubbed her hand up and down my arm. I cleared my throat and looked up the stairs at where her room would be. I looked her up and down. She was very, very pretty. She smelled so good. I started to take one step up, and before I could lift the other foot off the ground, it went right back on the ground. I took my other foot and also stepped down. "No, Ms. Betty. I think I'm gonna pass this time."

"Really? Are you sure about that, sweety?"

I reached in my pocket and pulled out a dollar. I handed it to her. I said, "Sorry to have bothered you, ma'am. I just can't right now."

"Well, if you change your mind, you come on back. I'll be right here, ready and willing."

"Yes, ma'am, I bet you will be," I said with some regret and sadness in my voice.

I tipped my hat toward her, looked around, turned, and walked out. Right then, I knew I was a changed man whether I would want to be or not.

I made my way back to the hotel room. Walking through the door, I saw Mr. Sapphire was standing behind the counter as he always was. "Mr. Sapphire," I said as I headed to the stairs.

"Man, Mr. Adams, you look sharp! Cleaned up. Pretty nice new duds you got there. I like that vest." I turned and headed his way.

"Thank you, thank you so much, Mr. Sapphire. I need to ask you a question."

He paused for a moment. "Well, okay."

"That Bible that's in that desk drawer up there, would you mind if I had that?"

He kind of looked puzzled. "Oh? There's a Bible in that drawer?"

"Yeah, you didn't know that?" He shook his head.

"No, sir. I didn't know there was one there. But regardless, you can have it if you want it."

"Yes, sir, I do appreciate it, Mr. Sapphire. Is there anywhere I can send a telegraph?"

"Yes, sir, the telegraph office is about four streets down. You take a right, go toward the west."

"Thank you, thank you, Mr. Sapphire." Deciding I didn't want to go to my room, I headed out and found my way to the telegraph office. The gentleman behind the counter greeted me as I walked in. Looking around, I saw there was a little girl playing on the floor with her doll. He said, "Suzie, Suzie, can you calm down? We've got a customer."

I waved my hands, "Ah, I don't mind her. She's just a baby, let her play."

"Yeah, she is. What can I do for you?"

"I need to send a telegraph to El Paso."

I wired my mother and asked her about my father. Hoping she was in town today, I waited there for about thirty minutes to see if I could get a response. While I was waiting, I asked the child, "How you doing, baby girl? You've got some pretty blond hair there!" She just smiled.

"My baby doll has been playing all day, and she's getting kind of tired. I'm going to put her to bed," she said.

"Little Suzie, don't bother the gentlemen," her father said.

I shot little Suzie a smile. "No, sir, it's me who's bothering her. I'm keeping her from her motherly duties! You go right ahead, little girl. You put that baby to sleep!" I watched as she walked over to her little chair and sat down and started rocking her babydoll. It was cute to see.

Realizing I wasn't going to get a response, I straightened up and headed to the door. "Well, Mr. Telegraph man, I'm gonna be over at the Sapphire Hotel. I'm gonna be there tonight and tomorrow if you happen to get a wire back for a Mr. Elijah Adams, then please send it over to me."

"I'd be happy to, Mr. Adams! I'll bring it right over."
Patting my pocket, I asked, "What do I owe you, sir?"

"You owe me one bit," he answered.

So I paid the man, waved at little Suzie, and told her,
"You be a good momma!"

Lifting up her chin and tilting her head to one side
with a large grin on her face, she answered, "I always am!"
Then she continued to rock her baby doll.

I stepped out on the walkway and looked around. I
made my way back toward the hotel and came up to the
Sunlight Bar and stepped inside. I walked up to the barkeep and asked, "How're you doing today?"

"Not too good, sir, not too good."

"Really? What happened?" I asked.

"Well, you were here, you know what happened last
night. The saloon girl, she quit on us. Said she's gonna get
another job, said she couldn't do this anymore. And now
it's got me questioning if I wanna do this."

"Yeah, I understand barkeep. I understand."

"Well, if business doesn't pick up, I may have to shut down anyhow."

"In a big town like this, you don't have much business?"

"Well, I got a strong feeling," said the barkeep. "With that reverend around, I may lose a lot of patrons. They may stop coming around."

"Well, I know alcohol doesn't taste the same to me since last night, but how about just a little bit of beer just to see what it tastes like?"

So he poured me a little bit, and I took a sip. Sure enough, it was alright, but I just didn't think I would ever be able to do liquor again. "Well, here's to you, bartender." I sat my glass down and paid the man. "I'm gonna make my way back to the hotel. Good seeing you, sir. By the way, the good reverend is having a church meeting at ten o'clock down there at the fort."

"The fort? Pickers?"

"Yes, sir. He's their new pastor."

"Really?"

"Yes, sir. I'm gonna be there in the morning. Maybe you'd like to come?"

"Interesting," said the bartender. "Very interesting."

After I arrived at the hotel, I made my way up to my room. I walked over to my bed, sat down, and took my gun off and hung it over the bedrail. I opened up the drawer of the table beside my bed, and there was that Bible. I opened it up to the only passage I ever remembered in my life: John 3:16. "For God so loved the world that he gave his only begotten Son, that whosoever believeth in him should not perish but have everlasting life."

That has become so clear to me right now—truly clear to me. With those thoughts on my mind, I lay back and fell asleep.

The next morning, after a good night's sleep, I made my way over to the reverend's door. "Reverend, you in there?"

His door was locked, so I locked my door up to protect my Spencer rifle that was still in there. I wasn't sure whether I should wear my six-shooter or not. I decided not to since I was going to church. I walked back to my room. Once inside, I hung it over the bed rail, walked out, and locked my door back. When I reached the bottom of the stairs, I looked over, and there was the clerk again.

"Mr. Sapphire," I said.

"Good morning to you, sir!" he said with a smile on his face.

"Well, I'm gonna walk down over here to Flo's and grab me a bite to eat and then head on over to the church."

"Down at the fort? The picker fort?"

"Yes, sir, the good reverend will be preaching his first message down there today."

"Well, I don't think you'll be eating at Flo's today because she's not open on Sundays."

"Oh, really?"

"Yes, sir!"

"Oh well, any other restaurants around here?"

"Yeah, there's a few on the other end of town that are open today. My wife made me a couple of biscuits right here. Got some bacon and some boiled eggs if you'd like. You're welcome to them." He reached behind him and pulled out some containers with the food in it. He walked them over to a table with a few chairs around it that was off to the side.

"I think I'll take you up on that. Thank you so much!"

"Come on, sit down here, we'll have breakfast together. Even got some coffee right here." He walked back to behind the counter and through a door that was not far behind it and came out a few minutes later with two steaming cups of coffee.

"Thanks a lot, Mr. Sapphire. By the way, what about that proposal to come to church with me?"

"You know what, considering you and the reverend are my only two customers at the moment, I'll go with you."

"Sounds good to me, sir." Sometime later, we finished our food and cleaned up. He locked up his hotel, and we made our way down to the picker fort is what they called it. As we walked, we started seeing all the people coming out of different buildings and walking toward the church. I pulled out my pocket watch and looked at it. Mr. Sapphire pulled out his pocket watch and also looked at his.

"By the way, what time is it, Mr. Sapphire?" I asked.

"It is ten minutes till ten." He looked over at me just as we reached the church.

"I think we're right on time," I said as we headed inside.

Mr. Johnson was just inside the door greeting and introducing Reverend Williams to everyone. Looking around, I could see a great many people were already seated. Even the Harrises were there. As soon as Mrs. Harris saw the reverend, she threw her arms around him. "It is so good to see you!" she exclaimed. "I thought we would never see you again!"

All the children started to surround the reverend and hug him. Mr. Johnson stood there, smiling. "I think we've got some here that really appreciate you being here."

"Not as much as I love having them. How you doing, kids?" The reverend hugged each one of their necks.

Mr. Harris shook the reverend's hand and then Mr. Johnson's. "Good to have you here, Reverend."

I walked up to Mr. Harris and patted him on the back. "How are you doing there, Mr. Harris?"

Mr. Harris turned around, his eyes widening as well as his smile. "Well, Mr. Adams, you're here too!" He nodded at Mr. Sapphire.

Mr. Johnson stepped over and said, "Mr. Harris, this is Mr. Sapphire. He owns the hotel in town, the Sapphire Hotel.

Mr. Jonson grinned and nodded. "Yes, sir, Mr. Johnson. You don't mind if we sit through the service today, do you?"

"No, sir, Mr. Sapphire! You and Mr. Adams are more than welcome! Well, are you about ready to get started?"

"Yes, sir, yes, sir. I'll talk to your children in just a little bit, okay?"

Mrs. Harris hugged him one more time, and the family walked over and took their seats. As I walked over to take my seat near the front, about third row back, along with Mr. Sapphire, I noticed the saloon girl was there seated next to the bartender. Two other gentlemen who were at the bar that night that the Holy Spirit fell on the place were also there. It was awfully funny when you see white people at a black church service. It's very different in this day and age. I didn't think I would ever witness this in my life. Mr. Johnson stood up to speak.

"Brothers and sisters, community, I'm sure you all have heard of the horrible loss of our beloved Reverend Simms. Continue to keep his family and close friends in your prayers. God has blessed us with a gift, our new brother in Christ. So I would like you all to help me welcome our new reverend. I know most of you have already met him, but this is Mr. John Williams. Reverend John Williams. He is going to be our new pastor and our new schoolteacher for your children.

"Looks like we are going to have some white brothers and sisters for service! Hopefully they will join us from now on. As the reverend has told me many times since I've met him a couple of days ago, there is no color in God's eyes. So let's enjoy the service together."

As the reverend stood up, he picked up a hymnal and then said, "Together now, let's all sing 'Amazing Grace.'" It was such an amazing place to be that morning. No hatred, no hostility—just a sweet presence of the Holy Spirit and our Lord Jesus Christ. Mr. Sapphire and I also attended the evening service. Instead of a service, they laid the late Reverend Simms to rest. Everyone sang, and the reverend gave the eulogy. It was just as peaceful as the morning service had been.

Everyone who was there that morning also attended that evening. Even Flo was there. I gave her a hard time for not being at the restaurant so I could have some of her mighty fine biscuits.

She laughed aloud. "You show up in the morning before you catch that train, and I'll make sure you have some biscuits!"

"I'm gonna take you up on that! I truly am!"

"As a matter of fact, you can have some biscuits today because we put a meal together for the reverend to welcome him. All you fine people are welcome to come! It's at Mr. Johnson's house. All the ladies of the church got together and made a fine meal for all of us."

We all got together later that evening and ate together. I ate so much I was on the lookout for that outhouse one more time. Afterwards, I went to my room to clean up a bit and went over to say hi to the reverend. The reverend was walking out as I stepped out of my room.

"Reverend, where are you going?"

"Souls out there. I need to go and see if I can find some more people to come to church with us!"

"Really, Reverend? We've had church all day and that mighty fine meal!"

"Mr. Adams, there's no rest for God's workers."

"You're right, Reverend, you are right. Well, Reverend, I probably won't see you in the morning. I won't disturb you 'cause I know you've been busy all day. Let me shake your hand. I'm gonna say goodbye to you right now. In the morning, I'm gonna be going to the train depot to load up Rosie."

"Yeah, I think I'll be selling my horse and my mule and making this place my home. This is my last night here. Tomorrow I'll be moving to the parsonage down at the church."

"Well, Reverend, it's been an honor to know you. And I'll say it one more time, I've never met a man like you. Probably never will again."

"If I don't see you on this side of glory…"

"Eh, you will, Reverend, you will. Like you say, Reverend, God will let our paths meet again."

"Yes, they will! I'm not shaking your hand, brother. I'm hugging your neck!"

He reached over and gave me a big bear hug. I'm not much for hugging, but I had to pat him on the back.

"You're a good man, Reverend, a good man. These fine people need you. I know that God has led you here to be their minister."

"I believe that with all my heart, Mr. Adams. Thank you so much, dear Jesus, for leading me to these people. Thank you for allowing me to find them. I feel at home here." He prayed.

"I bet you do, Reverend, I bet you do."

"Well, send the love to your mom, all your other family members, and Tammy when you get back home if she's not married."

"Well, I don't know about Tammy, I'll find out when I get there."

"Yes, sir, you will."

The reverend made his way out. I stepped back in my room and turned in for the night. It was pretty tiring going to church all day, not to mention that big, nice meal I had with Flo's biscuits. It has been a good day here. I had such good dreams again that I slept like a baby once more. I woke up the next morning, packed my stuff up, went downstairs, and bid farewell to Mr. Sapphire. I made my way down to the livery and picked up Rosie, saddled her, and rode her down to the train depot. I walked up to the lady sitting behind the counter. "I need a ticket to El Paso."

"The train will be here any moment, just have a seat," she said.

"How much is it to take my horse too?" I asked.

"It'll be ten dollars."

I handed her the money.

"Thank you, sir. Here's your tickets. The train conductor will show you where to load when he gets here. Please have a seat. The train should be pulling up at any moment."

It wasn't long before I heard the whistle of the train and the thundering of the wheels on the tracks. It came to a screeching halt when it showed up just a little later. I untied Rosie from outside and walked her around to the cargo compartment. The conductor opened it up. Inside there were other horses in there, along with a cow on one end. A casket and some luggage sat on the other side, away from the animals. I loaded Rosie into the cargo and the conductor threw a little more hay in there and filled the water trough. I walked up front and stepped aboard. No sooner than I stepped on the train did I look over and noticed somebody I had seen before. I was trying to remember where I had seen him before. It was a little white man sitting right beside a picker woman. Right across from him were two black ladies. I looked at him, and it dawned on me.

"I remember you!"

"S'cuse me?"

"You're Mr. Germany. We met you at Patterson's!"

"Patterson's? That dumpy restaurant?"

"Yes, sir! We were walking in while Mr. Patterson was throwing you out. You remember?"

"He's thrown me out a bunch of times, I don't remember seeing you."

"Yes, sir, you remember what you told us when we walked in there?"

"I don't remember nothin'!" he said in a gruff voice.

"Ladies, I'm sorry you're having to sit with this grumpy old guy."

"What are you talking about? I'm the one having to be stuck beside these pickers."

They all looked at him. I leaned over and sniffed him.

"Sorry, ladies, that he smells like a bucket full of buttholes."

I turned around and began walking over to my seat. He became so angry he jumped up and started to walk up behind me. I looked over my shoulder toward him and shook my finger at him as if to say, *No no*. He turned around and sulked back to his seat. He sat back in his seat, pouted, and looked out the window.

Chapter 13

I continued to have a conversation with the ladies while we rode on the train for quite a while. Time and time again, I would notice Dwight would be staring at one of the young light-skinned women that was sitting with me. We continued enjoying our company together as Dwight stepped out of his seat and walked toward the rear of the train car. He made his way to the laboratory where a young lady was exiting. He made some rude comments toward her. In response, she slapped him and stormed by me and the ladies. Dwight continued on in. A few minutes later, the conductor was brought back by the young lady that was offended by Dwight. Apparently, she was very upset. As the conductor made his way toward us, he looked to me and asked if the three picker ladies were with me. I responded with confidence, "They are not with me, I am with them."

"Either way," the conductor responded, "the blacks must sit in the rear of the train, not here in the passenger car." So we stood and made our way toward the rear of the train. Before I could go too far, the conductor spoke up and said, "You can stay, but they cannot.

"I took a minute to respond and looked him right in the eyes. "If they aren't welcome in this car, then neither am I!"

As we were departing, Dwight exited the laboratory. The young lady with the conductor pointed at him and said, "That is the rude man!" Immediately, after she said that, the conductor grabbed Dwight by the arm and escorted him to the end of the train where we were heading. We slid open the door of the car and stepped to the platform. I opened the door for the last car and held it for the ladies to enter. We could hear Dwight cursing the conductor and yelling that he had done nothing wrong. So once the ladies and myself entered the car, I slammed the door right in Dwight's angry face. He yanked the door back open, and the conductor pushed him inside. He continued to curse everyone and everything around him! I moved hay around that they kept for the horses so that the ladies had a comfortable place to sit.

Dwight stormed around kicking hay and the wall, making his way to the horses that were tied on one side of the car. As he came near my horse, Rosie, he swatted at her with his hat, and out of reaction, she kicked him in the stomach. He flew back, hitting his head against the coffin, almost turning it over. Then he collapsed unconscious. The ladies and I made our way to help Dwight. We dragged him away from the horses. The young attractive girl made a pillow of hay wrapped with a potato sack and placed it under his head. I gave her my bandana. She sat next to him and wiped his brow with water and made sure he was alright.

After about twenty minutes, Dwight opened his eyes. He never said a word; he just stared at the pretty young lady wiping his brow. I noticed that he was quite infatuated with her. She was not looking at him when he opened his eyes. She was singing a tune to herself—"Amazing Grace," I do believe. Once she noticed he was awake, she stopped singing and started to move away.

"Please don't stop," Dwight responded in a whisper. The young lady, not knowing what to make of the request, looked up once again at the ceiling and began to sing once again.

I made my way toward them and helped the young lady up, thinking it was my place to show her she did not have to stay there if she did not want to. I helped her to sit by the other ladies, then I kneeled by Dwight, who was staring at the girl, and said, "She is quite fetching, isn't she?" He mumbled something I couldn't quite understand. I thought he said, "Beautiful," but I was not sure. His eyes made contact with my eyes, and he snorted and turned away like he was disgusted with himself. So I sat down beside him.

The ladies were having their own conversation on the other side of the room. I was trying to have one with Dwight, but he had his back turned toward me and was acting like he wasn't listening. "You know, Dwight, that there is nothing wrong with thinking that young lady is beautiful because she is. Just because you have been raised to believe the blacks are below you doesn't make it true. You know that young lady stayed with you, wiping your brow the whole time you were unconscious and was afraid you were injured. I saw you and her had made eye contact when we were in the passenger car. Even though you were rude when she and the other ladies first came aboard, I think she likes you."

He slowly turned his head and looked at me. Then he slid from a lying position to a sitting position and grunted as he sat up. I continued to talk to him. I asked, "Why would she do that, Dwight, knowing the way you feel about her people?" He made eye contact with me once again. He continued to rub the place where his thumb used to be reminding me that he was the man whose finger I shot off at the lynching that never took place.

Dwight finally broke his silence, asking me, "What business is it of yours how I feel about those nig…" He coughed, then cleared his throat and said, "Ladies?"

I answered quickly, "It's not my business. My business is to keep you from being rude to them and to make sure you're not injured." As I said that, he glanced around once again at that pretty young lady.

He seemed like he was distracted, but I couldn't tell if it was from the concussion or another injury. I asked if he would be okay, and he said he was very thirsty. I waited until he was making eye contact and said, "If you promise to be good, I will send that pretty gal over here with some water. He kept eye contact with me and nodded his head yes. I walked over to the ladies and asked the young girl if she would bring him a glass of water. She agreed. I looked back at Dwight, and he was straightening his shirt up and combing his hair with his fingers.

Dwight had a sort of crooked smile on his face as she approached. She smiled right back at him. They were quiet as he drank the water. Then he spoke up and said, "I really like your singing." She smiled and began to sing lightly. He stared with infatuation. When she finished, she immediately began to sing a second song. I noticed as she sang Dwight's eyes seemed to fill with tears. He didn't want her to see him that way, so he faked turning away from the pain in his gut. I noticed it all, though. As she kneeled beside him, he slid a little closer to her. I listened closely to make sure he said nothing wrong. Surprisingly, he was a perfect gentleman. He asked what her name was, and she responded with "Zuri."

"Dwight." He pointed to himself in response.

She smiled and said, "I like your name. It's very American." Then he asked her what her name meant, and she said, "My great-grandfather named me after his mother, who lived in Africa. He told me the first time he saw me after I was born that God spoke my name into his heart. After his mother, Zuri Kiswahili. My grandfather told me it means 'beautiful woman.'"

Without pause, I heard him say, "Yes, you are!" Then Dwight immediately looked at me, and his face turned blood red. He looked at the ground, and I saw him swallow hard as if he was ashamed of what he just said.

Zuri reached over and rubbed his face gently and said, "You're flushed. Are you sure you're alright? Do you need some more water?"

Dwight responded, "No," and looked at her with a lot of embarrassment on his face. "I've never actually had a talk with a picker—sorry, women like you before. I was always taught to think we are different, but I am feeling that we are more alike than I thought. This is the reason I'm flushed." He then reached up and took her hand from the side of his face and held onto it for a few seconds. She withdrew her hand from his and giggled quietly.

Dwight was getting to know Zuri, while I was getting to know the two ladies I was sitting with. I found out they were Zuri's aunts, the sisters of her mother. Zuri was a beautiful, light-skinned young lady, but her aunts were dark-skinned. Their names were Mary and Lussa. Mary would speak to me, but Lussa would not speak. She told me she had been living on a plantation that they had been freed from because they had nowhere else to go. They had heard from a relative living in Texas, so I invited them to travel with me. Apparently, the plantation owner, even though their master recognized them as free, was not happy that they had decided to leave even though they were given their freedom. He did want them to leave because at one time, he was in love with Zurri's mother. She had been with him for over twenty years before she passed from a fever last summer. Zuri was eighteen now.

After a while, I decided to make my way to the front to get us some food. The train had started to slow abruptly, causing everyone to sway forward. There were cries of fear and panic from all over the car. The conductor that had forced us to the back compartment ran by me toward the front car, shouting for us to stay calm and stay in our seats. He explained briefly as he ran that he would see what was going on and let us know soon. Believing that I might be of some help, I began to follow him forward. I was thinking that a tree might have fallen on the track or maybe me being a sheriff might help. After a few steps, I began to look around and noticed the scared faces of the other passengers. That made me think about the ladies in the car with Dwight and how they might be as scared as the rest of the passengers. I turned and made my way back to the car to help protect and comfort them if needed. When I arrived, they all seemed to be fine, so I explained that I wanted to go see what happened and help if needed. Dwight spoke up, saying he was better now and wanted to accompany me. As we made our way toward the front, we soon found out this was a robbery! Apparently, the train was stopped due to a wagon with two horses parked on the tracks.

This train was full of women and children as well as older people. Because the women in the back car were all picker women, they may be in a higher danger than the other women on this train. I grabbed Dwight and pulled him down behind one of the seats. I told him I would distract the robbers so he could help in hiding the ladies in the back. I instructed him to hide them under the hay behind the horses. He nodded his head and headed immediately to the back. I stayed in the car just before the last one to make sure no one would get past me to the back.

I made my way to the car ahead to put two cars away from the last. All the other passengers were down on the floor, hiding. With my gun out of my holster, I eased forward, looking from one car to another, until I could see the masked men toward the front of the train. They had the head conductor at gunpoint. All the other conductors were also in that front compartment. Only passengers all around me lay on the floor. A gunman was walking toward where I was hiding, shouting for everyone to stay down and no one would get hurt.

One man had a sack collecting valuables from the passengers. As he came closer to me, I took a seat beside a lady and her frightened child. I started to console them, saying everything would be fine if we all gave them what they wanted. They were almost completely under the seats on the floor, so I slid off the seat beside them like I was a scared child also.

As the masked men approached, I looked as close to their eyes as I could, trying to recognize them. I knew none of the men. All I knew was, if I made a move, it could lead to others being killed. As they walked closer, they shouted very loudly, "Give me all your valuables! Watches, gold, paperbacks, anything of value. If not, we will take something from you one way or the other!"

One masked man reached over and whispered to the man in the lead, "I don't see her." I was not sure what that meant; this looked like a robbery only.

I kept my hand on my revolver, not sure what I should do. Should I try to stop them or continue to submit to keep everyone safe? It seemed they were not going to hurt anyone. Then I remembered something the reverend had said to me, "When in doubt, pray! Always call upon God, and he will help you." The Holy Spirit that lived inside of me now was beckoning me to pray, so I took my hat off my head and prayed in the midst of all this happening around me. *Dear heavenly Father, in Jesus Christ's mighty name, tell me what I need to do? Give me your strength to deal with this situation. Ease my heart and guide me.* As I opened my eyes, I knew to take my hand off my gun and just surrender. I pulled my wallet from the inside of my jacket packet. As I grabbed my wallet, I felt the small Bible in that same pocket. I pulled the money from my wallet, which was about seven or eight dollars. The lady beside me had nothing to offer. As they grabbed the money from my hand, they must have thought she was my wife and left her alone.

They began to shout, "If anyone tries anything, we will shoot the women and children first." One man stayed in the car with us, watching us while the others went toward the car where Dwight and the ladies were hiding. My heart started to pound! At the same time, I felt a calm as if God had given me a new heart and confidence after I prayed. Not only did I feel comfort in knowing that no one was going to be hurt, but I also felt God at work here! As the masked men eased forward into the last car, I could hear a little ruckus. Dwight stepped out, trying to protect the women when he was hit on the head. One man shouted, "Come on, let's go, we got the package." Within a few seconds, they jumped from the back car, and others jumped from the other cars. They gathered the horses from the waiting men outside, saddled up, and rode off! Once they departed, I stood up to make my way to the back car to check on the ladies and Dwight. When I walked into the back car, I noticed the horses were fine, but Dwight was lying on the ground, two ladies over him. Zuri was not with them. I scanned the room, but she was nowhere to be found.

I asked, "Where is Zuri?"

The one aunt shouted and cried, "They took her! They knocked this young man out because he was trying to protect her."

"God's grace, they didn't kill him! The fool!" I said.

The one lady said, "He was very, very brave, stepping up to them as they grabbed Zuri! As he fought with the masked man. I got a glimpse of that man. I recognized him. I know who he is."

"What do you mean you know him, Mary?"

"Mr. Adams, he is from the plantation where we were before we left. I didn't tell you before, but Zuri is the massa's daughter. Her mammy, my sista, was his slave. Favorite slave, if you know what I'm sayin?" She huffed in disgust. "He never claimed to be Zuri's pops. My sister told me how he took her many times, forcing her to come into his room! At least until she gots pregnant. When the baby started to show, even up until the baby was born, he wouldn't have any more to do with her, but he did have a fondness for Zuri. He always treated her differently than the rest of the young girls on the plantation, never letting the other workers touch her. He always kept a close eye on her."

"What was the name of this plantation? What was your master's name?"

"James Carter of the Carter Plantation. He raised peanuts there. The man that took Zuri, his name is Sand. I don't know his last name, but he worked for Mr. Carter. He never questioned what he was asked to do. He slung me and sista around. He didn't want to hurt us. When he hit that young man, he just did what he had to do so we wouldn't know who he was. I's know her papa's tryin to just get her back. He was very upset when we left, but there was nothing he could do. We's was freed. We snuck away in the middle of the night. We ended up at that train station with monies we had been collecting from the time I was a small one. Mr. Carter's daughter, Belinda, loved us. She would always send us to the mercantile to gather things and never ask for her change back. If we tried to give it, she would just smile and say, 'One day, you will need this.' If Ms. Belinda knew what was happening right now, she would be highly upset. If her

Maw had been alive, Zuri would have never been born to Mr. Carter. Zuri's moms was very beautiful. It made clear sense why he would take her to be with her. My sista was always the prettiest and the sweetest, which made all men like her. When she passed that year, Mr. Carter mourned. He never came out of his room for weeks. When he did, he was drunk every single time as if he missing her. He was always kind to us, but we wanted our freedom. Once we learned of our family in Texas, it was natural we should travel to be with them." She got up and began to pace around.

"I agree, Mary! If you are good, I will leave Dwight with you so I can try to follow and find these men. I'll check with the passengers to see if I can get some help." I went to head for the door, but she stopped me with a hand to my arm.

"I know you're a good, God-fearing man. Would you want to pray for this man since he has been knocked out more than once today? We may want to pray with him to make sure he is fine."

We knelt down next to Dwight and put our hands on his head. "Yes, ma'am, I am new to this prayer. I'll let you do the praying."

She bowed her head and explained, "I will pray, sir, I can always talk to my Jesus. He always hears me. If we want Jesus to bless our ways, we must always cry out to him! Dear Jesus, I know we are not worthy of what you can do for us, but we ask it all the same. This young man needs a touch from your heaven. He's hurtin' and needs youn to move on him like yous did in the deep and made this world. Now, Lord, nothin' is impossible with your mighty healing powers. Please, in Jesus's name, we's ask. Amen!"

Once Mary finished praying, I noticed Dwight was breathing normally. Amazed as I was, I stood up to continue my mission of finding this girl before it may be too late to do so. I walked toward my horse to check her out and grab my saddle. "Ladies, I need to be on the path of those bad men who took Zuri. I hope to be able to recover your niece soon. Please take care of the boy until I return for him." Just as I turned to leave, Dwight opened his eyes.

"Take me with you!" he cried out." I took a second to study the man. By the look on his face and the determination in his eyes, I knew he would be going with me. Out of curiosity, I still had to ask, "What do you mean, Dwight? This is a girl you barely know!"

"It's not the girl," he said. "They took my grandfather's pocket watch. It's been in my family for the last three generations. I've got to have it back." This left me confused about where he stood.

Shaking my head, I replied, "If I catch them, I will recover your watch. You don't worry about that."

He got up and stomped over to the other horse next to mine. He then said more vehemently, "I have to go!"

"You have been knocked out twice today. We thought you were not going to make it after being hit with a revolver." He continued to insist on going with me, so I agreed. We walked our horses off the back of the train, and I quickly threw on the saddle blanket and turned to look at him. He again asked loudly, "Just let me ride with you. I'm fine!"

I gestured for him to mount up, saying, "Very well, do as you please. Is that even your horse? If not, I'm sure whoever owns it will not mind as long as we bring it back after we recover Zuri." I started to check my saddle, making sure the stirrups were right and the saddle were tight, cinching up the girth. Everything was ready. Dwight slapped a saddle while pulling on the latigo strap. After pulling on the girth, he was up in that saddle quicker than I could get into mine.

"Do you have a rifle?" he asked.

"Yeah, I have a rifle!" I held it up, and he had a curious look on his face as he looked at my Spencer. Then he rubbed his nub where his thumb used to be, looking puzzled as though he had seen a ghost. He remembered it was a Spencer rifle that blew his thumb off, but he didn't know it was this very rifle that took the finger from him.

"Let's go! Ladies, shut this door behind us once we leave." They both stood in the open doorway, and Mary yelled, "May the good Lord bless you, guide you, and protect you both." Then we jumped off the platform to the ground, following hard after the trail that was pretty easy to follow. There had to be six or seven, according to the tracks. They were heading west. I took what Mary had said. West is the general direction she was sure was where they would be heading. She was certain the girl was taken by her father, Mr. Carter. They staged this robbery and didn't hurt anyone. If they really didn't want to be found, they would have killed these two ladies. Apparently, this plantation owner had a fondness for these ladies, maybe out of a love for the aunt's sister who was no longer with us.

The Carter Plantation happens to be in Charlotte County, just south of where we are at now. We followed the tracks south, still not knowing where they led or what they led us into. We heard the door shut on the train car behind us as we rode away. Other than that door slamming behind us, there was an eerie silence, except for the sound of our horse hooves hitting the dirt. Dwight was very quiet.

It had been dry for the last week or so. There was a dust trail the riders made so we would be able to see from far away. We followed the trail, and it was clear where they were going. This Carter Plantation was supposed to be a large place—easy to find was how Mary described it. Growing pecans, peanuts, and evil or whatever we may find when we get there. *James Carter better have answers when I do get there!* I thought.

As we rode, I broke the silence, asking Dwight, "Are you ready for this?"

Dwight answered, "I will be if you let me carry the Spencer rifle in my scabbard. I think I can help you there."

As I handed it to him, I replied, "My six-shooters should be enough to suffice." Then I asked, "Have you ever used a Spencer rifle?"

Dwight replied, "Yes, everyone used the Spencer where I came from." He turned it this way and that and then answered, "Yeah, it's a popular rifle. We may be in need of these guns when we meet those cowboys."

As we rode away from the train, we slowly saw the train fading in the distance. It was a wide-open-range area. We could see fields everywhere and we could see in the dry dirt the tracks from the riders. Horse tracks were easy to follow, which kept us following for six hours. They must have been traveling pretty steady due to not seeing horse dust in the distance. I thought we would at least start to see a fire when it turned dark, so we continued.

I continued to wonder why Dwight had accompanied me on this journey. I had asked him a few times, and he would only say it was about retrieving his grandfather's watch. I asked if this could have anything to do with that pretty young Zuri, and he would just keep silent and shrug off my question. Maybe he thought because she was not white, he could not admit to having feelings for her. You can lie to other people and try to lie to yourself, but you can't lie to your heart! He was fighting a battle in his own mind and heart. We have all fought this battle in more ways than one. It doesn't matter if you are the most prejudiced boy like Dwight or even an ex-slave owner who loves a daughter even if she was the offspring of a slave. We all have hearts that will never recognize color or the truth that we all are the same race. The reverend would say the Bible says from one bloodline all races were born! I can hear him say that again and again. We all see people of a different color and think differently about people who are of a different color. That is a cruel thing that should never have existed in this world. From one bloodline all races were born. That girl that we are looking for is no different than any of us. Her blood is the same color as mine or Dwight's. This is a fact no one can deny! Thanks to the grace of God and the help of a preacher. I truly believe the only difference is the color of our skin. Preacher told me the Christ who died on that cross was not a white person like myself but that he was also a person of color. People from Israel are not the same color as I am. He died for every one of us no matter what color you are.

As I was explaining these things to Dwight, he turned from squeamish to listening intently. I could feel that burning inside my chest when I spoke of these things the same as I did when the preacher would speak them to me. As the preacher would pour out into me, I now was pouring out into Dwight. "Freely you received now freely give," Preacher John said many times. Quoting Peter, he would often reply to me.

Talking with Dwight, I found out his family was very active with the Klan. This was the only reason he had joined this activity. It was normal to a young poor influential boy from the South raised among this kind of thinking—treating the pickers as though they were like animals, beating them sometimes as though they owned them like a common dog. This I could tell he pondered in his head because of the feelings he was having for this girl whom he barely knew. Through the one conversation he had with such a sweet, beautiful girl that changed his way of thinking forever. Funny how your heart can lead you down a different path that you would have never taken until Christ steps in and changes you forever the way only God can do.

This girl, Zuri, was not a normal pretty! Far above what we have seen in this area, she was light-skinned, smelled like flowers from a meadow—fresh smell—and as sweet a girl as I had ever met.

This must have been overwhelming for Dwight, to wake up to this kind of angel looking down on him when he had awakened on that train car. It was an instant attraction whether he wanted it to happen or not.

We rode until dark was upon us. We made our camp on the same trail we had been following just before we ran completely out of daylight.

I dismounted and tied Rose to a nearby bush. Dwight also dismounted to tie his horse. He started to gather some wood to make a fire. I retrieved matches from my saddlebag. Once the fire was blazing, I also gathered firewood to keep this fire going for at least an hour or so. Dwight brought the remainder of the biscuits. Out of concern, I replied, "Not sure if those biscuits are still good, they are pretty old." He just shrugged and then took a bite." A little tough but still good to me. I heard a crunch as he bit into that biscuit, discouraging me from partaking in the last of them.

We started to discuss what we were about to face and the possible outcomes we may be facing in the near future. I had to ask if he had ever met this Jesus who had saved and changed my life. Something had happened in that bar! Such an overwhelming presence of the Holy Spirit filled that place completely, from one wall to another! Something had knocked me to my knees and broke the man. It was crushing everything I was and remaking me into someone

I would not recognize a month ago. I felt a pounding in my heart, a fire from within overtaking my entire being as never felt before in or out of church!

As I shared this with Dwight, he tearfully said he had been in church when he was a child but never felt anything like what I was describing. "I am feeling something that I hadn't felt when I was a kid. This feels like your words are sticking a knife into my soul!" His tears fell to the ground as the words continued to flow from my mouth like a fire shot up in the depths of my heart. The presence I had felt in the bar that night was all around us. I explained to him that Christ gave His life for each and every one of us so all would have a chance of salvation. If Christ so loved the whole world regardless of the color of our skin, shouldn't we do the same? If Christ sees us all the same, then we should all be looking through His eyes. This is the way I see God's creations now—clearer than I ever had. I only pray you can see this also. He died so we all can have a chance to live in His kingdom. "For God so loved the world that He gave his only begotten son so through Him none should perish but have everlasting life!"

"Preacher told me this more than once while I traveled with him." I lay my hand on Dwight's shoulder to ask if he was ready to surrender to the will of Christ and make him his Lord and savior. He was frantically wiping the tears from his eyes and cheeks. He jumped up and shouted, "I'm not sure," as he walked away from the fire into the darkness in more ways than one. Once I composed myself, I said a short prayer for Dwight and Zuri, taking my last drink of coffee from earlier, and then I lay down after throwing a few more pieces of wood on the fire. I laid my head on my saddle and pulled my blanket from my saddle over myself. I was asleep within minutes.

I was awakened after only minutes of sleep to Dwight still weeping. "How do I get to find Jesus the way you did?" he asked me.

Without hesitation, I asked, "Have you prayed before?"

"I did when I was a little kid," he answered.

"That's how we do it today. You are about to make the most important decision you will ever make. Pray after me, Dwight, and mean it from your heart! Dear Lord, please put Your hand on Dwight's heart to see what is truly happening to him right now. Repeat after me, Dwight.

"Dear heavenly Father, please forgive me for all the evil things I have done in my life. Each and everything I have come against your will for my life. I know You died on that cross to take away the sins of this world, and I am one of those sinners. I believe You died on that cross for me and came back to life after three days. Please come live inside my heart. Make me the man you made me to be. I turn away from the ways I have done and will walk in your steps as much as I can. In Jesus's name I pray. Amen!" As I opened my eyes, I saw Dwight mumbling to himself then speaking up to say amen after I did. I knew he had spoken every word I had just said. Then I wiped the tears from my eyes as he did earlier. Now he had changed and he should be able to be true to himself and the feelings he had for this girl we were trying to rescue.

We turned in after this, maybe to arise as different men in the morning. We both had coats on. Dwight had no blanket to cover up with. I lay on one with my saddle blanket over me. I spoke up to Dwight to look on the back side of the saddle under my head where the other blanket I had was tied. He retrieved the blanket and then lay down in a quiet and solemn manner. As Dwight fell asleep, I glanced around one last time to see both horses sleeping, standing there, and Dwight shivering. I arose, took my blanket I lay on, and spread it over this young man. As it just touched his body, he tucked it under his side. I threw one more log on the fire, covered up once again with the saddle blanket, and fell asleep.

Chapter 14

———◆◆◆———

I awoke to find the men we had been following to be standing over us with guns pointing at our heads. The first man spoke up and asked why we were following them. I was still trying to get my wits about me. Dwight just lay there, not sure what to do.

I spoke up and asked, "What are you talking about? We were traveling and bedded down for the night when we had run out of daylight." I did see Zuri was not with these men.

"You know exactly what I'm talking about. You two have been following us for the last few miles. We noticed your fire and turned back to find you sleeping here."

I spoke up again. "I just told you we are just traveling and needed to camp for the night, and this was as good a place as any. We don't know who you men are! I suggest you put your guns down before you do something you may regret since I am a lawman from Tennessee in pursuit of robbers making their way toward the west."

"Oh yeah? What's the name of the desperadoes? It doesn't matter if you are coming with us to meet the boss! He will decide what to do with you."

I spoke up once again. "You are about to be facing federal charges if you take us without our consent. These are serious charges in a federal court! Judge Trapper may see you men hang for standing in the way of law men doing their duty to capture our prisoners." The leader of these outlaws would not believe anything I was telling him.

"We will be taking you to see the boss! Now shut your mouths before I put a bullet in you and feed you to our pigs!" So we held our peace.

We rode about an hour, arriving at a large plantation. Because it was so close to where they had overtaken us, this would explain why Zuri was not with them. They had dropped her off but turned back to make sure they had not been followed. Yes, we were close enough this made them think we had been following them.

The plantation was a large white home with three barns, I assume for all the peanuts that were processed and brought in at harvesttime. There were also three large silos for storing the peanuts and many workers—maybe former slaves working for the plantation now or maybe some who were still kept in slavery. Not sure but I was sure we would find out once we spoke to Mr. Carter.

As we stepped up on the porch of the large home, we noticed whips hanging on the side of the porch. I could only imagine that they were used for the slaves before or even now to remind the workers of punishment, if needed. We did not know, so we did not say anything unless we were asked.

This large home was apparently where Mr. Carter lived. Shortly after entering the home, an older white-haired gentleman came into the room. The men who had been talking among themselves suddenly became very quiet—out of respect, I assumed. As he walked into the room, I noticed he was a large man, around three hundred pounds or so, but not overweight! He was more muscular than fat and in a six-foot-three-inch-tall frame. He was a giant of a man, "intimidating," and a gray long beard fell below his neckline.

He looked as though he was once a rough man, a brawler, and his shoulders were very wide. He took his rather large hat off and laid it to the side in one Queen Anne chair and sat in the other matching chair. Both chairs were expressively upholstered with wood showing on the legs around the edge and the bottom. The handles also had fine wood for handrests. Wood also ran along the back top of the chair—something you would expect to see in a king's palace. It was not common to me nor to the men that worked for him.

The leader of the cowboys spoke up, saying, "These men were following us, although they claim they are lawmen on a mission working for the federal government. We believe they followed us from the train! This young man looks like the man we encountered on the train who tried to stop us from taking Zuri. We found them on the trail we rode in on. I decided to bring them to you to let you make the call as to what to do with them."

This was the man whom Mr. Carter trusted the most. He was probably the ranch foreman. He continually addressed Mr. Carter as sir. "Not boss, not Master, but sir."

At this time, Mr. Carter loudly cleared his throat. He had a rough, deep voice but was highly intelligent. "Can I ask you why you might be here and why my men say you are lawmen on a federal case? Explain to me why I should believe you."

"As we told your men, we are on a federal case looking for men who robbed a bank back in Alexandria, Louisiana.

To be precise, we were just passing through here when your men found us bedded on the same trail they were on. We would appreciate you letting us go to do our jobs."

"Oh, really?" Mr. Carter replied. "If you're on a federal case, then you will have warrants for the men you're pursuing. You do have those warrants, do you not? What's to make me believe what you're saying is true?"

"No reason to believe," I said. "Why would I tell you any different?"

Angrily, Carter demanded, "Where's your proof that you are telling the truth! I think you were on this train my men just left from and why you were on this trail and the reason you will never leave here alive! I think you know about the little girl we brought back here. I think her aunties told you why we brought her back here. This is none of your business, has nothing to do with you. Why you have decided to follow her back here is beyond me. This is none—I repeat—none of your affair. No longer are we having this conversation. You will be locked up until I decide what to do with you or at least your bodies… Take them away, lock them in the outer barn. I will come up with a decision soon."

We were taken to a barn where they slaughtered their animals. I had a strong smell of death and rotting blood. The smell was so horrible Dwight threw up soon after arriving. To be honest, I almost followed his lead, but I would not give them the satisfaction of knowing I was bothered by our location. I hoped that was the smell of animals and not humans. I had been to slaughterhouses many times and didn't remember it being bad. We knew only that we were now captives.

The foreman gave orders to another man, who was also on the train earlier, to tie us up, and he kept us in a small stall in the corner of the barn. We sat on top of dried horse hay. "Keep an eye on them and shoot either if they try to escape," he demanded.

After the stall was closed and locked, the man watching us left. So we sat there together, not knowing what was about to happen. We both were a little concerned about what tomorrow holds.

Dwight looked as scared as any child I had ever seen in my life, even though Dwight was his age. He was a young man but he was old enough to know better.

It entered my mind immediately after that stall closed, and now I shared with Dwight that God will take care of his children. He can open up doors when doors need to be opened. He can also close them when doors need to be closed! Dwight nervously said, "I'm not very worried because what's going to happen to us will not matter anyhow. All I'm concerned about is what is happening to Zuri right now." He breathed heavily as if he had a weight on his chest from the worry he said he didn't have.

"Are you truly concerned about Zuri? I knew you had feelings for her. I didn't know they were that strong."

He said honestly, "Sheriff, I do have feelings for her. She is the most beautiful, kind girl I've ever known in my life. I felt her in my soul when she spoke to me. I knew she was my future from the first time I opened my eyes up and saw an angel."

"Whew, Dwight, never heard that before. You must be a truly changed man."

"When God touched me last night, everything started to change on the inside. All the feelings of hate disappeared. All the things I had done before started to come to my mind last night in my dreams. When I awoke, I prayed to God to forgive me for all the wrongdoings. That's why I have been completely quiet this entire time, praying. I can no longer hide how I feel. I must be completely open so God can bless me. Christ has changed me like you said in your prayer last night."

"Dwight, I am so happy to hear about your changed heart. Did you ever go to church when you were young?" I asked.

"Yes, sir, we went all the time," he said as he nodded his head. "Do you remember some of the songs they sang when you were in church?"

Nodding his head a little more excitedly, he replied, "I do remember some. I was young but I do remember some."

"I want to tell you. Dwight, I was in a little bar in Alexandria, Louisiana, and the preacher I was traveling with sat down at a piano in that bar and started playing 'Holy, Holy, Holy.' That song lit that whole bar on fire!" Dwight's eyes were wide. He asked if I meant it burnt to the ground. I replied, "It burnt the sin out of men's hearts all the way to the ground. Because the Holy Spirit moved that day stronger than I remember ever seeing or feeling such a strong presence of God's power in my life. My father was a preacher. It moved so strongly that it changed my life and my heart. I can no longer be the same man I was before that happened. I can sing this song, but it won't compare with what I heard at that bar. There was a little girl there that sang so sweet that came straight from her heart and touched everyone in that bar. Sing with me."

Amazing grace how sweet the sound
That saved a wretch like me,
I once was lost but now I'm found,
Was blind but now I see.

As I sang, Dwight joined in as if we both had been in church our entire lives. I could feel the Holy Spirit move. When we finished that song, another song poured out of both of us. We sang many songs of praise. The walls seemed to be shaking from the presence of the Holy Spirit. It was so strong! As it began to shake the entire barn, the door on the stall just opened on its own as though an angel had opened it from the outside.

When these things took place, I told Dwight we may need to escape while we had a chance! Like a bolt of lightning, Dwight spoke up to say if God can open this door, then he can save us from this place.

The man that was in charge of watching us came running into the barn, and noticing the stall door was open, he frantically started to look around like we had run off. He was so nervous thinking we had escaped. We could see this through the boards on the stall we were still in. Out of fear from the repercussions from him not watching us and letting us escape, he would have been beaten. The man pulled his pistol from his holster and put it to his head.

Dwight noticed the man was about to kill himself, so he yelled out. I also shouted out, "Brother, stop! Don't do this! We are still here."

He stepped into the stall, asking, "Why are you still here? I thought you had escaped!"

"No," I proclaimed. "We are still here praising God! Thanking God for everything He is doing for us. He will lead and guide us to where Zuri is."

Looking shaken and confused, he asked, "So you are trying to find this girl?"

"Yes, we are here to save the girl. We were on the train. Yes, we followed you men to the place we were captured."

"Why would you not let me just kill myself? That's what I would have done. If you men had escaped, they would have killed me anyhow for allowing it to happen."

"Are they truly that evil?" Dwight asked.

"I've witnessed this many times in such cases," the cowboy answered.

I patiently looked at the man and was guided to tell him. "I'm not sure what he would do to you, but I know what my God will do for me. His presents moved all around us. He moved on this door and opened it. We were compelled to stay here just like Paul and Silas were freed from their prison bars and they stayed." I then told him of the story of Paul and Silas and the goodness of the Lord.

As we poured out into this cowboy's life, his heart was touched. He said, "You have truly moved me. Instead of running away, you stayed here to introduce Christ to me. This has truly moved me. I would like to know this Christ you have been talking about."

Saying a prayer of thanks to the Lord and feeling the joy of bringing another soul to Christ. "You can know him from within your heart. The way he has touched mine and this young man's heart, he can truly touch yours if you desire to follow Him. What is your name, cowboy?"

My name is Thomas Robinson. I have been working for Mr. Carter for several years. I need to change my life. My family also needs to know this true Jesus! I'm going to help you get out of here. I will take you out of here to stay with my wife so I can keep you safe! I'll take you home to wait until I can bring this girl Zuri home to you. You will have to trust me."

Dwight and I both looked at each other. "What other options do we have, sheriff," Dwight said.

We left, making sure no one was around so as not to be seen. As we got a little distance from the barn, it was starting to turn dark. Thomas said, "We will travel west. I live about three miles from here."

This Thomas was surely becoming a brother in Christ to us. He was risking not only his safety but also the safety of his family. His heart was changed, and we had not led him through the sinner's prayer yet. His heart was changed because he was changed in his mind. Thomas insisted on waiting for his wife to pray the prayer of salvation with him.

We arrived at his home. It was a small cabin with wood planks on the outside for siding. Someone had planted a small flower garden on both sides of the steps leading into the front porch. Once we entered the home, Thomas insisted we tell his wife what we had told him. Her name was Edna. She was a fairly attractive lady standing about five feet and six inches, only about two inches shorter than her husband. We all sat down when we started to share how Thomas had helped us leave, and by the power of Christ, he was now a part of the family of God. Edan spoke up, explaining how she had been saved since she was a child and had been praying for her husband for many years. So I asked, "Ma'am, do you want to lead your husband in the Sinner's Prayer?" She gladly did.

Immediately after, Thomas started to say his goodbyes so he could get back to the plantation. "I will return soon." He spoke loudly so everyone could hear. I watched him as he kissed his wife goodbye. I walked with him until he was out of earshot of his wife and asked quietly, "Will you be alright? You were so fearful when you thought we had escaped. How can you be so sure of what you are doing?"

He walked out to his horse, and before he got on, he said, "I feel it in my spirit what I need to be doing." I nodded my head and stepped back. He quickly mounted his horse, took a quick look around, smiled at his wife, and rode away.

I turned toward the house and headed to Edan to apologize for her being in this situation. I could tell she was a godly woman. She was singing hymns to herself as the preacher did on the trails as we traveled. She spoke with a feeling of strength that God was in control of this situation and all would be fine.

She walked over to tending to the children before returning to the kitchen to make food. She was still singing to herself about the glory of God and his goodness. The children surrounded us when I entered the house. They asked us a hundred questions. The children were about four to six years old. They were just "babies," so curious about everything we had been through. As Dwight talked to the children, I was now worried if we had followed the right path to let the father of these babies help us. Looking back, I could see the hand of the Lord in all that had happened so far, and I knew that I had to continue to put my trust in Him.

We struggled in our minds as we spoke to one another about whether Thomas was going to be okay and return to his wife and children. We were trying to decide if we needed to go help him. We were standing up to leave when Ms. Edna said, "He will be fine. I have prayed for him as I always have. I would feel in my spirit if anything bad had happened. God has always spoken to me on these matters. Now that Thomas is a believer, he has not only my protection in prayers but also the promises of the Bible covering him." She finished stirring something in a large pot and walked to where the children were sitting on the couch, watching us. One of them climbed onto her lap when she sat, and she stroked her fingers over the little one's hair.

"When Thomas was a younger man, he struggled with alcohol. I prayed for quite a while. God moved! He quit drinking. He was not a very good husband or father! I prayed for him to change! God moved! He became the most dedicated husband and father I could ask for. A good man. I prayed for years that he would give his heart to Christ—for years! God moved! Now he is a believer. I've prayed for him to return home safely. God will move!" So this true woman of faith calmed us down instead of us calming her down. We did believe, as she had helped us to strengthen our faith!

She fed us all a fine meal of stew with cornbread and, after that, a mixed berry pie with coffee. As we put the dishes in the sink, we heard hooves outside. So I grabbed my gun and walked to the edge of the front door, waiting to see who was outside. I looked over to see Dwight standing by the window, pulling the curtain back. He abruptly dropped the curtain and ran toward the door as if he was overly anxious! I whispered, "What, Dwight? What is it?" He never looked my way. He just threw the door open and ran outside!

It was Thomas and Zuri! Dwight, without an invitation, ran to Zuri, grabbed her, and then hugged her. She was surprised, to say the least. Once she pushed back a little, Dwight, Thomas, and Zuri came into the house where the children and Mrs. Robinson surrounded Thomas. You could feel the love in the room. Dwight was apologizing for his behavior. "I was just overwhelmed when I saw you, miss."

Zuri smiled up at him. "That's quite alright after what Mr. Thomas told me you have done for me."

Thomas interrupted, "We have got to go our separate ways. It has surely been noticed that she and you are missing! I will head back to the plantation and join them in the effort to find you." To me, he said, "I need you to step outside." As we did, he asked me to hit him.

"Why would I do that?" I asked.

He told me, "It has to look like you jumped me and knocked me out escaping."

I nodded my head in understanding. He turned his face to the right, asking me to hit the left side of his face.

Everyone knows he had a bad left eye, and he would not be able to see if someone snuck up on him on the left. Yes, that would make sense, I thought. I hit Thomas hard enough to put a bruise on his face and also bust his lip open. He staggered and grabbed his mouth to find the blood on his lip. Great job, sheriff. Now I have to go." He turned, jumped on his horse, and rode off.

"Sheriff? Zuri and myself are ready to go if you are." I turned to see everyone watching me from the front porch.

"Yes, Dwight, I am ready." I turned to Mrs. Robinson. "Ma'am, thank you so much for your hospitality. I will be praying for Thomas to come home safely. God will take care of us. He always does."

"Always has!" she said with a smile on her face. She reached over and hugged me as I started to leave. "Be blessed, sheriff."

Dwight, Zuri, and I rode about five miles away from Thomas's cabin. They believed Thomas apparently. We never saw Thomas's wife or children again, but Thomas was a different story. We rode as hard as we could even in the darkness. They had the upper hand in knowing the area and all the shortcuts. We ran into the ranch foreman, and all the cowboys were with him. They rode hard upon us until we were overtaken about three miles after they saw us. When they captured us, I knew we were going to be killed shortly. Even before our horses had a chance to stop, Dwight and I were dragged off them, and we were beaten. They then dragged us over to the base of a tree and tied us up. There was no reason why we were not killed, I thought. The foreman stood a few feet in front of us and informed the rest of the men that we were to wait until Mr. Carter arrived.

They had sent one of the younger men to retrieve Mr. Carter. After just a little while, the men threw two ropes over tree limbs, and at the end of the ropes were nooses tied. We knew what was in store for us. No surprise there.

Chapter 15

We had been sitting in the same position for the last few hours while the men around us pulled out a deck of cards to kill time while we waited. My arms and hands were almost numb from being tied behind my back. I was bleeding from my nose and mouth. Dwight was bleeding from one of his ears. His right eye was swollen shut. Zuri had been tied up but left alone on the ground next to the tree. She had tears streaming down her face when everything had happened, but she did not say a word in hopes of not making things worse. She was still silent now, even maybe a little scared. From the moment they tied us up, I had begun to pray for God to have the glory in this situation. I knew the Holy Spirit was with us, and He had a plan for our lives. I just had to keep trusting in Him.

I closed my eyes to give them a rest, but they popped open when we heard the sound of a wagon and horse hooves. Mr. Carter had arrived. When Mr. Carter's wagon finally came to a stop, one of the men went over to help him step down. He was a very heavy man. When he stepped off the wagon, it raised up about six inches. Mr. Carter and the foreman came together in the dark and spoke for about five minutes. All you could see was their silhouettes in the moonlight. Mr. Carter made his way over. The men were holding torches all around us.

"Well, Lawman, I guess you were not after bank robbers after all. My men were right, and you are a liar! You were on the train. You did come for Zuri. This little girl belongs to us. This is none of your affair! Those ropes there are going to settle this once and for all." He leaned over us with a smug look on his face and pointed over to the ropes as he spoke.

"I know this is your daughter and I know you sent these men to recover her for you because you love her!" As I said these words, his eyes squinted at me like I have no right to even talk about this. Carter was very angry. "You have no right!" I spoke up again. "She may be your daughter, but she is not your slave or your property! You have no right to hold her captive. You and I can talk about this situation where your men do not need to hear the things we are talking about. We can discuss this as civilized men. There is *no* reason whatsoever in this world you would need to harm us or this girl."

Mr. Carter took a step closer to me and angrily said, "You shut your mouth now! You know nothing of my affairs and this girl's affairs!" he shouted. "Your information comes from two women that have no right to speak of any of the things they had no knowledge of. In no way will I put up with your divisive attitude! Keep your mouth shut, or that noose will be a slow death instead of the quick one that is about to happen."

Before Mr. Carter could finish speaking, we heard a low sound of singing.

Just as I am without one plea, that Thy blood was shed for me…

It was Zuri in a quiet voice; we could barely hear, but it sounded like an angel singing. Zuri had Carter's attention turned toward her. All of his anger was gone as he looked in amazement at the sound of this angel's voice that had captured all of our attention. We all turned, looking at Zuri still lying on the ground. As she continued to sing, she slowly rose from the ground, making eye contact with Mr. Carter. She made her way over to him, tears still rolling down her face as she came within one foot of him. She spoke faintly, saying, "Papa, Papa please don't hurt these men. You know that Mammy was a Christian woman. She would not want you to do this, and I know you cared about her. Papa, you have always treated me special. Now I know why. I never knew why you were so kind to me the whole time I was growing up. Now I know. As God is my witness, I love you. I've always thought of you as my father. I cannot stand here and let you hurt these men who are only trying to help me."

All the men around stood silent, their guns now pointing at the ground instead of at us. I was in awe of what was going on. Dwight's one eye was still shut, but the other one was in tears from listening to Zuri crying out to her father.

As Zuri continued to speak, Mr. Carter's heart softened. He was a different character altogether. "Now, girl, I don't care what you have been told. Yes, I cared deeply for you and your mother. I know she is in heaven. A godly woman. There's no hope for me, girl. Whether I kill these men or not, there is no hope for me."

Zuri spoke up. "Papa, there's hope for everyone. Room in God's kingdom for us all. Mammy always read from the Bible. She always told me there are many rooms in God's mansion in His heaven. Room for you, me, and these two men. Room for us all." She took a step closer to the tree where we were still sitting on the ground. "The sheriff and Dwight, they were so kind to me, Papa. They treated me as good as any white woman ever was!"

"You are, girl!" Carter said in a defensive voice. "You are as good as any white woman, and I'll not let anyone treat you any differently. That's why you need to stay with me."

She closed her eyes for a moment and then looked him in the eyes and said, "Papa, I can't. I'm a grown woman now. It's time for me to make my way in this world without your protection." She was glancing toward Dwight as she spoke. "Zuri, my girl there is no way I could protect you if you weren't here. There will be times when you need a papa. You will need a father. I can't be there to protect you the way I couldn't protect your mother from that sickness. Your mammy died, and it almost killed me. I can't let that happen to you. That's why I had these men stage the train robbery to bring you back here for my protection. Those foolish aunties of yours. They dragged you off with these wild ideas of freedom. I can't stop you but allow me to help you." He pleaded.

"But, Papa, God is my protector! God will always be my protector. You are my papa, but God is my Father!"

"Girl, I can't just let you leave. I care too much for you. God can't do anything for me because there's no hope for someone like me. I've done things that would never let me enter heaven."

I felt such a stirring in my heart that I had too. I spoke up with authority. "Mr. Carter, Christ will forgive you for everything you have done. I know this isn't the first time you have heard this. Zuri's mother told you this before. You might have ignored it, but she planted a seed, and God can make that seed grow inside your heart. Find it inside you to allow God to move, to touch your heart. God can forgive you for everything you have done." I could feel the strong presence of the Holy Spirit all around us as the Lord spoke through me. The words flowed from deep within me like water from a cistern.

"Silent, sheriff, you have no say-so here," Mr. Carter snapped at me. The burning of the Holy Spirit I felt must have been overwhelming for him enough to make him want to stop the strong feelings he was not used to. I could tell Mr. Carter was really struggling with his emotions right now. Inside of his heart, there was a burning I knew because I recognized in him the feelings I felt in the bar back in Alexandria and the night Dwight made his choice to accept Christ in his heart. The moving in the hearts of men sometimes takes a strong breaking of the walls down that we build up our whole lives.

Zuri spoke up. "Papa, God is calling out to you. His spirit is trying to touch your heart right now. He is trying to change everything in your life right now that is not of him. Everything in your past that you have done can all be forgiven if you cry out to God."

Still fisting his hands now at his side, he yelled, "Girl, I'm beyond help! Now keep your mouth shut. I have business to attend to. He instructed the foreman to take her away because she doesn't need to see what's about to happen.

Dwight and I held our own. We didn't fight what was about to take place. We were tied on our horses. We stayed calm. They led us over to where the nooses were at. Two men held our horses. One man put the nooses around our necks. Zuri had been led off. We were about to be hung just for trying to help this girl.

Mr. Carter stood beside his wagon quietly. Very quietly, his head was bowed. He looked in my direction, not making eye contact. He was looking at my saddle horn. He would not look at me or Dwight. Not sure why he would not look at me. He turned swiftly toward his wagon. Walking to the wagon, he climbed in and sat down. He looked back at my saddle and then the ground, like he did not want to see what was about to happen.

One of the men asked, "Sir, you give the orders. We will take care of this problem." Mr. Carter would not speak. He was silent for a good two to three minutes, looking down at the ground and then back at us and then to the ground again. He refused to look at us, just the saddles we were sitting on. I did recognize confusion when I saw it. I knew there was a battle going on in his mind.

Mr. Carter raised his hand in the air, his right arm. I knew he was about to drop his hand to give the order to smack the horses right out from under us. After two minutes, his hand was still raised in the air, and he wasn't moving.

He stood back up, pointed his hand toward me, and said, "Take the ropes off their necks." About that time, we heard a horse galloping up very fast. It was Zuri!

I don't know how fast she was riding, but it spooked the horse on the wagon. The horse started to run. Mr. Carter, who was still standing, fell from the wagon! The noose that was around my neck had already been removed. Dwight still had the rope around his neck. Both horses spooked and reared up, dumping me off mine, and ran off. Dwight was hanging by the neck. Even with my hands still tied, I was able to grab Dwight's legs to hold him up on my shoulder. One of the men who took the noose off my neck was still there, but his horse was also spooked. It reared up, but he stayed in his seat until he could settle it down. This man swiftly cut the rope, allowing Dwight to fall to the ground on top of me. The man who cut the rope dismounted to help me and Dwight up. In amazement, we noticed it was Thomas, Thomas Robinson.

Three men were trying to help Mr. Carter. Zuri also had made her way to Mr. Carter, who was lying on the ground unconscious. She dismounted from her horse and almost fell on top of him.

"Papa, are you hurt?" she cried out. Mr. Carter was unconscious. The foreman rode up between the men standing around. He saw what had happened when Zuri rode in. He saw Mr. Carter fall from the wagon. He knew why his boss was lying there. As he rode up, he started giving orders. "Catch that wagon!" he shouted. "Bring it back so we can load the boss!"

It only took minutes to catch the horse, and Zuri refused to leave Mr. Carter's side. When the wagon rode off with him, she was right there beside him holding his hand. The foreman took his coat off and gave it to Zuri to put under Mr. Carter's head. Dwight and I gathered our horses. Not sure what to do, we followed them back to the plantation.

We all arrived back at the plantation. Mr. Carter, Zuri, us, and all the cowboys hurried into the home. Dwight and I helped carry Mr. Carter inside and put him on his bed. This was in a large room, the size of most cabins. The bed was a large extravagant bed with a canopy top and large wooden legs, like something a king or a president may have.

One man ran out the door, ordered by the foreman to go retrieve the doctor.

You could hear Zuri's small pleading voice as she remained at her father's side. "Papa? Please speak to me, Papa." The room was silent except for Zuri's cry. All the cowboys stood around the room; even the foreman stood silent. After a while, though, he looked around and, spotting us, pointed to a few of the men, ordering them, "Keep an eye on those two! I don't know why these men followed us back, so keep an eye on them!" He then turned his attention to Zuri. "Girl, you claim this man is your father. I know you're a believer in God, so I ask that you start praying."

Zuri responded, "I am, sir."

I started feeling that burning inside my heart once again, the same feelings I felt in the field earlier. I spoke up. "Mr. Carter, if you can hear me, speak to me. Mr. Carter, we need you to speak to me now!"

The foreman said, "You keep your mouth shut, mister!"

Zuri stood up immediately, saying, "In the name of Jesus, you let him speak right now. Jesus is all we have, and His saving and healing power is all we have." She was standing tall now and was bolder than I've ever heard her. "Sheriff, Papa needs you to pray for him." As she said this, the foreman took a few steps back as if he was pushed! Startled, he motioned with his hand toward Mr. Carter, giving me permission to pray for him. As I stepped forward, he reached down, touched his gun with his hand, and then looked at me. I made eye contact with him and then his gun. Shrugging, I turned my attention back to Zuri and Mr. Carter. Opening my coat, I turned to where the foreman could see what I was reaching for and retrieved the Bible the preacher had given me. The bullet hole was very visible. I held it up so the whole room could see what I had. The tension in the room became very calm.

I opened my Bible up to Isaiah 53 and read, "He was wounded for our transgressions, He was bruised for our iniquities. The chastisement for our peace was upon him, and by His stripes we are healed." Then I lowered my Bible and laid it on Mr. Carter's chest. Then I prayed, as I heard the preacher say while we traveled on that trail. "I command this spirit of sickness and the spirit of death to leave right now! Every sickness or brokenness to leave in the name of Jesus!"

The room was very silent. The power of the Holy Spirit was very thick in the room. Every eye in the room had tears. It looked as you would think the upper room would look on the day of Pentecost. I believe even the foreman had his head bowed in prayer. All the men were praying. You could hear the sounds of mumbling of prayers from all over the room. As I opened my eyes, so did Mr. Carter. When he opened his eyes, he looked straight at Zuri.

"Girl, I've seen something I have never seen before." He swallowed hard and looked slowly around the room. "I've seen a picture of hell. I saw hellfire everywhere.

Demons torturing people. Men from my past I knew who had gone to hell!" He looked startled, frightened from the very depths of his soul. Mr. Carter explained hell with vivid detail. He was sweating profusely. He shouted out, "I know there is a God because all the people there were crying out to Him. 'Jesus! Lord, help me,' I could hear over and over all around me! It was pitch black. All you could see was flames from the lake and people trying to climb out of these flames! Tears and screaming all around that horrid place. 'Lord, help me! Lord, help me!' Screams! Screams all around! I don't want to be there, girl. Pray for me!"

"Papa, oh, Papa, you need to pray. You need to ask Jesus to come into your heart to be your Lord and savior. We have been praying for you. The sheriff prayed that your injuries would be healed, but, Papa, it takes you to cry out to God before He will save you."

He reached out to grab Zuri's hand. "Yes, girl, it does. Help me, girl. Help me, sheriff. Help me to pray. Help me to pray, Zuri! Help me! Someone, help me!" He was so terrified to his very core!

I took a step forward and laid my hand on his shoulder. "Mr. Carter I'll help you." Bowing my head, I said, "Repeat after me, brother. Mean this from your heart, and Christ will heal your pain. He will hear this prayer. Dear heavenly Father, please forgive my sins, which are many. Please take away everything that comes against you. All the bad I've done against you. Everything in my past that has let you down! I know you died on that cross for my sins. You rose the third day for me. Just for me! I repent of all my sins. Please be my Lord. I will make you the Lord of my life. I will always proclaim you, Jesus, the Lord of my life from this day forward." Mr. Carter repeated every word after me, and he truly meant it. Loudly, he called out to the Lord.

As Mr. Carter called out to Jesus. I saw a different man step forward. The expression on his face was different. Even the foreman had tears running down his face. I think he prayed the same prayer Mr. Carter prayed. The power of the Holy Spirit was in this room more so than when Dwight gave his heart up. Zuri was also in tears as she hugged her papa.

She was whispering to him, but we all could hear. "Papa, I'm so happy. Now we can be in heaven with Mammy one day. I know this was ordered by God. Your men capturing me and bringing me back, the capture of the sheriff and Dwight, the hangings that didn't happen, you falling from the wagon, and the vision you had! This was all in God's plan to bring you to Him. I know God did this to bring you to him. The vision you had was not just from you, it was from God to change your life."

Mr. Carter smiled up at his daughter. "My life has changed. My heart is changed. I feel like a great weight has been lifted off my life."

"Papa this is what I prayed for all these years, even before I knew you were my papa. You were mean to a lot of the other slaves, but you were never mean to me. I could always feel you were protecting me. For that, I love you, Papa."

"I love you too, girl. I always have. I also loved your momma. Your mammy was one of the best women I have ever known in my life. Even though I was mean to her and forced myself onto her, I knew she loved me back. If times were different, she could have been my bride. She wasn't just my slave. She was always more than that. My love! I cared for that woman deeply," he whispered this to Zuri with tears in his eyes.

Zuri reached down and hugged him. We could all feel the love of a father to his daughter. It was different now. Mr. Carter was a completely different man.

We knew now life was going to be good for them. Still uncertain what was going to be for us, Mr. Thomas spoke up. "Sir, these men are still uncertain of their fate. What should we do with them? Should I let them go free?"

Mr. Carter glanced over and said, "Follow your heart, son. Follow your heart." So Thomas walked over to Dwight and said, "You're a good boy." He had a slight smile on his face as he did so. He shook my hand and whispered, "I'm happy for you and Dwight. I was not sure what to do when they were going to hang you."

"It all worked out for the best, Thomas. It confirmed that I knew we were still on the same team."

Chapter 16

We all gathered together outside where we sat around a huge firepit. Mr. Carter and Zuri sat together with their heads close together as they talked among themselves. There was a calmness now with all the men, and even the foreman, who had been very vocal before, was now a quiet man. Instead of anger and hatred, there was a sense of peace that surrounded everyone. I spoke of the change that God made in my life over the last weeks. I shared all the amazing things that had happened on my journey to get home to my family. I told them of the reverend I left in Alexandria and the adventures we had gone through. There was a true change in my life after the experience in the bar in Alexandria. Some of the men opened up and told us about their lives and what had brought them to be who they had become. They spoke of the peace they now felt in their souls and how some of them couldn't wait to get back to their families to share the peace with them. These men opened up to us. We were more like companions than we were former enemies.

After we sat there for some time, the foreman rose to his feet and suggested that we all get some sleep. He offered the barn for us to sleep in. He said there were horse blankets to lay on if we wanted to. Dwight and I took him up on his offer and found the blankets. Once we got things laid out, we both fell fast asleep.

Unfortunately, I only slept for about three hours. As I awoke, I looked around the large barn where both our horses were kept. I walked over to where Dwight was asleep and woke him up too. Brain still in a fog from sleep, Dwight woke up, asking in a rough, sleep-filled voice, "You ready to go, sheriff?" Instead of answering right away, I walked over and spoke to Rosie as I began to saddle her. Dwight rose and I believe I heard him praying as he saddled his horse. When I didn't hear anything for a little bit, I asked, "In a good mood, Dwight?"

He finished positioning his saddle and answered, "Things seem to be getting better, sheriff. I feel like God has something good in store for me."

We both grabbed the reins and walked outside with the horses in hand. As we stepped out, there came that pretty sweet girl, Zuri, walking toward us from the big house. She had a bag in one hand and my little Bible with the hole in it in the other. With a smile on her face, she walked right up to Dwight and said, "Papa said I can go with you. He instructed me to wire him if I ever needed anything." The smile that spread across Dwight's face was a sight to see. "That is great news, Zuri. Now you can start the life you have always wanted to now."

She shifted slightly. "I am excited to move on to other places where I will be looked at as another of God's creations." She glanced toward Dwight. He lit up when she looked at him. He said excitedly, "You're going with us? Why would you go with us since you finally found your papa, and he is a different man now? I want you to go, but I am confused."

She reached over and put her hand on Dwight's arm. "I want to have a life that I will make with a new family," Zuri explained.

Dwight lit up once again. "Your family?" he asked.

"My aunties and whoever God puts into my life." Her hand tightened on his arm. "God has a plan for my life, and I will follow His lead to wherever He leads and to whomever He leads me to."

Dwight looked down at Zuri with true love in his eyes and with an intention of making her his, if at all possible. Dwight cleared his throat and asked, "Zuri, I would be honored if you would ride beside me till we get to the train and get to your aunts. We can ride the train together since we are all going that way."

She smiled and said, "I would be happy to ride beside you, Dwight."

I rode in silence since I was not able to talk to either of them. They were lost in conversation between themselves. They were really getting to know each other. Not sure how Zuri was feeling, but this Dwight, who once was disgusted by people that were different from him, was now falling in love with this beautiful girl. The heart only sees one color. The blood that we all bleed is the same color, especially when it's the color of the blood Jesus shed on that cross so long ago. The same blood we all have in our veins as we rode on this trail to El Paso! Christ's blood covering the El Paso trail! Thank you, Lord, for that covering.

As we rode, I could hear Dwight become tongue-tied here and there as his blood would run a little hot now and then. His face would turn red from the excitement and from the attention of this beautiful girl.

I rode along, contemplating what had taken place since the beginning and what may take place at the old homestead. How my mother was doing now that my father was gone. Or maybe not. I would not find out until we arrived in El Paso. The reverend said he was supposed to take the pastorship over the same church my dad was pastor of for years since the former pastor had passed away. Not only losing my father, but how was my mother doing? She had been married to my father for over fifty years. I was not sure what I would find when I got there. All I knew was she would truly be needing me now more than ever.

We rode for a couple of hours until we came upon the train that was surprisingly still waiting there for some unknown reason. We could see in the distance the two aunties laughing, smiling, jumping up and down, and shouting, "Praise Jesus! Praise Jesus!" as they threw their hands in the air!

"Thank God you're alive." The two aunts were very excited to see Zuri. So with tears running down all three women's faces, Zuri climbed off the horse and hugged both of them.

We did not know why the train was still here and had not departed to its destination, so we made our way to the front of the train to ask the conductor what was going on. "Why was the train not moving?" I asked the conductor.

Looking a bit stern, he explained that the little women were very convincing as to why we needed to wait till you and their niece returned. They said you were a mighty important sheriff and that you would be returning with their niece. They are very convincing! We gave them until four o'clock to pull out, and here you are. A miracle that you made it on time." He pulled out an old pocket watch on a chain, checked it, and then clicked it shut. "Yes, sir, it was a miracle more than you can know," I said.

"We need to make a report when we arrive at the next town of the robbery that was no robbery that took place.

Everyone is saying nothing was taken but this young lady. Those men left the bag of the valuables they took on the train when they rode off. Now you have brought her back. I'm not sure we need to make a report."

I just stared at him for a moment then asked, "All the valuables, you say? Was there a watch in those items?"

He responded, "No, there wasn't."

I looked over to where Dwight was standing not too far behind me. "Well, I guess something did get taken."

Right then, Dwight pulled his watch from his pocket. "I just wanted to come along to get Zuri, and it was a good excuse."

"I thought that was the case," I agreed.

"Well, Mr. Conductor, we will need to because of the time that was lost in your train schedule."

The conductor picked up his journal and told us that was all the report that needed to be made. "As far as anything missing, I can say there is nothing, and no one will be the wiser. Well, since you're on the train safely, you can get your horses loaded up. We will be on our way."

Dwight and I made our way back to load our horses.

Rosie and the other horse refused to load, so we got two boards from inside one of the cars. We put it behind Rosie, and then Dwight pulled her lead line while I pushed with the boards braced in the door, opening behind her. I was behind her, smacking her on the hind quarters, trying to get her into the train car. They were reluctant but did load one at a time. Once Rosie loaded, the other horse followed her lead.

With my stubborn horse, it took us over thirty minutes to get them loaded. I heard the engine of the train start to roar as it started to move. Black smoke rolled through to the back of the train. Wind softly blew from the front to the back as we moved forward.

We made many stops along the way. Nothing exciting happened for the next four days until we arrived in El

Paso. Dwight had sat with Zuri the entire trip. From the time we left Louisiana till we made our last stop, he was sitting talking to Zuri. They seemed to be inseparable. I sat across from Zuri and Dwight making conversation with the two aunts. After a couple of days, I invited everyone to come stay with us at the family farm—hopefully to help my mother. Reluctantly they accepted my invitation. Zuri and Dwight led the drawing of the aunts into the decision. Both women were very sweet. Zuri was the kindest, most pure-hearted girl I may have ever known. I could under-stand the attraction Dwight had for this young lady.

We would talk for hours on end until night. We would retire to our Pullman sleepers every evening. Dwight and I would take turns as lookouts throughout the night to make sure what had happened before would not catch us off guard again. This continued every day until the last day; while in the great territory of Texas, the terrain was differ-ent—it was drier. Desert was everywhere, as well as cactus and tumbleweeds. We saw many black-tailed lizards, jack-rabbits, and prairie dogs all over as we traveled through.

The many days we traveled, Dwight and Zuri became close—very close. They were holding hands by the third day. He was more captivated by her every day.

Once we arrived in El Paso, I just stood there with Dwight. He asked, "What do you think we will find here once we arrive at your family's farm?"

Shaking myself out of my melancholy mood, I answered, "Our next great adventure, Dwight. Life and family are the greatest adventure there is. I'm not sure what awaits, but we will do it as a family." I put my hand on his shoulder and smiled at him. He smiled back with his slightly crooked smile.

I made my way to the back of the train car to take Rosie out. I instructed Dwight to stay with the ladies while I went to purchase a wagon to travel the ten miles to the family farm.

God provided plenty of money through the preacher. I was able to purchase a road buggy big enough to carry all three ladies with Dwight leading the team of two Quarter Horses. I also wanted to pick up supplies for the next month. As I departed the livery and made my way toward the general store, I saw someone I had not seen since I left years earlier.

Tammy was walking on the path between two buildings. She was slightly older but just as pretty as I remembered her. The one difference I could not overlook was the person holding her hand. A small child about three years old was walking with them. She was the spitting image of her mother. She made eye contact with me as I rode by. She stopped in her tracks and stared at me. Before I could stop, a man appeared behind her, his presence turning her attention away from me. That closed the door I was not sure was still open or not.

I loaded up the supplies from the general store and headed to the depot with the wagon. We got the ladies and their luggage loaded into the road buggy. I untied Rosie, and we all headed out with me leading the way. It was a long ride after being on that train for so many days.

When we arrived at the family farm, I dismounted from Rosie and went to find my mother and what may be waiting. I handed the reins of Rosie to Zuri. "I'll be right back," I told everyone as I ran into the home where I found no one. A fear came over me, although it didn't last long. A calmness was right behind it. Closing my eyes for a few minutes, I said a small prayer. Something told me to look in the backyard. I made my way out to the backyard and stopped short. Over by the huge tree that used to have a swing were two graves.

I was overcome with grief! There lay my father and my dog whom our family had for half of my life. Beside the graves was my mother setting their flowers on both graves. When she noticed me, she immediately started to cry. I ran to her, picked her up, and cried with her. It was so good to see her face. I always remembered her with a smile on her face. But now, she was covered with bittersweet pain and joy from seeing me and the loss of my father.

I walked her into the house where I introduced her to our new family of Dwight, Zuri, and the two aunties. Mom was more than welcoming to everyone, as she always was. She was older with more white in her hair than I remember but just as sweet to everyone. She loved the thought of having all the help and the new family. She thought she had lost the chance at having a family when my father passed. Sometimes, when we lose one dream, God creates a new one for you to keep the faith alive.

The end.

About the Author

First-time author Bill Handy fulfilled a lifetime desire of sharing one of the many Christian Western stories that mold his way of thinking. A love for God and the Western area have driven the writing a story that has developed over a three-year period. A father of three and grandfather of six. He is a very dedicated husband and has been a successful manager for over thirty years as a leader.

www.ingramcontent.com/pod-product-compliance
Lightning Source LLC
Chambersburg PA
CBHW071658120626
46550CB00001B/27